Adequacy of Retirement Income after Pension Reforms in Central, Eastern, and Southern Europe

Adequacy of Retirement Income after Pension Reforms in Central, Eastern, and Southern Europe

THE WORLD BANK
Washington, DC

ERSTE Stiftung

1818 H Street NW
Washington, DC 20433
Telephone: 202-473-1000
Internet: www.worldbank.org
E-mail: feedback@worldbank.org

ISBN: 978-0-8213-7781-9
eISBN: 978-0-8213-7780-2
DOI: 10.1596/978-0-8213-7781-9

Library of Congress Cataloging-in-Publication Data

Holzmann, Robert.

Adequacy of retirement income after pension reforms in Central, Eastern, and Southern Europe: eight country studies/Robert Holzmann and Ufuk Guven.
    p. cm.
    ISBN 978-0-8213-7781-9 (alk. paper) — ISBN 978-0-8213-7780-2
    1. Retirement income—Government policy—Europe, Eastern. 2. Retirement income—Government policy—Europe, Central. 3. Pensions—Government policy—Europe, Eastern. 4. Pensions—Government policy—Europe, Central. I. Guven, Ufuk, 1972- II. Title.
HD7164.7.H647 2009
331.25'2094—dc22

2008041837

Cover photos: Couple in Czech Republic/Corbis; Couple in Romania/Corbis; Couple by Water/Getty.
Cover design: Naylor Design, Washington, DC

Contents

Preface   *xv*
Acknowledgments   *xvii*
Abbreviations   *xix*

Chapter 1 **Introduction, Summary, and Policy Conclusions**   1
               Motivation for Reform and Policy Trends   3
               Characteristics of Reformed Pension Systems   10
               Assessment of the Performance of Pension Systems   37
               Conclusions   52
               Notes   56
               Bibliography   58

Chapter 2 **Bulgaria**   61
               Motivation for Reform   62
               Characteristics of Bulgaria's Pension System   64
               Assessment of the Performance of Bulgaria's
                   Pension System   73
               Conclusions   84
               Notes   85
               Bibliography   87

Chapter 3	**Croatia**	**89**
	Motivation for Reform	90
	Characteristics of Croatia's Pension System	91
	Assessment of the Performance of Croatia's Pension System	100
	Conclusions	110
	Notes	111
	Bibliography	113
Chapter 4	**The Czech Republic**	**115**
	Motivation for Reform	116
	Characteristics of the Czech Republic's Pension System	117
	Assessment of the Performance of the Czech Pension System	127
	Conclusions	141
	Notes	143
	Bibliography	145
Chapter 5	**Hungary**	**147**
	Motivation for Reform	148
	Characteristics of Hungary's Pension System	150
	Assessment of the Performance of Hungary's Pension System	162
	Conclusions	173
	Notes	175
	Bibliography	177
Chapter 6	**Poland**	**181**
	Motivation for Reform	182
	Characteristics of Poland's Pension System	184
	Assessment of the Performance of Poland's Pension System	195
	Conclusions	204
	Notes	206
	Bibliography	207
Chapter 7	**Romania**	**211**
	Motivation for Reform	212
	Characteristics of Romania's Pension System	213

	Assessment of the Performance of Romania's	
	Pension System	223
	Conclusions	234
	Notes	235
	Bibliography	237

Chapter 8	**The Slovak Republic**	**239**
	Motivation for Reform	240
	Characteristics of the Slovak Republic's	
	Pension System	242
	Assessment of the Performance of the	
	Slovak Pension System	252
	Conclusions	262
	Notes	264
	Bibliography	265

Chapter 9	**Slovenia**	**267**
	Motivation for Reform	268
	Characteristics of Slovenia's Pension System	269
	Assessment of the Performance of Slovenia's	
	Pension System	278
	Conclusions	288
	Notes	289
	Bibliography	291

| **Index** | | **295** |

Box

| 1.1 | Taxation of Retirement Savings | 15 |

Figures

1.1	Projected Pension System Fiscal Balances before	
	Reform in Eight CESE Countries	4
1.2	Old-Age Dependency Ratios, 2000–50,	
	by World Region	5
1.3	Gross Replacement Rates for Male Full-Career	
	Workers in Eight CESE Countries	41
1.4	Net Replacement Rates for Male Full-Career	
	Workers in Eight CESE Countries	43

1.5	Net Replacement Rates for Male Partial-Career Workers in Eight CESE Countries	45
1.6	Impact of Indexation on Income Replacement (Active Earnings Units) in Eight CESE Countries	47
1.7	Projected Pension System Fiscal Balances after Reform in Eight CESE Countries	50
2.1	Projected Fiscal Balance of Bulgaria's Public Pension System before Reform, 2001–50	63
2.2	Projected Old-Age Dependency Ratio in Bulgaria, 2005–50	64
2.3	Sources of Gross Replacement Rates in Bulgaria, by Income Level	78
2.4	Sources of Net Replacement Rates in Bulgaria, by Income Level	79
2.5	Net Replacement Rates for Male Full-Career Workers in Bulgaria, Europe and Central Asia, and the World, by Income Level	80
2.6	Net Replacement Rates for Male Middle-Income Partial-Career Workers in Bulgaria, by Career Type and Exit Age	81
2.7	Projected Fiscal Balance of Bulgaria's Public Pension System after Reform, 2001–50	82
2.8	Net Replacement Rates for Men in Bulgaria before and after Benefit Adjustment	84
3.1	Projected Old-Age Dependency Ratio in Croatia, 2006–50	91
3.2	Sources of Gross Replacement Rates in Croatia, by Income Level	105
3.3	Sources of Net Replacement Rates in Croatia, by Income Level	106
3.4	Net Replacement Rates for Male Full-Career Workers in 2040 in Croatia, Europe and Central Asia, and the World	107
3.5	Net Replacement Rates for Male Middle-Income Partial-Career Workers in Croatia, by Career Type and Exit Age	108
3.6	Projected Fiscal Balance of Croatia's Public Pension System after Reform, 2005–40	110
4.1	Sources of Gross Replacement Rates in the Czech Republic, by Income Level	132

4.2   Sources of Net Replacement Rates in the Czech
        Republic, by Income Level   133
4.3   Net Replacement Rates for Male Full-Career
        Workers in the Czech Republic, Europe and
        Central Asia, and the World, by
        Income Level   134
4.4   Net Replacement Rates for Male Low-Income
        Partial-Career Workers in the Czech Republic, by
        Career Type and Exit Age   135
4.5   Net Replacement Rates for Male Middle-Income
        Partial-Career Workers in the Czech Republic, by
        Career Type and Exit Age   136
4.6   Net Replacement Rates for Male High-Income
        Partial-Career Workers in the Czech Republic, by
        Career Type and Exit Age   137
4.7   Projected Fiscal Balance of the Public Pension System
        in the Czech Republic after Reform, 2009–50   139
4.8   Projected Old-Age and System Dependency Ratios
        in the Czech Republic, 2005–50   139
4.9   Net Replacement Rates for Male Full-Career Workers
        in the Czech Republic before and after Benefit
        Adjustment, by Income Level   141
5.1   Projected Fiscal Balance of Hungary's Public Pension
        System before Reform, 2000–50   150
5.2   Projected Old-Age and System Dependency Ratios in
        Hungary, 2005–50   150
5.3   Sources of Gross Replacement Rates in Hungary, by
        Income Level   166
5.4   Sources of Net Replacement Rates in Hungary, by
        Income Level   167
5.5   Net Replacement Rates for Male Full-Career Workers
        in Hungary, Europe and Central Asia, and the World,
        by Income Level   167
5.6   Net Replacement Rates for Male Middle-Income
        Partial-Career Workers in Hungary, by Career Type
        and Exit Age   169
5.7   Projected Fiscal Balance of Hungary's Public Pension
        System after Reform, 2005–50   170
5.8   Net Replacement Rates for Male Workers in Hungary
        before and after Benefit Adjustment   172

6.1	Projected Fiscal Balance of Poland's Public Pension System before Reform, 2000–50	183
6.2	Projected Old-Age and System Dependency Ratios in Poland, 2005–50	184
6.3	Sources of Gross Replacement Rates in Poland, by Income Level	200
6.4	Sources of Net Replacement Rates in Poland, by Income Level	201
6.5	Net Replacement Rates for Male Full-Career Workers in Poland, Europe and Central Asia, and the World, by Income Level	202
6.6	Net Replacement Rates for Male Middle-Income Partial-Career Workers in Poland, by Career Type and Exit Age	203
6.7	Projected Fiscal Balance of Poland's Public Pension Scheme, 2004–50	204
7.1	Gross Replacement Rates in Romania, by Income Level	227
7.2	Sources of Net Replacement Rates in Romania, by Income Level	228
7.3	Net Replacement Rates for Male Full-Career Workers in Romania, Europe and Central Asia, and the World	228
7.4	Net Replacement Rates for Male Middle-Income Partial-Career Workers in Romania, by Career Type and Exit Age	229
7.5	Projected Fiscal Balance of Romania's Public Pension System after Reform, 2008–50	231
7.6	Projected Old-Age and System Dependency Ratios in Romania, 2008–50	232
7.7	Net Replacement Rates for Male Workers in Romania before and after Benefit Adjustment	233
8.1	Projected Fiscal Balance of the Slovak Republic's Public Pension Scheme before Reform, 2000–50	241
8.2	Projected Old-Age and System Dependency Ratios in the Slovak Republic before Reform, 2005–50	242
8.3	Sources of Gross Replacement Rates in the Slovak Republic, by Income Level	256
8.4	Sources of Net Replacement Rates in the Slovak Republic, by Income Level	256

8.5   Net Replacement Rates for Male Full-Career
       Workers in the Slovak Republic, Europe and
       Central Asia, and the World   257
8.6   Net Replacement Rates for Male Middle-Income
       Partial-Career Workers in the Slovak Republic,
       by Career Type and Exit Age   258
8.7   Projected Fiscal Balance of the Slovak Republic's
       Public Pension Scheme after Reform, 2005–50   260
8.8   Net Male Replacement Rates in the Slovak
       Republic before and after Benefit Adjustment   262
9.1   Sources of Gross Replacement Rates in Slovenia,
       by Income Level   282
9.2   Sources of Net Replacement Rates in Slovenia, by
       Income Level   282
9.3   Net Replacement Rates for Male Full-Career
       Workers in Slovenia, Europe and Central Asia,
       and the World   283
9.4   Net Replacement Rates for Male Middle-Income
       Partial-Career Workers in Slovenia, by Career Type
       and Exit Age   284
9.5   Projected Fiscal Balance of Slovenia's Public Pension
       Scheme, 2005–50   286
9.6   Projected Old-Age Dependency Ratio in Slovenia,
       2005–50   286
9.7   Net Replacement Rates for Male Workers in Slovenia
       before and after Benefit Adjustment   287

Tables

1.1   Characteristics of Multipillar Pension Reforms in
       Transition Economies   8
1.2   Structure of Pension Systems in Eight CESE Countries   12
1.3   Taxation of Retirement Savings in Eight CESE Countries   14
1.4   Basic Pension Benefits from the Zero Pillar in Eight
       CESE Countries   17
1.5   Eligibility for and Benefits Provided by Old-Age
       Pensions in Eight CESE Countries   20
1.6   Eligibility for and Benefits Provided by Disability
       Pensions in Eight CESE Countries   28
1.7   Eligibility for and Benefits Provided by Survivor
       Pensions in Eight CESE Countries   31

1.8	Voluntary Pension Provisions in Eight CESE Countries	35
1.9	Health Care Provisions for Contributors and Retirees in Eight CESE Countries	36
2.1	Fiscal Balance of Bulgaria's Pension System before Reform, 1990–99	63
2.2	Structure of the Bulgarian Pension System	66
2.3	Parameters of Earnings-Related Schemes in Bulgaria before and after Reform	68
2.4	Characteristics of the Voluntary Scheme in Bulgaria	70
2.5	Eligibility Conditions for and Benefits Provided by Disability Pensions under the First Pillar Earnings-Related Scheme in Bulgaria	72
2.6	Eligibility Conditions for and Benefits Provided by Survivor Pensions in Bulgaria under the First-Pillar Earnings-Related Scheme	74
3.1	Projected Fiscal Balance of Croatia's Public Pension System before Reform, 1994–2000	90
3.2	Structure of the Croatian Pension System	93
3.3	Parameters of Earnings-Related Schemes in Croatia before and after Reform	95
3.4	Characteristics of the Voluntary Scheme in Croatia	96
3.5	Eligibility Conditions for and Benefits Provided by Disability Pensions in Croatia	99
3.6	Eligibility Conditions for and Benefits Provided by Survivor Pensions in Croatia	101
4.1	Fiscal Balance of the Czech Republic's Pension System before Reform, 1994–2000	117
4.2	Structure of the Czech Republic's Pension System	119
4.3	Parameters of the First-Pillar Earnings-Related Scheme in the Czech Republic before and after Reform	121
4.4	Characteristics of the Voluntary Scheme in the Czech Republic	123
4.5	Eligibility Conditions for and Benefits Provided by Disability Pensions in the Czech Republic under the First-Pillar Earnings-Related Scheme	126
4.6	Eligibility Conditions for and Benefits Provided by Survivor Pensions in the Czech Republic under the First-Pillar Earnings-Related Scheme	128
5.1	Fiscal Balance of Hungary's Pension System before Reform, 1991–96	149
5.2	Structure of Hungary's Pension System	152

5.3   Parameters of Earnings-Related Schemes in Hungary
       before and after Reform   155
5.4   Characteristics of the Voluntary Scheme in Hungary   158
5.5   Eligibility Conditions for and Benefits Provided
       by Disability Pensions in Hungary under
       the First-Pillar Earnings-Related Scheme   160
5.6   Eligibility Conditions for and Benefits Provided by
       Survivor Pensions in Hungary under the First-Pillar
       Earnings-Related Scheme   162
6.1   Fiscal Balance of Poland's Pension System before
       Reform, 1992–99   183
6.2   Structure of Poland's Pension System   186
6.3   Parameters of Earnings-Related Schemes in Poland
       before and after Reform   189
6.4   Characteristics of the Voluntary Scheme
       in Poland   192
6.5   Eligibility Conditions for and Benefits Provided by
       Disability Pensions in Poland under the First-Pillar
       Earnings-Related Scheme   194
6.6   Eligibility Conditions for and Benefits Provided by
       Survivor Pensions in Poland under the First-Pillar
       Earnings-Related Scheme   196
7.1   Fiscal Balance of Romania's Pension System before
       Reform, 1992–98   213
7.2   Structure of Romania's Pension System   215
7.3   Parameters of Earnings-Related Schemes in
       Romania before and after Reform   217
7.4   Characteristics of Romania's Voluntary Scheme   218
7.5   Eligibility Conditions for and Benefits Provided by
       Disability Pensions in Romania under the First-Pillar
       Earnings-Related Scheme   221
7.6   Eligibility Conditions for and Benefits Provided by
       Survivor Pensions under Romania's First-Pillar
       Earnings-Related Scheme   222
8.1   Fiscal Balance of the Slovak Republic's Pension
       System before Reform, 1995–2002   241
8.2   Structure of the Slovak Pension System   244
8.3   Parameters of Earnings-Related Schemes in the
       Slovak Republic before and after Reform   247
8.4   Characteristics of the Voluntary Scheme in the
       Slovak Republic   248

8.5   Eligibility Conditions for and Benefits Provided
       by Disability Pensions under the First-Pillar
       Earnings-Related Scheme in the Slovak Republic   251
8.6   Eligibility Conditions for and Benefits Provided by
       Survivor Pensions under the First-Pillar Earnings-
       Related Scheme in the Slovak Republic   251
9.1   Fiscal Balance of Slovenia's Pension System before
       Reform, 1992–99   268
9.2   Structure of Slovenia's Pension System   271
9.3   Parameters of First-Pillar Earnings-Related Scheme
       in Slovenia before and after Reform   272
9.4   Characteristics of the Voluntary Scheme in Slovenia   274
9.5   Eligibility Conditions for and Benefits Provided by
       Disability Pensions in Slovenia under the First-Pillar
       Earnings-Related Scheme   276
9.6   Eligibility Conditions for and Benefits Provided by
       Survivor Pensions in Slovenia under the First-Pillar
       Earnings-Related Scheme   277

Preface

The former transition countries of Central, Eastern, and Southern Europe (CESE) inherited defined-benefit public pension systems financed on a pay-as-you-go basis. Under central planning, these systems exhibited fiscal strains that worsened during the early years of the transition and became unsustainable under a market economy. Recognizing that short-term fiscal pressures and incentives would worsen over the long term as a result of population aging, many CESE countries introduced reforms. Although approaches varied—particularly with regard to the choice between parametric and systemic reforms and over the introduction of funding—reforms typically focused on sustainability rather than benefit adequacy.

At the request of—and with cofinancing from—the ERSTE Foundation, Vienna, World Bank staff prepared individual studies for eight CESE countries (Bulgaria, Croatia, the Czech Republic, Hungary, Poland, Romania, the Slovak Republic, and Slovenia). The objectives were (a) to identify their motivations for reform against the backdrop of the trend toward multipillar arrangements, (b) to document their key provisions and compare them in the context of the World Bank's five-pillar paradigm for pension reform, (c) to evaluate the sustainability and adequacy of reformed pension systems in the face of population aging, and (d) to provide a basis for recommendations to address gaps and take advantage of opportunities for further reforms. Benefit adequacy was assessed by estimating future gross and net replacement rates along both income and contribution record dimensions under steady-state conditions approximated by the year 2040. These eight studies are presented in this report.

The report's introduction summarizes the case-study findings and discusses several broad conclusions that emerge from them:

• Fiscal sustainability has improved in most study countries, but few are fully prepared for the inevitability of population aging.
• The linkage between contributions and benefits has been strengthened, and pension system designs are now better suited to market conditions.
• Levels of income replacement are generally adequate for all but some categories of workers (including those with intermittent formal-sector employment or low lifetime wages). Addressing the needs of those groups will require macroeconomic and microeconomic initiatives that go beyond pension policy.
• Further reforms to cope with population aging should focus on extending labor force participation by the elderly to avoid benefit cuts, which could undermine adequacy, or very high contribution rates, which could discourage formal-sector employment.
• More decisive financial market reforms are needed for funded provisions to deliver on the return expectations of participants.

These country studies were undertaken to inform policy makers, pension providers, researchers, future retirees, and other stakeholders inside and outside the region about the status of future benefit adequacy in the region as well as the tasks that still lie ahead. We hope that the methodology and comparability of analysis across countries contribute to a more informed pension reform discourse and better outcomes for the retirees of the future.

Acknowledgments

This report was prepared by Robert Holzmann and Ufuk Guven of the World Bank. Robert Holzmann was responsible for the overall direction of the project. He provided technical guidance and review and wrote the first chapter. Ufuk Guven wrote the eight country studies.

Both authors wish to express their deep appreciation for the advice and technical input provided by Zoran Anusic, Mukesh Chawla, David Robalino, Anita Schwarz, and other World Bank staff members; the suggestions of Edward Whitehouse, of the Organisation for Economic Cooperation and Development (OECD) on the use of the Analysis of Pension Entitlements across Countries (APEX) model; the analytical work of Sergiy Biletsky, of the World Bank, who ran the APEX model; and the editing of Christopher Bender. They also wish to express their gratitude to the ERSTE Foundation for initiating and cofinancing the report and to its representatives, Rainer Munez and Karl Franz Prueller, for their seamless cooperation.

The authors also thank the country experts who provided invaluable comments and suggestions on drafts of the case studies. They include Jordan Hristoskov, of the National Social Security Institute (Bulgaria); Georgi Shopov, of the Institute of Economics, Academy of Sciences (Bulgaria); Ljiljana Marusic, of the Agency for Control of Financial Services (Croatia); Jiri Kral, of the Ministry of Labor and Social Affairs (the Czech Republic); Erzsebet Kovacs, of Corvinus University of Budapest (Hungary); Gábor Orbán, of the Economics Department of Magyar Nemzeti Bank (Hungary); Péter Holtzer, of ORIENS IM (Hungary); Agnieszka Chlon-Dominczak, of the Ministry of Labor and Social Affairs (Poland); Marek Lendacký, of the Ministry of Finance (the Slovak Republic); and Tine Stanovnik, of the faculty of Economics and Institute for Economic Research, Ljubljana (Slovenia). Although this report was subjected to the World Bank's internal review process, the findings, interpretations, and conclusions expressed herein are those of the authors and do not necessarily reflect the views of the World Bank, its affiliated organizations, its executive directors, or the governments they represent.

Abbreviations

APEX	Analysis of Pension Entitlements across Countries
CESE	Central, Eastern, and Southern Europe
EET	exempt-exempt-taxed
EU	European Union
GMI	Guaranteed Minimum Income
GDP	gross domestic product
HZZO	Croatian Institute for Health Insurance
ILO	International Labour Organization
NDC	notional defined-contribution
NHIFA	National Health Insurance Fund Administration (Hungary)
NSSI	National Social Security Institute (Bulgaria)
PDII	Pensions and Disability Insurance Institute (Slovenia)
PROST	Pension Reform Options Simulation Toolkit
REGOS	Central Registry of Insured People (Croatia)
ZUS	Social Insurance Fund (Poland)

CHAPTER 1

Introduction, Summary, and Policy Conclusions

All of the former transition economies in Central, Eastern, and Southern Europe (CESE) inherited from the era of central planning traditional defined-benefit pension systems financed on a pay-as-you-go basis. Like many pay-as-you-go public pension systems elsewhere in the world, CESE pension systems were in need of reforms to address short-term fiscal imbalances and longer-term issues relating to population aging. Reforms were also needed to adjust benefit and contribution structures to meet the challenges of—as well as to take advantage of opportunities relating to—the transition to a market economy, including the widespread adoption of multipillar designs with improved risk-sharing across funded and unfunded pillars. By 2006, most countries in Europe and Central Asia had introduced a voluntary private pension scheme. By 2008, 14 countries—roughly half of all countries in the region—had legislated mandatory private pension schemes, and all but one of those schemes (the one in Ukraine) had been introduced. These reforms shared a number of common objectives, in particular putting the systems on a sounder financial footing and better aligning them with the (very different) incentives of a market economy.

Most observers would probably agree that while most countries have made progress, many of the reforms seem to have focused more on the sustainability of the systems than on the adequacy of their retirement benefits. A pension system that delivers adequate benefits is a system that prevents old-age poverty and provides a reliable means of smoothing life-time consumption for the vast majority of the population. Indeed, this is one of the paramount objectives of pension system design.

The perception that reforms placed undue emphasis on sustainability, in combination with the widespread move toward multipillar arrangements and funded provisions, has raised concerns about the adequacy of benefits at a time when many new retirees are receiving comparatively modest benefits. Moreover, reforms that improved but did not fully resolve issues of fiscal sustainability only heighten concerns about benefit adequacy for future generations of retirees.

The population is aging rapidly in all of the CESE countries. This makes issues of sustainability and adequacy particularly important, because the inevitable consequence of the ongoing process of population aging—characterized by low and declining fertility rates and rising life expectancy—is that in the absence of reforms, public pension expenditures will need to rise to accommodate the larger beneficiary pool that will result from current benefit provisions and retirement ages. This is especially challenging for CESE countries with unfunded systems, because pension spending is already very high relative to gross domestic product (GDP), even though some reforms have already been enacted and the number of contributors across most age groups has fallen considerably (a drop that has not reversed, even as economic growth had picked up in some countries prior to the current financial crisis). Because many people currently of working age may not be eligible for pension benefits when they are ready to retire, governments may be compelled to consider providing them with some sort of social assistance benefits. These costs will add to the burden of paying pensions for those who do qualify for contributory benefits.

This chapter summarizes the country-level evaluations presented in subsequent chapters of the adequacy of retirement income in eight middle-income countries in the region: Bulgaria, Croatia, the Czech Republic, Hungary, Poland, Romania, the Slovak Republic, and Slovenia. Six of these countries (Bulgaria, Croatia, Hungary, Poland, Romania, and the Slovak Republic) introduced systemic reforms involving mandatory funded pension schemes (of varying sizes and with different rules for the inclusion of current workers), together with parametric reforms to their traditional defined-benefit schemes. In Croatia, Romania, and the Slovak Republic, parametric reforms involved the introduction of a point system (described later); Poland went further, introducing a nonfinancial (or notional) defined contribution (NDC) scheme. The Czech Republic and Slovenia are not actively working on reforms involving NDCs or mandatory funded schemes, although policy dialogue remains ongoing in both countries.

This chapter is organized as follows. The first section discusses the motivation for reform across the eight countries included in the study against the backdrop of the regional (and global) trend toward multipillar pension arrangements. The second section summarizes the key provisions of the reformed systems in the eight countries within the World Bank's five-pillar framework for pension system design. The third section summarizes pension system performance against the two crucially important dimensions of adequacy and sustainability. The last section provides some policy recommendations for addressing gaps in reforms and taking advantage of further opportunities.

Motivation for Reform and Policy Trends

CESE countries share several common motivations for reforming their pension systems. These include the need to restore fiscal sustainability to traditional pay-as-you-go pension systems, align benefit structures, improve economic incentives, diversify risks for all parties, and (in common with countries from other regions) create a vehicle for promoting financial market development (Barr and Rutkowski 2004; Holzmann 1997b; Nickel and Almenberg 2006; and Schwarz 2007).

Issues of fiscal sustainability existed in many CESE countries before 1990; they were exacerbated by the transition from central planning to a market economy as a consequence of the high level of coverage under the old system (which resulted in large numbers of beneficiaries, many of whom became eligible for benefits at a relatively young age) coupled with the sharp drop in the number of contributors as a result of the initial fall in economic output, decline in labor force participation and formal employment, and rise in unemployment. The level of pension expenditures in CESE countries was typically very high relative to the level of development (as measured by GDP per capita). At the same time, their capacity to collect contributions and taxes was increasingly compromised. The resulting gap between expenditures and revenues led many CESE countries to consider reforms early on, but until the second half of the 1990s, fiscal pressure was accommodated largely by ad hoc measures, such as adjustments in indexation procedures and some initial parametric reforms. Prereform fiscal balances and (in some cases) projected prereform fiscal balance for the public schemes of the eight study countries indicate that deficits were invariably projected to increase over time (figure 1.1).

Figure 1.1   Projected Pension System Fiscal Balances before Reform in Eight CESE Countries

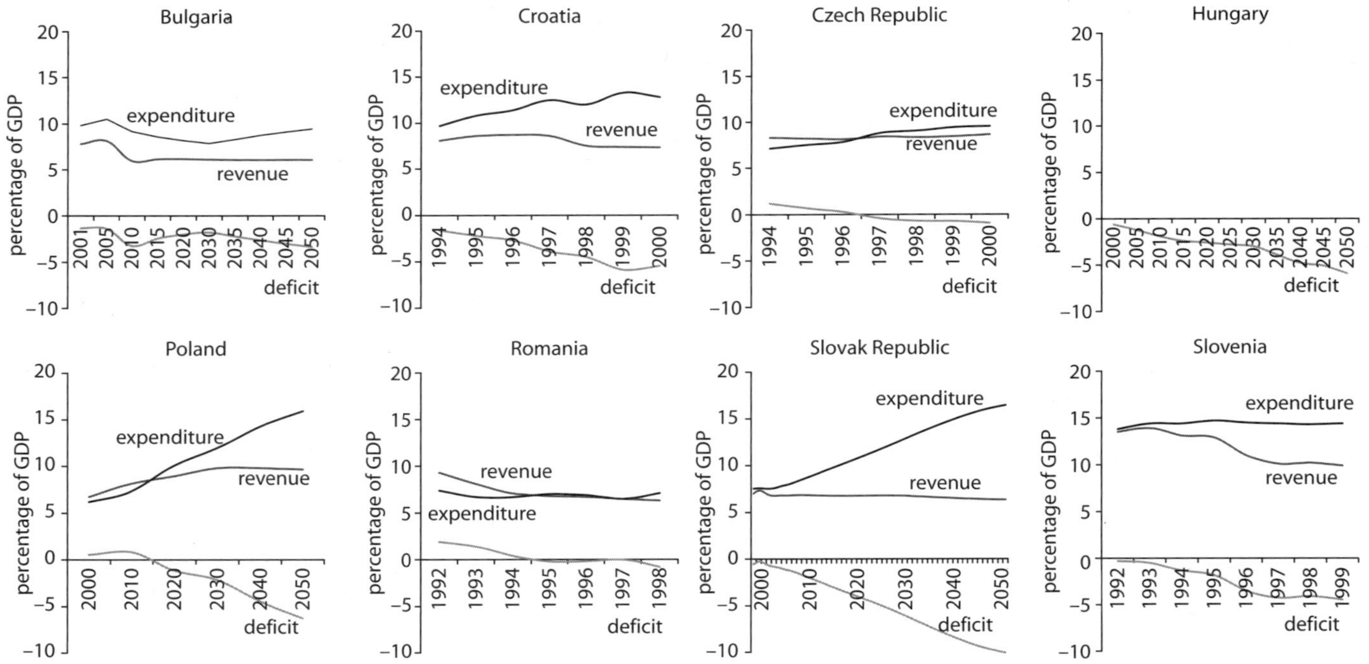

Sources: European Commission 2007, national ministries, and national social security institutions. For details, see individual country chapters.
Note: Projections of prereform expenditures and revenues were not available for Hungary; historical data are provided.

4

The long-term deterioration expected in the fiscal balances of the pension systems of the eight study countries will ultimately be driven by further population aging, a phenomenon common to all countries in the region. Projections of old-age dependency ratios (that is, the ratio of the population age 65 and older to the population age 15–64, a good proxy for the impact of aging on pay-as-you-go pension schemes) for six groups of countries is shown to highlight the relative magnitude of aging in the region (figure 1.2). These projections show that while aging in Central Europe and the Baltic region and in South Eastern Europe is currently less pronounced than it is in the EU15 countries (members of European Union before 2004), the rate of aging is higher, so that by 2050 the old-age dependency ratio in Central Europe and the Baltic region is expected to surpass that of the EU15, more than doubling in less than 50 years. For many of the countries in the region, old-age dependency ratios actually underestimate the impact of aging on their pay-as-you-go pension systems, because retirement ages in most of these countries are well below 65 and the number of pension system contributors, which declined during the transition, has shown no indication of returning to anywhere close to pretransition levels.

Figure 1.2   Old-Age Dependency Ratios, 2000–50, by World Region

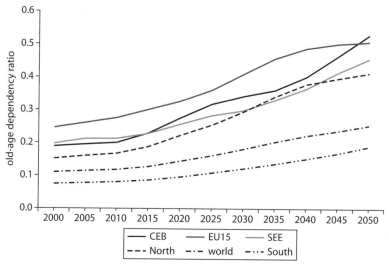

Source: Authors' estimates based on UN 2007.
Note: The old-age dependency ratio is the ratio of the population age 65 and older to the population age 15–64.
CEB = Central Europe and the Baltics; EU15 = members of European Union before 2004; SEE = Southeastern Europe.

In addition to the need to address issues of short- and long-term fiscal pressure, another common motivation for reform in CESE countries was to better allow their pension systems to function in a market economy. Their inherited pension systems shared a number of common features, including the use of unfunded (pay-as-you-go) financing based on contributions levied on wages; benefit formulas based on wages at retirement, with little linkage to lifetime contributions and often with a redistributive objective intended to support low-income earners; low retirement ages; and many privileges for special groups, despite the fact that most CESE countries had a single scheme that also covered civil servants and farmers. The special treatment given to many groups and the structure of benefits may have been conceptually aligned with public ownership of enterprises and centralized contribution payments. It became increasingly dysfunctional in a market economy with the privatization of large state enterprises and the emergence of small and medium-size enterprises and the self-employed. Moreover, the use of pay-as-you-go financing placed all risk on plan sponsors—that is, governments—which were also faced with the rapid aging of their populations. For their part, individuals were deprived of the opportunity to profit from the diversification of risk and the investment of their savings in emerging financial sectors.

At the beginning of economic transition, the financial sectors in CESE countries consisted only of state-owned banks. These banks catered to public enterprises and were essentially an arm of the central planning process. The financial instruments available to individuals and small enterprises were limited primarily to cash, often held in foreign currencies, and savings accounts yielding low nominal returns. Although the reform of banking systems (including bank privatization) and the establishment of insurance and securities markets were part and parcel of the reform process in all CESE countries, the development of financial systems takes time. Even today, the financial sectors of many CESE countries are less developed than those in countries elsewhere with similar income. This recognition contributed to the consideration of reforms, including the introduction of funded pension pillars, that were expected to accelerate financial market development, as they did in Chile (Holzmann 1997a).

Against this backdrop, all countries in the region initiated a process of pension reform motivated by the need to reform their existing systems and, in many (but not all) cases, by the trend toward multipillar structures, which started in Latin America. The publication of the World Bank's seminal report *Averting the Old-Age Crisis* (World Bank 1994), motivated in part by the reform challenges faced in Latin America, supported this trend. After reviewing the limited alternatives then being proposed by the literature—and then and now by the International Labour Organization—many reformers concluded that a more radical approach, including a move toward multipillar systems with mandatory fully funded, defined-contribution pension schemes, was required.[1]

Several transition economies have introduced multipillar pension systems. Hungary and Kazakhstan were the first to do so, in 1998. By 2008, 13 countries in the region had introduced funded pillars, with Ukraine conditionally scheduled to follow in 2010 or 2011. All CESE countries have undertaken parametric reforms, some significant, others basic. Some countries, including the Czech Republic and Slovenia, have resisted introducing mandated funded pillars; their pay-as-you-go schemes require additional parametric reforms to become sustainable. In Armenia, Montenegro, and Serbia, the debate over funded pillars continues. Albania, Azerbaijan, Bosnia and Herzegovina, the Kyrgyz Republic, and Turkmenistan have yet to undertake major reforms; they may need to defer consideration of funded pillars until preconditions have been met.

The countries that have undertaken multipillar reforms may have been inspired by the examples of Chile and other Latin American countries, but each of them has taken its own approach (table 1.1). Of the 14 countries that have legislated reforms, 12 have retained a main pay-as-you-go (first) pillar scheme. Mandatory funded (second-) pillar schemes supplementing first-pillar schemes are expected to diversify risk while providing roughly half of retirement income. The decision to retain first-pillar schemes was driven primarily by the major financing needs a full transition, such as Chile and Mexico implemented, would have called for.

The institutional arrangements for private pension funds vary across CESE countries; in most cases, they diverge from the Latin American examples with regard to sponsoring institutions and supervision. A number of CESE countries have taken innovative approaches to reforming their first-pillar schemes and have tried to learn from the experiences of Latin American countries in keeping the costs and fees of their funded second pillars low. The first-pillar reforms fully introduced in Latvia and Poland and partially introduced in the Russian Federation were inspired by the example of Sweden, which pioneered the use of NDCs, which mimic defined contribution schemes while remaining largely unfunded (see Holzmann and Palmer 2006). The introduction of a point system in Croatia, Romania, Serbia, the Slovak Republic, and Ukraine was inspired by the German and French systems. This system behaves like an NDC scheme but lacks many of its strengths.

Table 1.1 Characteristics of Multipillar Pension Reforms in Transition Economies

Country	Starting date	First (or zero) pillar	Size of second pillar (percentage of payroll)	Projected pension fund assets in 2020 (percentage of GDP)	Share of workforce in funded pillar in 2008 or earlier (percent)	Switching of rules to new system
Bulgaria	January 2002	Pay-as-you-go defined benefit	5.00	~25	70	Mandatory for workers under age 42
Croatia	January 2002	Pay-as-you-go defined benefit	5.00	25	80	Mandatory for workers under age 40, voluntary for workers age 40–50
Estonia	July 2002	Pay-as-you-go defined benefit	6.00	20	75	Voluntary (optout + 2)
Hungary	January 1998	Pay-as-you-go defined benefit	8.00	32	45	Mandatory for new entrants, voluntary for others
Kazakhstan	January 1998	Basic pension	10.00	35	82	Mandatory
Kosovo	January 2002	Universal/minimum consumption basket level	10.00	8	30	Mandatory
Latvia	July 2001 (NDC January 1996)	Pay-as-you-go defined contribution/ nonfinancial defined contribution	4.00, growing to 10.00 by 2010	25–30	72	Mandatory for workers under age 30, voluntary for workers age 30–50
Lithuania	January 2004	Pay-as-you-go defined benefit	5.50	35–40	55	Voluntary

Country	Date	First pillar			Second pillar
Macedonia	January 2006	Pay-as-you-go defined benefit	7.12	26	25	Mandatory for new entrants
Poland	January 1999	Pay-as-you-go defined contribution/ nonfinancial defined contribution	7.3	34	70	Mandatory for workers under 30, voluntary for workers 30–50
Romania	Registration completed; contributions began June 2008	Pay-as-you-go defined benefit	2 in 2008, growing gradually to 6 by 2016	9	65	Mandatory for workers under 35, voluntary for workers 36–45
Russia	January 2002	Pay-as-you-go defined contribution/ nonfinancial defined contribution	(6 in 2008)	—	33	Mandatory for workers under 50
Slovak Republic[a]	January 2005	Pay-as-you-go defined benefit	9	20	75	Mandatory for new entrants
Ukraine	July 2009 or January 2010	Pay-as-you-go defined benefit	2, growing to 7	16	—	Mandatory for new entrants

Source: Holzmann 2009.
— Not available.
Note: Data are as of January 2008. Systems are operating in all countries except Ukraine, where reforms have been partially legislated.
a. Made optional for new entrants in January 2008; participants were given six-month window to opt out (or in) of the second pillar.

The only CESE countries to follow Chile's approach to pension reform are Kazakhstan and Kosovo. Both countries rely exclusively on a basic (zero) pillar (a noncontributory scheme intended to provide a minimal level of income protection) and a mandated funded (second) pillar. In Kazakhstan, all workers were enrolled in the new scheme, although their rights under the old pay-as-you-go scheme were recognized (Hinz, Zviniene, and Vilamovska 2005). In Kosovo, after the conflict the new authorities had neither the means nor the records to recognize accrued rights. A special feature of the Kosovo scheme is that all assets are invested internationally, because the domestic market is not yet considered ready for local investing (Gubbels, Snelbecker, and Zezulin 2007).

Characteristics of Reformed Pension Systems

An accurate assessment of the adequacy and fiscal sustainability of a pension system must start from a clear understanding of its design. This section summarizes the key provisions of the reformed pension systems in the eight study countries as of January 2008. These provisions include the structure of the individual pillars of social insurance; the rules governing pension taxation; institutional structure; coverage; and the rules governing old-age, disability, and survivorship pensions. These provisions are then discussed within the framework developed by the World Bank, which generally recommends including a funded component if conditions are appropriate but which increasingly recognizes that a range of choices is available to policy makers to provide effective old-age protection in a manner that is fiscally responsible.

The World Bank suggests that pension systems be composed of some combination of five basic pillars:

- a noncontributory (or zero) pillar (in the form of a demogrant, social pension, or social assistance benefit) intended to provide a minimal level of income protection;
- a first-pillar contributory system linked to earnings, which seeks to replace a portion of preretirement income;
- a mandatory second pillar (essentially, individual savings accounts), which can be designed in various ways;
- a voluntary third pillar, which is flexible and discretionary (this pillar, too, can take a variety of forms); and
- a fourth pillar of informal intrafamily or intergenerational sources of financial and nonfinancial support to the elderly, including access to health care and housing (Holzmann and Hinz 2005).

Pillar Design

All of the reformed pension systems of the eight study countries provide old-age income support through some combination of all five of these pillars (table 1.2). All countries have a zero pillar, the purpose of which is to alleviate poverty among the elderly. In most countries, the zero pillar is part of a broader scheme of social assistance available to everyone, regardless of age, intended to guarantee a minimum income level. Three countries (Bulgaria, Hungary, and Slovenia) provide an age-related social pension specifically for the elderly. Zero pillars are all means tested (to target lower-income groups), universally publicly managed, noncontributory, and financed with general tax revenue. The amount of the benefit is typically adjusted to ensure that total household income meets some minimum state-defined level, which is often related to other forms of assistance and adjusted for inflation (or wage growth) on an ad hoc basis. The relation between the income level and the poverty line is often tenuous, and poverty lines vary widely across countries.

All eight countries reformed their existing pay-as-you-go, first-pillar schemes, all of which are earnings related in the sense that benefits in retirement depend, in varying degrees, on earnings received and contributions paid while working. The structure of their reformed schemes differs across countries. Bulgaria, the Czech Republic, Hungary, and Slovenia rely on a traditional defined-benefit design in which benefits depend on (a) some measure of assessed income, (b) an annual accrual rule (the percentage of assessed income that is replaced in benefits for each year of contributory service), and (c) the length of contributory service. In contrast, Croatia, Romania, and the Slovak Republic replaced their defined-benefit schemes with a system based on points. When appropriately implemented, such a system is functionally equivalent to a reformed defined-benefit system in which lifetime income is revalued relative to the average wage. Poland replaced its defined-benefit scheme with an NDC scheme that functionally mimics a funded defined-contribution system while remaining financed on a pay-as-you-go basis (plus a reserve fund). Contributions to the scheme are earmarked to individual accounts and remunerated with (notional) interest. At retirement, account balances in combination with conditional life expectancy are used to determine initial benefits.

Provisions for the remaining pillars are as follows:

- Six of the eight countries (Bulgaria, Croatia, Hungary, Poland, Romania, and the Slovak Republic) reduced first-pillar benefits for future

Table 1.2 Structure of Pension Systems in Eight CESE Countries

Country	Zero pillar (noncontributory) Provision (Public)	Type (MBB)	Function (Poverty)	First pillar (mandated, earning related) Provision (Public)	Type	Function (Insurance)	Second pillar (mandated, earnings related) Provision (Private)	Type	Function	Third pillar (voluntary) Provision (Private)	Type (FDC)	Function (Insurance)	Fourth pillar (health care) Provision (Public)	Function (Insurance)
Bulgaria	X	X	X	X	NDB	X	Private	FDC	Insurance	X	X	X	X	X
Croatia	X	X	X	X	NPS	X	Private	FDC	Insurance	X	X	X	X	X
Czech Republic	X	X	X	X	NDB	X	n.a.	n.a.	n.a.	X	X	X	X	X
Hungary	X	X	X	X	NDB	X	Private	FDC	Insurance	X	X	X	X	X
Poland	X	X	X	X	NDC	X	Private	FDC	Insurance	X	X	X	X	X
Romania	X	X	X	X	NPS	X	Private	FDC	Insurance	X	X	X	X	X
Slovak Republic	X	X	X	X	NPS	X	Private	FDC	Insurance	X	X	X	X	X
Slovenia	X	X	X	X	NDB	X	n.a.	n.a.	n.a.	X	X	X	X	X

Source: Unpublished World Bank pension database.
Note: MBB: means-tested basic benefit; NDB: nonfinancial defined benefit; NPS: nonfinancial point system; NDC: nonfinancial (notional) defined contribution; FDC: financial defined contribution.
n.a. Not applicable.
X Countries have these pillars.

12

beneficiaries and complemented their first-pillar schemes with mandated earnings-related, funded second-pillar schemes. These schemes are defined-contribution schemes that rely on privately managed pension funds for administration and asset management.

- All eight countries introduced voluntary funded, third-pillar schemes to provide individuals with a mechanism for supplementing the benefits paid by the mandatory pillars. These schemes rely on private-sector financial institutions—such as insurance companies, mutual funds, and pension funds—for administration and asset management.
- All eight countries provide health insurance on a contributory basis to the active population. Health insurance schemes extend to retirees receiving public pensions. Access to this fourth pillar is crucially important for the design of a pension system and its target levels of income replacement.

Taxation of Contributions and Benefits

The taxation of contributions and benefits for each pillar of a pension system has major bearing on the adequacy of pension benefits and the degree to which take-home pay is actually replaced in retirement. The difference between gross replacement rates (the ratio of benefits disbursed to pretax preretirement earnings) and net replacement rates (the ratio of benefits actually received to posttax preretirement earnings) is usually substantial. What matters for the elderly is the amount of their net pension, because it is on this basis that they finance their consumption in retirement. Taxation of pension contributions, investment returns (during the accumulation phase of funded schemes), and benefits upon disbursement range widely across the eight study countries and across the individual pillars of their pension systems (table 1.3).

Among pension policy experts, there is consensus that earnings-related schemes should be subject to some form of taxation; there is less agreement on whether earnings-related schemes should be subject to comprehensive income taxation or expenditure (consumption) taxation. Such taxation is generally considered to be less distortionary with regard to savings decisions (decisions relating to whether to consume now or in the future).

Certain principles apply to the taxation of retirement "savings" (box 1.1). These principles are typically applied to funded schemes but should also be applied to unfunded schemes.

For noncontributory zero-pillar schemes, the first two opportunities for taxation do not exist, and means-tested benefits in all study

Table 1.3 Taxation of Retirement Savings in Eight CESE Countries

Country	First pillar (earnings related)			Second pillar (earnings related)			Third pillar (voluntary)			Fourth pillar (health care)		
	Contributions	Investments/ capital gains	Benefits	Contributions	Investments/ capital gains	Benefits	Contributions	Investments/ capital gains	Benefits	Contributions	Investments/ Capital Gains	Benefits
Bulgaria	Exempt	Exempt	Exempt	Exempt	Exempt	Exempt	Exempt[a]	Exempt	Taxed	Exempt	n.a.	Exempt
Croatia	Exempt	Exempt	Taxed	Exempt	Exempt	Taxed	Exempt[b]	Exempt	Taxed	Exempt	n.a.	Exempt
Czech Republic	Taxed[c]	Exempt	Exempt[d]	n.a.	n.a.	n.a.	Exempt[e]	Exempt	Taxed	Taxed	n.a.	Exempt
Hungary	Taxed	Exempt	Exempt	Taxed	Exempt	Exempt[f]	Exempt[g]	Exempt	Exempt[h]	Exempt	n.a.	Exempt
Poland	Exempt	Exempt	Taxed	Exempt	Exempt	Taxed	Taxed[i]	Exempt[j]	Exempt	Exempt	n.a.	Exempt
Romania	Exempt	Exempt	Taxed	Exempt	Exempt	Taxed	Exempt[k]	Exempt	Taxed	Exempt	n.a.	Exempt
Slovak Republic	Exempt	Exempt	Exemp	Exempt	Taxed	Exempt	Exempt[l]	Taxed	Taxed	Exempt	n.a.	Exempt
Slovenia	Exempt	Exempt	Taxed	n.a.	n.a.	n.a.	Exempt[m]	Exempt	Taxed	Exempt	n.a.	Exempt

Source: European Commission 2007, national ministries, and national social security institutions. For details, see the individual country chapters.

Note: All benefits under the noncontributory (zero) pillar are exempt from taxation.

n.a. Not applicable.

a. Contributions up to 10 percent of earnings are exempt from the taxation. Contributions up to lev 60 per worker per month paid by employers are exempt from the corporate income tax base.

b. Contributions up to HRK 12,000 a year can be deducted from personal income for tax purposes.

c. Since January 1, 2008, contributions paid to the first pillar are part of the income tax base, consistent with the tax reform that introduced a flat tax of 15 percent.

d. Pensioners are provided with a large tax allowance on pension income. Pensioners with total taxable income of less than 80 percent of average earnings do not pay income taxes, exempting pensions from taxation for all pensioners except those with substantial supplementary income. Pensioners who are taxed pay a rate lower than that levied on earnings. Pensions thus pay substantially less in taxes than workers with the same total income.

e. Contributions of CZK 6,000–2,000 and employer contributions up to 5 percent of wage are tax exempt.

f. There is great uncertainty regarding the taxation of benefits after 2013.

g. Thirty percent of contributions are tax deductible up to an annual cap of HK$100,000.

h. Benefits are exempt from tax if taken as a qualified annuity and the accumulation period is at least 20 years. If the accumulation period is 10–20 years, benefits are partially taxed.

i. Employer contributions to the third pillar are deductible from the employer's taxable income.

j. Employees are granted tax relief up to 150 percent of the average wage, above which they must pay taxes for capital gains and retirement savings.

k. Up to EURO 200 per year per participant is tax exempt.

l. Up to Sk 12,000 annually is exempt from taxation.

m. Up to 24 percent of contributions to the first pillar are tax exempt.

Box 1.1

Taxation of Retirement Savings

Like other forms of savings, retirement savings can be taxed when contributions are made; as investment income and capital gains accrue (except, of course, in pay-as-you-go pension schemes); or when benefits are actually paid. Four of the eight possible combinations are examined in the table below for a hypothetical contribution of 100 units of currency made five years before a worker's retirement. Investments are assumed to earn a 10 percent annual rate of return; the tax rate is assumed to be 25 percent.

Table   Retirement Benefits Paid under Various Tax Regimes

Item	Exempt-exempt-taxed (EET)	Taxed-taxed-exempt (TTE)	Taxed-exempt-exempt (TEE)	Exempt-taxed-taxed (ETT)
Initial contribution	100	100	100	100
Taxes levied on contribution	0	2	25	0
Initial account balance	100	75	75	100
Investment returns net of taxes	61	46	33	44
Ending account balance	161	121	108	144
Taxes paid on distributions	40	0	0	36
Pension net of taxes	121	121	108	108

Source: Whitehouse 1999.

In this stylized illustration, the first two regimes—exempt-exempt-taxed (EET), in which contributions and investment income are exempt from taxation but benefits are taxed, and taxed-exempt-exempt (TEE), in which contributions are taxed but investment income and benefits are exempt from taxation—provide the same level of postretirement income. Both also provide the same present value of tax revenues, although the revenues under EET (a classic expenditure tax) are deferred until the worker retires whereas revenues under TEE (a prepaid expenditure tax) are received earlier. The remaining two regimes (both comprehensive income taxation) provide equivalent levels of postretirement income and tax revenues. Relative to expenditure taxes, however, they yield more taxes and lower overall rewards for saving.

countries are low enough that they are not subject to income taxes, making zero-pillar schemes effectively fully exempt from taxation in the eight study countries.[2]

Taxation of first-pillar schemes varies. Bulgaria and the Slovak Republic fully exempt benefits from taxation; Croatia, Poland, Romania, and Slovenia have classic expenditure taxes. The Czech Republic and Hungary have prepaid expenditure taxes. All countries but one that have introduced mandatory second pillars apply the same rules to their second-pillar schemes as they apply to their first-pillar schemes. The exception is the Slovak Republic, where the first pillar is fully exempt from taxation but investment income and capital gains under the second pillar are taxed.

Taxation of voluntary third-pillar schemes varies widely across the eight study countries (as well as with respect to the way in which first- and second-pillar schemes are taxed). All eight countries exempt contributions, investment income, and capital gains (except the Slovak Republic); all countries except Hungary and Poland tax benefits (consistent with an expenditure tax approach). Because voluntary schemes are more popular with higher-income groups, the exemption of benefits is regressive. All countries except the Czech Republic tax health care contributions; all countries exempt health care benefits from taxation.

Benefits from Zero-Pillar Schemes

All eight countries provide minimum old-age benefits, aimed at alleviating poverty among the elderly. In most countries benefits are part of a broader noncontributory program of social assistance available to everyone, regardless of age, intended to guarantee a minimum income level, independent of other individual characteristics (table 1.4). Such means-tested programs were necessary in transition economies, because only certain categories (such as people with disabilities) were eligible for social assistance under central planning; everyone else had access, in principle, to paid employment followed by a pension. Once central planning was abandoned, this was no longer the case.[3]

With the abolition of most categorical benefits and the introduction of a guaranteed minimum income level for everyone, most CESE countries have been reluctant to address the problem of poverty among the elderly with social pensions. Social pensions provide an income guarantee, but they apply only to people of a certain age. Moreover, while benefits are typically higher than general social assistance benefits, means-testing is typically less intrusive.

Table 1.4 Basic Pension Benefits from the Zero Pillar in Eight CESE Countries

Country	Benefit	Coverage/Eligibility	Year	Benefit level	Indexation	Number of beneficiaries	Total expenditure (percentage of GDP)
Bulgaria[a]	Social pension	Individuals above age 70 who are not collecting a pension; average income per family member must be lower than the guaranteed minimum income for full 12-month period	2006	63 leva (17.75 percent of average wage)	50 percent prices, 50 percent wage growth previous year	4,592 (0.2 percent of total pensioners) in 2005	—
Croatia	Guaranteed minimum income	Individuals with income below guaranteed minimum income	n.a.	Percentage of state-defined subsistence allowance	Ad hoc	2.7 percent of population in 2005	0.22
Czech Republic	Guaranteed minimum income	Individuals with income below guaranteed minimum income	2006	3,126 koruny	Prices	About 4 percent of households	—
Hungary	Old-age allowance	Individuals age 62 and older with income below 80 percent of minimum old-age pension	n.a.	Supplements actual income to reach 80 percent of old-age minimum pension	Old-age minimum pension	6,679 beneficiaries (0.4 percent of population age 62 and older) in 2003	0.01
Poland[b]	Guaranteed minimum income	Individuals with income below guaranteed minimum income	2006	About 16 percent of average wage	Regular increases based on social assistance legislation	—	—

(continued)

Table 1.4 Basic Pension Benefits from the Zero Pillar in Eight CESE Countries (continued)

Country	Benefit	Coverage/Eligibility	Year	Benefit level	Indexation	Number of beneficiaries	Total expenditure (percentage of GDP)
Romania	Guaranteed minimum income	Individuals with income below guaranteed minimum income	2006	RON 92 (9 percent of average wage)	Changes in consumer price index	834,000 beneficiaries in 2005	0.2
Slovak Republic	Guaranteed minimum income	Individuals with income below guaranteed minimum income	2006	Sk 4,980 (about 27 percent of average wage)	Minimum subsistence level (close to consumer price index)	182,479 beneficiaries in 2007[c]	0.45
Slovenia	State pension	Individuals 65 and older who do not qualify for a pension from the first-pillar pension scheme[d]	n.a.	One-third of minimum pension assessment base	Growth of minimum pension assessment base	—	—

Source: European Commission 2007, national ministries, and national social security institutions. For details, see individual country chapters.

— Not available.

a. Another noncontributory source of income support for the elderly comes from the guaranteed minimum income, which provides a means-tested benefit.

b. There is also a minimum pension guarantee under the old-age pension system. For pensioners who contributed for at least 25 years (men) or 20 years (women) whose total pension falls below a certain threshold, the difference is topped up from the state budget. In 2008 the guaranteed benefit was Zl 636 per month. Minimum pensions are taxed according to the general PIT (Personal Income Tax) taxation rules.

c. About 21.2 percent of all beneficiaries (38,606 people) are of pensionable age.

d. Beneficiaries must also have lived in Slovenia for at least 30 years between the ages of 15 and 65.

Three countries (Bulgaria, Hungary, and Slovenia) offer social pensions in addition to the general social assistance scheme. In Bulgari,a social pensions are provided to individuals age 70 and older who are not collecting old-age or disability pensions. Eligibility is based on average income per family member. The allowance is means tested and adjusted in value such that the beneficiary's total income reaches the minimum threshold (roughly 18 percent of the average wage). In Hungary, eligibility is limited to individuals age 62 and older who can demonstrate that their total income falls below 80 percent (95 percent for couples) of the minimum old-age pension. In Slovenia, eligibility is limited to individuals age 65 and older who have lived in Slovenia for at least 30 years and who do not qualify for an old-age pension. Benefits are equal to one-third of the minimum pension assessment base.

Benefits from Earnings-Related First- and Second-Pillar Schemes

Earnings-related, first-pillar pension schemes in all eight study countries provide old-age pensions, disability pensions, and survivorship benefits. Second-pillar schemes are structured primarily to provide old-age pensions only. The key characteristics of each of these types of benefits across all eight countries are discussed in this section.

Old-age benefits. Earnings-related, first-pillar pension schemes—and (for countries that have them) second-pillar schemes—exhibit both similarities and differences in terms of eligibility conditions and benefit provisions across the eight study countries (table 1.5). The most significant of these conditions and provisions are vesting periods, contribution rates, contribution ceilings, benefit calculations, retirement ages, and benefit indexation.

VESTING PERIODS. Vesting periods (that is, the minimum period of contributory service needed to qualify for a pension upon reaching the minimum or normal retirement age) are typical of traditional defined-benefit schemes. They serve to prevent a form of arbitrage in which people work for only a few years to become eligible for a minimum (in some cases, a flat) benefit worth far more than the contributions they paid toward their benefits. In actuarially fair pension systems (that is, systems in which the lifetime value of a person's benefits is, by design, roughly equal on average to the lifetime value of his or her contributions), vesting periods are unnecessary, except for determining eligibility for a minimum pension. To

Table 1.5 Eligibility for and Benefits Provided by Old-Age Pensions in Eight CESE Countries

Country	Pillar	Vesting period	Contribution rate	Contribution ceiling	Benefit rate	Pension assessment base	Retirement age	Benefit indexation
Bulgaria[a]	First	15 years	TCR: 23.00 percent (14.95 percent by employer, 8.05 percent by employee)	Fixed annually in budget (1,400 leva in 2007, roughly 350 percent of average wage)	1 percent per year	Highest 3 of last 15 years before 1997 plus entire working period afterward	63 for men; gradually increasing to 60 for women by 2009	50 percent prices, 50 percent wage growth of previous year
	Second	No minimum	PCR: 5 percent (for people born after 1959)	Fixed annually in budget (1,400 leva in 2007)	Varies depending on life expectancy at retirement and rate of return	Accumulated funds	63 for men; gradually increasing to 60 for women by 2009	Income stream from conversion of capital accumulation
Croatia	First	15 years	TCR: 20 percent (all from employee)	5 times average wage	0.75 percent in 2008, decreasing over time (0.25 percent of average wage and 25.00 percent of Swiss-indexed point value for second-pillar participants)	Flat rate plus Swiss-indexed lifetime earnings for second-pillar participants	60 for women, 65 for men	50 percent prices, 50 percent wages
	Second	15 years	PCR: 5 percent (all from employee)	5 times average wage	Varies depending on life expectancy at retirement and rate of return	Accumulated funds	60 for women, 65 for men	Price-indexed annuity

Czech Republic	First	35 years at normal retirement age by 2019; 20 years for people who retire 5 or more years after normal retirement age	TCR: 28.00 percent (21.5 percent by employer, 6.5 by employee)	None	Flat benefit plus 1.5 percent per year	Gradually increasing to average of last 30 years' earnings by 2016	By 2030 65; for all men and for women with no or one child, 64 for women with 2 children, 63 for women with 3 children, and 62 for women with more than 3 children	Minimum of prices plus one-third of real wage growth
Hungary	First	15 years at age 62 under special (strict) conditions; 20 years normally	TCR: 33.5 percent (24.0 percent by employer, 9.5 percent by employee)	Employee: Set annually by government, at about 8 times minimum wage Employer: No maximum	Until 2013: 33.00 percent for first 10 years, 2.00 percent for 11–25.00 years, 1.00 percent for 26–36 years, and 1.50 percent beyond 36 years After 2013: 1.65 percent per year	Average lifetime earnings revalued by wage growth	62 for men; 62 for women by 2009	50 percent prices, 50 percent wages
	Second	No minimum	PCR: 8 percent (all from employee)	Employee: Set annually by government, at about eight times minimum wage Employer: No maximum	Varies depending on life expectancy at retirement and rate of return	Accumulated funds	62 for men; 62 for women by 2009	50 percent prices, 50 percent wage, indexed annuity

(continued)

Table 1.5   Eligibility for and Benefits Provided by Old-Age Pensions in Eight CESE Countries *(continued)*

Country	Pillar	Vesting period	Contribution rate	Contribution ceiling	Benefit rate	Pension assessment base	Retirement age	Benefit indexation
Poland[b]	First	No minimum; individuals are eligible for minimum pension after 20 years (women) and 25 years (men)	PCR: 19.52 percent (9.76 percent by employer, 9.76 percent by employee)	2.5 times national average wage	Varies depending on life expectancy at retirement and notional rate of return	Notional capital accumulation	Gradually increasing to 65 for men by 2014 and 60 for women by 2009	Mixed price-wage formula, in which wages account for 20 percent of indexation
	Second	None; individuals are eligible for minimum pension after 20 years (women) and 25 years (men)	PCR: 7.3 percent (all from employee)	2.5 times national average wage	Varies depending on life expectancy at retirement and rate of return	Capital accumulation	Gradually increasing to 65 for men by 2014 and 60 for women by 2009	Price-indexed annuity
Romania[c]	First	15 years	TCR: 29.75 percent (20.25 percent by employer, 9.50 percent by employee)	None	Based on number of wage-indexed points earned	Lifetime average indexed to nominal wage growth	Gradually increasing to 65 for men and 60 for women by 2015	Adjusted based on changes in point value (cannot fall below 45 percent of average wage)

	Second	Not established by new law	PCR: 2 percent increasing to 6 percent over period of 8 years	None	Varies depending on life expectancy at retirement and rate of return	Capital accumulation	Gradually increasing to 65 for men and 60 for women by 2015	Specific regulation does not yet exist
Slovak Republic	First pillar	15 years	PCR: 28.75 percent: 18.00 percent old-age (4.00 percent by employee, 14.00 percent by employer); 6.00 percent disability (3.00 percent by employee, 3.00 percent by employer); 4.75 percent reserve fund (100.00 percent by employer)	3 times average wage	1.19 percent per year (based on number of wage-indexed points earned)	Lifetime average indexed to nominal wage growth	62 for men; gradually increasing to 62 for women by 2016	50 percent prices, 50 percent nominal wage growth
	Second	10 years	PCR: 9 percent (all old-age) (all from employee)	3 times average wage	Varies depending on life expectancy at retirement and rate of return	Accumulated funds	62 for men; gradually increasing to 62 for women by 2015	Depends on options chosen

(continued)

Table 1.5   Eligibility for and Benefits Provided by Old-Age Pensions in Eight CESE Countries *(continued)*

Country	Pillar	Vesting period	Contribution rate	Contribution ceiling	Benefit rate	Pension assessment base	Retirement age	Benefit indexation
Slovenia	First	15 years	TCR: 24.35 percent (15.5 percent employee, 8.85 percent employer)	No maximum	35 percent for men, 38 percent for women for first 15 years of contribution; 1.5 percent per year beyond 15 years	Gradually increased to best 18 years in 2008	Gradually increasing to 63 for men by 2009 and 61 for women by 2023	Wage growth

Sources: European Commission 2007, national ministries, and national social security institutions. For details, see the individual country chapters.

Note: TCR = total contribution rate (including contributions to both the first and the second pillar, where applicable); PCR = pillar-specific contribution rate; n.a. = Not applicable.

a. In addition to the main (universal) defined = contribution scheme, there are also fully funded defined = contribution schemes as part of the second pillar.

b. The total contribution rate is 27.92 percent (19.52 percent for old-age pensions, 6.00 percent for disability pensions, and 2.45 percent for sickness and maternity benefits). Individuals participating in only the first pillar pay 19.52 percent to the first pillar for old-age pensions (split equally between employers and employees). Individuals participating in both the first and the second pillars pay 12.22 percent to the first pillar (9.76 percent paid by employers and 2.46 percent paid by employees) and 7.3 percent to the second pillar (paid entirely by employees). Employers pay contributions for work injury. The rate varies by industry.

c. Total contribution rate will be reduced to 28 percent (18.5 percent by employer, 9.5 percent by employee) in 2009.

avoid the payment of pensions on small amounts, lump-sum payments can be provided.

Of the eight study countries, only Poland—with its combination of an NDC first-pillar scheme and a defined contribution second pillar—has an actuarially fair system. As a result, it is the only country not to specify a vesting period, although eligibility for its minimum pension is subject to a minimum contributory period of 20 years for women and 25 years for men. In all other study countries, vesting periods for first-pillar benefits are 10, 15, 20, or 25 years.

Some countries (such as Croatia and the Slovak Republic) but not others impose vesting periods on second-pillar benefits. Because defined contribution schemes are, by construction, actuarially fair, vesting periods for second-pillar schemes are theoretically unnecessary; it is possible that they are imposed for administrative reasons or out of the desire for consistency with first-pillar rules. In practice, vesting periods tend to reduce incentives to enroll in voluntary schemes as well as the effectiveness of an actuarially fair structure with regard to labor supply decisions.

CONTRIBUTION RATES. Contribution rates for first-pillar schemes in most of the eight study countries collectively cover the cost of old-age and disability pensions as well as survivorship benefits. The exceptions are Poland, where old-age pensions have an earmarked contribution rate of 19.52 percent, and the Slovak Republic, where the contribution rate is 18 percent. Contribution rates in the other seven countries range from 20.0 percent (in Croatia) to 28.0 percent (in the Czech Republic) and 24.35 percent (in Slovenia), neither of which has a second-pillar scheme. Contribution rates for second-pillar schemes range from 5 percent (in Bulgaria and Croatia) to 9 percent (in the Slovak Republic). In most countries they are being phased in gradually. In Romania, for example, the contribution rate, initially set at 2 percent, is gradually being increased such that it will reach 6 percent by 2016. Assuming that the contribution required to fund disability benefits is roughly 6–8 percentage points of the total pension levy, second-pillar contribution rates in the study countries are roughly a third the size of first-pillar contribution rates for old-age pensions (including survivorship benefits).

CONTRIBUTION CEILINGS. Contribution ceilings differ widely across the study countries. Three countries (the Czech Republic, Romania, and Slovenia) have no ceilings. In three countries the ceiling is set as a multiple of the average wage (5 times the average wage in Croatia, 3 times the average wage in the Slovak Republic, and 2.5 the average wage in Poland). In Bulgaria and Hungary, the government sets the ceiling annually. Contribution ceilings limit the scope of a public pension scheme's mandate and create space for higher-income workers to diversify their retirement savings outside of mandated schemes. The absence of a ceiling, in combination with limits on the pension assessment base (that is, the wages on which benefits are based, an issue discussed below) introduces progressiveness, which has implications not only for retirement savings but also for labor supply decisions for higher-income workers.

BENEFIT CALCULATIONS.   Benefit calculations changed greatly in many of the study countries as a result of their reforms. By construction the pension assessment base in Poland (which introduced an NDC first-pillar scheme) and in Croatia, Romania, and the Slovak Republic (all of which introduced first-pillar schemes based on points) represents the revaluing of lifetime contributory income. The remaining four study countries, which introduced only parametric reforms, also extended the pension assessment, to 18 years in Slovenia, 30 years by 2016 in the Czech Republic, and lifetime earnings in Bulgaria and Hungary. Explicit and implicit rates of accrual (that is, the percentage of the assessment base that is effectively replaced in benefits for each year of contributory service) have also been reduced, particularly in countries that introduced second-pillar schemes. Benefits provided by funded second-pillar defined-contribution schemes will be based on accumulated contributions and investment income, net of fees and expenses, at retirement. In most cases the rules governing the payout of benefits and the institutional arrangements required for the payout phase have yet to be established, although most countries appear to envisage the provision of annuities by private life insurance companies.[4]

RETIREMENT AGES. Retirement ages are being raised in all of the study countries. Retirement ages for men have been increased (or are in the process of being increased) to 62 in Hungary and the Slovak Republic; to 63 in Bulgaria, the Czech Republic, and Slovenia; and to 65 in Croatia, Poland, and Romania. Retirement ages for women are also being increased (typically to 60), although they remain below those for men. Only Hungary and the Slovak Republic currently intend to establish gender neutrality.

BENEFIT INDEXATION. Benefit indexation for first-pillar benefits is now automatic in all eight study countries, although the form of indexation varies. Slovenia indexes benefits on the basis of nominal wage growth. Five countries use Swiss indexation (whereby benefits are indexed using a combination of inflation and nominal wage growth). These include Bulgaria, Croatia, and the Slovak Republic (which weight inflation and nominal wage growth equally); Poland (where inflation is given a weight of 80 percent); and the Czech Republic (where benefits are indexed on the basis of inflation plus one-third of real wage growth). Given that nominal wages tend to rise faster than prices, these differences have implications for the future adequacy of benefits and the fiscal sustainability of first-pillar schemes. Benefit adequacy tends to be negatively effected, fiscal sustainability positively.

The indexation of second-pillar benefits includes price-indexed annuities (in Croatia and Poland) and Swiss indexation (in Hungary). It has not yet been determined in all of the study countries.

Disability benefits. Disability benefits in all eight study countries continue to be provided almost entirely through first-pillar arrangements, in most cases with only tenuous integration with second-pillar schemes. The enduring linkage between provisions for disability and old-age pensions may merit reconsideration, because the risks of aging (including the risk that people might outlive their savings) need not be linked, practically or theoretically, with the risks of disability and should be assessed and priced independently (Holzmann and Hinz 2005). As a result of this enduring linkage, eligibility criteria and the design of disability benefits reflect the provisions of the old defined-benefit systems (table 1.6).

In all of the study countries, the vesting period for disability benefits increases with the age of the insured, typically reaching five years of contributory service by age 30 or (alternatively) one-third of an insured's working life from age 20 onward. Contributory service credit is awarded for service that would have been performed from the point of an individual's disability to the normal retirement age (the generosity of this credit varies across the study countries). Benefit eligibility requires an individual to have lost at least 30–67 percent of his or her working capacity, depending on the country. Some countries provide both partial and full disability pensions, while others provide only full disability pensions. Most countries have shifted from defining disability as the loss of capacity to perform a particular job to the loss of capacity to perform any job. Benefit determination—with regard to both the pension assessment base and the benefit rate—is based on

Table 1.6 Eligibility for and Benefits Provided by Disability Pensions in Eight CESE Countries

Country	Vesting period	Contribution rate	Eligibility	Benefit rate	Partial pension
Bulgaria	Under age 20: No minimum Age 20–25: 1 year Age 25–30: 3 years Over age 30: 5 years	No specific contribution rate	At least 50 percent loss in working capacity	1 percent per year	—
Croatia	Minimum coverage of one-third of working life above age 20 (26 for individuals with a university degree)	No specific contribution rate	Permanent loss in capacity for general disability pension; at least 50 percent loss in capacity for partial disability pension	1 percent per year for average worker	80 percent
Czech Republic	Under age 20: Less than 1 year Age 20–22: 1 year Age 22–24: 2 years Age 24–26: 3 years Age 26–28: 4 years Over age 28: 5 years	No specific contribution rate	At least 66 percent loss in capacity for full disability; at least 33 percent loss in capacity for partial disability pension	Full disability: Flat benefit + 1.50 percent a year Partial disability: Flat benefit + 0.75 percent a year	Flat benefit + 0.75 percent per year
Hungary	Under age 22: 2 years Age 22–24: 4 years Age 25–29: 6 years Age 30–34: 8 years Age 35–44: 10 years Age 45–54: 15 years Age 55 and above: 20 years	No specific contributions (estimated to be roughly 4 percent)	At least 67 percent loss in capacity to work	37.5–100.00 percent of average individual earnings, depending on level of disability and years of service	37.5–63.00 percent of average individual earnings

Country	Qualifying period	Contribution rate	Disability condition	Benefit calculation	Partial disability
Poland	Under age 20: 1 year Age 20–22: 2 years Age 22–30: 4 years Over age 30: 5 years	6.00 percent (4.5 percent by employer, 1.5 percent by employee), up to ceiling of 2.5 times average wage	Total or partial incapacity to work	Flat benefit of 24.00 percent of reference wage + 1.30 percent for each year of contribution + 0.07 percent for each noncontributory year	75 percent of total disability pension
Romania	Under age 25: 5 years Age 25–31: 8 years Age 31–37: 11 years Age 37–43: 14 years Age 43–49: 18 years Age 49–55: 22 year Over age 55: 25 years	No specific contribution rate	At least 50 percent loss in capacity to work	Calculated on the basis of number of points	Reduced benefits based on level of disability
Slovak Republic	Under age 20: Less than 1 year Age 20–22: 1 year Age 22–24: 2 years Age 24–26: 3 years Age 26–28: 4 years Over age 28: 5 years	6 percent (3 percent by employer, 3 percent by employee), up to ceiling of 3 times average wage	At least 40 percent loss in capacity to work	1.19 percent per year	Prorated if disability is 40–70 percent
Slovenia	Contributed at least one-third of the period between age 20 and time of disability	No specific contributions	At least 30 percent loss in capacity to work	Based on level of disability: 10–24 percent of minimum pension for full pension qualifying period	Pro-rated on the basis of level of disability

Sources: European Commission 2007, national ministries, and national social security institutions. For details, see the individual country chapters.
— = Not available.

old-age benefit formulas. This is also true for indexation policies. Disability benefits from second-pillar schemes generally take the form of lump-sum distributions or annuities. In some countries (such as Croatia), accumulated funds in second-pillar accounts are transferred to the accounts of the first-pillar scheme when first-pillar disability benefits exceed the combined benefit that would have been paid under both the first and second pillars.

Survivor benefits. Survivor benefits in all eight study countries continue to be closely linked to provisions governing old-age pensions (table 1.7). Eligibility is tied to the eligibility of the deceased for an old-age or disability pension. Eligible survivors include widows, widowers, children, and in some countries parents and siblings who were dependent on the deceased. The benefit rate varies but is typically about 50 percent, with supplements for additional eligible survivors. Total family benefits generally cannot exceed the benefit to which the deceased was entitled. For children eligibility generally ends when they start work, finish their studies, or reach age 25 or 26. For spouses eligibility depends on whether the spouse is capable of working (that is, not disabled, not caring for a child, and not too old work). If spouses are capable of working, benefits can be limited to a year (as they are in the Czech Republic, Hungary, Poland, Slovak Republic, and Slovenia). Rules regarding remarriage vary: eligibility ends only for spouses below retirement age in Hungary, and ends immediately in Bulgaria. Accumulated assets in second-pillar accounts are typically disbursed in a lump sum or installments if the deceased was of working age. If the deceased was already receiving an annuity, continuation of benefits depends on whether a single or joint annuity had been purchased. Overall, reforms left provisions governing survivorship largely intact, although in some cases eligibility criteria were tightened.

No efforts have been made by the study countries to integrate survivor benefits with second-pillar provisions (Holzmann and Hinz 2005). Given that female participation in the workforce is likely to expand and divorce rates are expected to continue to rise, survivor benefits for spouses may merit reconsideration.

Structure of Third- and Fourth-Pillar Schemes
Both the availability of voluntary retirement savings programs to supplement the benefits of mandated schemes and access to health care are central to the design of a pension system. This section examines both.

Table 1.7   Eligibility for and Benefits Provided by Survivor Pensions in Eight CESE Countries

Country	Eligibility	Spouse replacement rate	Benefit duration	Remarriage test	Orphan age limit	Orphan replacement rate	Total family benefit
Bulgaria	Eligibility of deceased for old-age or disability pension	One survivor: 50 percent Two survivors: 75 percent Three or more survivors: 100 percent or 20 percent of pension of deceased spouse as supplement to surviving spouse's personal pension	For life if spouse is disabled or has reached retirement age	Pension ceases if survivor remarries	26	One survivor: 50 percent Two survivors: 75 percent Three or more survivors: 100 percent	100 percent regardless of number of survivors,
Croatia	Eligibility of deceased for old-age or disability pension; minimum of 5 years of coverage or 10 years of qualifying periods by the deceased	70 percent if spouse is only survivor	For life unless spouse remarries; also for life upon remarriage if spouse remarries but is older than 50 and disabled	Pension ceases if survivor remarries and is younger than 50 unless disabled	26	70 percent if orphan is only survivor	One survivor: 70 percent of deceased's pension Two survivors: 80 percent Three survivors: 90 percent Four or more survivors: 100 percent
Czech Republic	Eligibility of deceased for old-age or disability pension	Flat benefit + 50 percent deceased's pension	For life if spouse is 70 percent disabled, taking care of a child or a dependent parent, or is 55 (women) or 58 (men); otherwise one year	Pension ceases if survivor remarries	26	Flat benefit + 40 percent	No maximum

(continued)

Table 1.7 Eligibility for and Benefits Provided by Survivor Pensions in Eight CESE Countries (*continued*)

Country	Eligibility	Spouse replacement rate	Benefit duration	Remarriage test	Orphan age limit	Orphan replacement rate	Total family benefit
Hungary	Eligibility of deceased for old-age or disability pension	50 percent of deceased's pension (20 percent if receiving own pension)	For life if spouse is disabled, caring for at least two children, or is past retirement age; 12 or 18 months if spouse is caring for a child	Remarriage test before retirement age, none thereafter	25	30 percent; 60 percent of higher of the two pensions if orphan lost both parents	Cannot exceed benefit to which deceased was entitled
Poland	Eligibility of deceased for old-age or disability pension	85 percent deceased's pension if sole surviving relative	For life if spouse is disabled, taking care of a child, or above age 50; otherwise one year	Benefits paid even if survivor remarries	25	85 percent if sole survivor	Two survivors: 90 percent Three and more survivors: 95 percent
Romania	Eligibility of deceased for old-age or disability pension	50 percent of deceased's pension if married for 15 years; 0.5 percent for each month less than 15 years up to a minimum of 10 years; 50 percent of deceased's pension if spouse is disabled and married for at least one year; 50 percent if spouse has children under age 7	For life if married for 15 years; married for 10 years with benefit reduction; disable and married for at least one year. Otherwise and with children, temporary until youngest child reaches age 7. Else for 6 months if none of spouse replacement conditions is met	Benefits paid even if survivor remarries	26	50 percent if sole survivor	Two survivors: 75 percent Three or more survivors: 100 percent

Slovak Republic	Eligibility of deceased for old-age or disability pension	60 percent of deceased's pension	For life, if spouse is 70 percent disabled, is caring for a child, or is at retirement age; otherwise, for one year	Pension ceases if survivor remarries	26	40 percent	100 percent, regardless of number of survivors
Slovenia	Eligibility of deceased for old-age or disability pension	70 percent of deceased's pension if sole beneficiary; 15 percent of deceased's pension if receiving own pension	For life, if spouse is 70 percent disabled, is taking care of a child, or is at retirement age; otherwise, for one year	Benefits cease if survivor remarries before reaching retirement age, unless incapable of working	26	70 percent if sole beneficiary	100 percent, regardless of number of survivors

Sources: European Commission 2007, national ministries, and social security institutions. For details, see the individual country chapters.

Voluntary old-age schemes. By 2006, all eight study countries had introduced voluntary private pension schemes. The primary public-policy purpose of these schemes was to offer individuals a credible vehicle for saving for retirement and to provide incentives for them to actually do so. To safeguard the role of these savings schemes in providing old-age income support, their products (and the providers who sell them) are typically subjected to more rigorous regulation and supervision than are nonretirement savings programs.

The provisions governing these schemes are similar across the study countries (table 1.8). All are tax-advantaged, but most countries impose limits on preferential tax provisions. Individuals are either allowed to deduct contributions from their taxable income or provided with other sorts of subsidies. In all countries but Croatia, employers who contribute on behalf of their employees are allowed to deduct contributions from income subjected to enterprise taxation. In all countries but Bulgaria and Croatia, schemes are subjected to vesting requirements (minimum participation periods). In all countries but Hungary, individuals must reach a minimum age to access the funds in their accounts. None of the countries imposes special rules on disbursement; all allow funds to be withdrawn as a lump sum.

Health care provisions for retirees. Access to health care is critically important to the issue of pension adequacy, because (in the absence of affordable health care) many elderly people would be forced to spend a main share of their retirement income on private health insurance, if one assumes such coverage were even available. The adequacy of pension benefits is affected by official out-of-pocket costs (including copayments for doctor visits and pharmaceuticals) and unofficial costs (including the enduring tradition from the communist era of paying tips to staff members of the health care providers).

All study countries provide mandatory health insurance for their active populations, including the self-employed (table 1.9). Health insurance schemes are financed by contributions from employers and employees. Benefits include cash payments (for example, sick pay), in-kind health care services, pharmaceuticals, and other items. Elderly people receiving a public pension (and their dependents) have access to the same benefits as the active population, but they typically pay a lower contribution rate (part or all of the difference is paid by the government or by the pension authority on their behalf).[5] The share of private expenditures in total health care expenditures in the study countries falls roughly in line with

Table 1.8 Voluntary Pension Provisions in Eight CESE Countries

Country	Vesting period	Retirement age	Tax advantages to participants	Contributions tax deductible by employers	Lump-sum payments possible in retirement
Bulgaria	No	58 (men), 55 (women)	Yes	Yes	Yes
Croatia	No[a]	50	Yes	No	Yes
Czech Republic	5 years	60	Yes	Yes	Yes
Hungary	10 years	No set retirement age[b]	Yes	Yes	Yes
Poland	5 years	60	Yes	Yes	Yes
Romania	90 months	60	Yes	Yes	Unknown[c]
Slovak Republic	10 years	55	Yes	Yes	Yes
Slovenia	10 years	58	Yes	Yes	Yes

Sources: European Commission 2007, national ministries, and national social security institutions. For details, see individual country chapters.
a. There is no specific vesting period. Benefits can be collected once an individual retires from the mandated schemes or upon reaching age 50.
b. Benefits can be withdrawn after 10 years.
c. Regulations related to the payout phase have not yet been issued.

Table 1.9 Health Care Provisions for Contributors and Retirees in Eight CESE Countries

Country	Contribution rate (percent) Active population			Retirees	Total 2005 health expenditure as percent of GDP	Public and private expenditure on health as percent of total health expenditure Public	Private	Out-of-pocket expenditure as percent of private expenditure on health
	Employer	Employee	Total					
Bulgaria	3.0	3.0	6.0	None	7.7	60.6	39.4	96.3
Croatia	15.0	0.0	15.0	None	7.4	81.3	18.7	93.6
Czech Republic	9.0	4.5	13.5	13.5 percent of state-defined wage level, paid by the government	7.1	88.6	11.4	95.3
Hungary	4.0	11.0	15.0	None	7.8	70.8	29.2	86.8
Poland	0.0	9.0	9.0	9.0 percent of pension	6.2	69.3	30.7	85.1
Romania	7.0	7.0	14.0	7.0 percent of pension	5.5	70.3	29.7	85.0
Slovak Republic	10.0	4.0	14.0	14 percent of minimum wage, paid by the government	7.0	74.4	25.6	88.1
Slovenia	6.56	6.36	12.92	5.0 percent of pension	8.5	72.4	27.6	45.0

Source: European Commission 2007, national ministries, and national social security institutions. For details, see individual country chapters.
Note: All eight countries provide public health insurance.

the shares observed in Organisation for Economic Co-operation and Development (OECD) countries, but—in contrast to OECD countries— private expenditures are related largely to out-of-pocket costs, not to the cost of private health insurance.

Assessment of the Performance of Pension Systems

The primary objectives of the eight country studies was to assess the performance of their reformed pension systems in a steady state (that is, as if their reforms had been in operation for long enough that current workers had always been subjected to the new rules). Because such an evaluation cannot be conducted ex post for many years, analytical tools had to be designed and applied specifically for this purpose, and benchmarks had to be developed against which performance could be evaluated. Given that earnings trajectories vary across countries (as a result of which, average benefits can vary across countries even if their pension systems rely on exactly the same provisions and average earnings are the same), the evaluation also required the development of a methodology for assessing countries both individually and collectively in a way that permitted comparisons across the sample.

The World Bank has established four principles for evaluating public pension systems, which together should guide the process of pension reform (see Holzmann and Hinz 2005). Broadly speaking, these principles include the adequacy and security of benefits, the affordability of contributions, the sustainability of the system over time, and the robustness of the system in the face of demographic changes and macroeconomic shocks. This section focuses primarily on the adequacy of benefits and the financial sustainability of the first- and second-pillar earnings-related pension schemes. The remaining principles are mentioned only briefly. Adequacy is analyzed through the lens of net replacement rates. Financial sustainability is evaluated using projections of pension expenditures and revenues.

Benefit Adequacy

Replacement rates are a useful yardstick for measuring the adequacy of pension benefits, because they express benefits relative to preretirement earnings, thereby indicating the degree to which income is replaced when workers retire. Two variants are commonly used. Gross replacement rates compute income replacement as the ratio of gross benefits paid to pretax preretirement earnings. Net replacement rates compute income replacement as the ratio of benefits received (that is, after the payment of taxes and other levies, including contributions for social insurance) to posttax preretirement earnings. In general, net replacement rates are a more useful measure of benefit adequacy, because they capture the degree to which actual take-home pay is replaced when workers retire.

Replacement rates are a function of the formula governing pension benefits; an individual's contribution history; and, in the case of net replacement rates, the rules of income tax, social security contributions, and other relevant levies. The benefit formula establishes the degree to which the system redistributes income across individuals of different levels of preretirement earnings. Progressive systems provide higher levels of income replacement to people with lower levels of preretirement income. In general, the degree to which a system is redistributive depends on (a) the existence (and value) of flat transfers and minimum pension guarantees, (b) the degree to which benefits are earnings related, and (c) the existence of ceilings on earnings subject to contributions. An individual's contribution history can be characterized by his or her age of entry into the labor force, contribution density, and decisions regarding the timing of retirement. To some degree, these three factors are influenced by the incentives embodied in the pension system. The tax and contribution system influences net replacement rates through the progressiveness of the income tax formula, which taxes (higher) income during a worker's active life more than it taxes (lower) pension benefits in retirement. In addition, social security levies (for pensions; unemployment; health care; and, at times, housing and family benefits) are typically reduced or eliminated altogether in retirement. These benefits are particularly important for low- to middle-income groups.

Benchmarks need to be established to evaluate the adequacy of the income replacement provided by the earnings-related pension schemes. Unfortunately, there is no consensus on what constitutes adequacy. According to one widely respected definition, pensions are adequate when they are sufficient to prevent poverty among the elderly and to provide the vast majority of people with a reliable mechanism for smoothing income over their lifetime. Even with a definition, however, establishing benchmarks is problematic, because attitudes vary across countries as a result of social and cultural perceptions. Moreover, benchmarks ignore the other factors that affect the welfare of the elderly—and that also vary across countries—including the existence and generosity of health insurance and long-term care, the cost of housing, the structure of traditional living arrangements, the presence of informal intrafamily or intergenerational sources of financial and nonfinancial support, and the availability and security of other mechanisms for people to save for their own retirement.

One reputable nine-country study (OECD 2001) observes that living standards are roughly comparable for people 10 years older than the normal retirement age and people 15 years younger than the normal retirement age when retirees have disposable income equal to roughly 80 percent of the disposable income of working-age people. In part, this is attributable to the fact that retirees have no work-related expenses (they do not have to commute or buy special clothing or uniforms, for example). This finding, however, does not imply that mandatory first-pillar pension schemes should actually target an 80 percent net replacement rate. To the contrary, in middle- and high-income countries, one can reasonably expect individuals to save for their own retirement—and the empirical evidence suggests that, in practice, they do so.[6] There is also some evidence to suggest that the ratio between pre- and postretirement income is somewhat independent of the income replacement mandate of the public pension system. Put simply, individuals tend to save more in countries with more modest mandates (and vice versa).

Because mechanisms for saving—such as voluntary pension schemes—exist in all of the study countries, it would seem reasonable to expect middle- and higher-income workers to save enough to finance at least 25 percent, if not closer to 50 percent, of this 80 percent income replacement target. Given this, three benchmarks are provided: a 40 percent net replacement rate (which implies that individuals would be expected to save enough to finance half of the total income replacement target); a 60 percent net replacement rate (which implies that individuals would be expected to finance a quarter of the target); and an 80 percent net replacement rate (which implies that individuals, most of whom would be low-income earners, would not be expected to contribute anything toward the target).[7] In the analysis conducted for each of the eight country-specific studies, the results of which are summarized below, adequacy is evaluated against these three benchmarks, as well as in conjunction with the average net replacement rate observed in 53 countries; the average net replacement rate observed for selected countries in Europe and Central Asia; and the average poverty line for the reviewed countries.[8]

In order to estimate gross and net replacement rates, we use the APEX model to consider two critical dimensions: earnings levels and contribution periods.[9] This model generates estimates for replacement rates under steady-state assumptions (that is, as if the rules of the reformed pension scheme had been in place over the entire active life of the individual).

Because life expectancies at retirement are projected to increase over time—which will affect the benefits paid by defined-contribution pension schemes—a reference year must be chosen. For this study, 2040 is used, because it provides a sufficiently long contribution period over which to approximate steady-state conditions. Gross and net replacement rates are considered both across incomes (where the income spectrum is expressed relative to average earnings, ranging from half the average to twice the average) and as a function of patterns of contributory service (which are captured by the age at which someone is assumed to enter the workforce, the degree to which he or she works continuously or with interrupted service, and the age at which he or she elects to leave the workforce permanently). Full-career workers are considered first, followed by partial-career workers (that is, people with intermittent patterns of formal-sector employment).

Income replacement for full-career workers. For this analysis, a full career is defined as continuous employment from age 20 to the retirement age in effect once reforms have been fully implemented. For men, this age ranges from 62 to 65 across the eight study countries.

GROSS REPLACEMENT RATES. Gross replacement rates were estimated using total benefits from all mandated pension provisions (that is, second-pillar benefits are included in the analysis for countries with second-pillar schemes).[10]

Figure 1.3 shows gross replacement rates as a function of preretirement income relative to the economywide average earnings. Analysis of figure 1.3 yields the following observations:

- Gross replacement rates differ substantially across the study countries—and the variation widens as earnings increase. At half the average earnings, gross replacement rates range from 50.00 percent (in Croatia) to 74.8 percent (in Bulgaria). At twice the average earnings, gross replacement rates range from 30.1 percent (in Czech Republic) to 74.8 percent (in Bulgaria).

- Countries have introduced reforms that impose greater actuarial neutrality (that is, NDC schemes, point systems, and similar parametric reforms). Bulgaria, Romania, Poland and the Slovak Republic provide gross replacement rates that are flat across the income spectrum but at different levels. Adding a second pillar does not change this result,

Figure 1.3   Gross Replacement Rates for Male Full-Career Workers in Eight CESE Countries

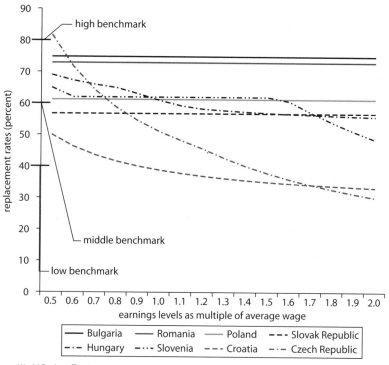

Source: World Bank staff estimates.

because the benefits paid by defined-contribution schemes are, by construction, directly determined by contributions.

- As a result of flat benefit provisions intended to affect income redistribution, gross replacement rates fall as income rises in Croatia (which has a two-tiered first-pillar point scheme) and the Czech Republic (which has a two-tiered first-pillar defined-benefit scheme). Slovenia's pension scheme is also progressive, but only at higher income levels. The Hungarian system has recently become progressive, as a result of the (recently introduced) net income base used to calculate benefits.

Gross replacement rates for countries with second-pillar schemes are time dependent, because second-pillar benefits are computed as annuities, which vary based on conditional life expectancy. Because life expectancy is increasing (at the rate of roughly two years per decade), the value of annuities will fall accordingly. if one assumes that funded schemes provide roughly a third of total gross income replacement, an increase in life expectancy of 10 percent per decade reduces total gross replacement rates by roughly 2 percentage points for individuals of the same age who retire 10 years apart. A similar reduction in gross levels of income replacement can occur in first-pillar schemes. Indeed, one of the objectives of an NDC scheme (such as the one introduced in Poland) is to reduce the vulnerability of pension systems to the uncertainties surrounding future changes in life expectancy. When the impact of rising life expectancy on both pillars is considered, an increase in life expectancy of 10 percent per decade reduces total gross replacement rates by some 6 percentage points over 10 years.

In Croatia, such a reduction is affected through the use of Swiss revaluation of the points an individual accumulates while working. However, because the flat benefit component of its first-pillar scheme is, by definition, revalued to be 25 percent of the average wage, rising life expectancy will have a smaller impact on gross replacement rates—less than 1 percentage point for the first pillar alone and roughly 3 percentage points for both pillars combined over a 10-year-period.

NET REPLACEMENT RATES. Gross replacement rates are of limited value in assessing the adequacy of retirement income. Net replacement rates are a better indicator. Figure 1.4 shows the net replacement rates that result from the gross replacement rates shown in figure 1.3 after the application of country-specific rules regarding income taxes and social security contributions.

Several observations emerge from analysis of figure 1.4:

- Net replacement rates are well above their corresponding levels of gross income replacement in all eight study countries. The Slovak Republic and the Czech Republic—with net replacement rates of 66 percent and 102 percent, respectively—define the range at half average earnings. At twice average earnings, the Czech Republic (42 percent) and Hungary (100 percent) define the range. Rising replacement rates in countries such as the Slovak Republic are due entirely to their progressive income tax rates, not to structural characteristics of their pension schemes.

- Net replacement rates for most countries remain broadly constant in the range of 60–100 percent, with some country-specific variation. In Croatia and the Czech Republic, net replacement rates fall substantially

Figure 1.4   Net Replacement Rates for Male Full-Career Workers in Eight CESE Countries

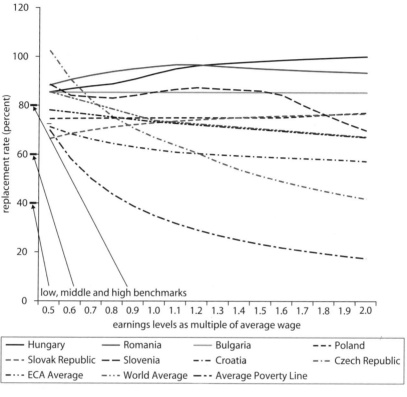

Source: World Bank staff estimates.

across the income spectrum. In Hungary and the Slovak Republic, net rates increase across the income spectrum. In Bulgaria and Poland net rates remain essentially flat.

- All of the study countries provide levels of net income replacement for full-career male workers that are higher than the middle benchmark (60 percent); in several countries (Bulgaria, Hungary, Romania and Slovenia), net replacement rates are close to or above the high benchmark (80 percent). Only in the Czech Republic at twice average earnings do net replacement rates fall near the low benchmark (40 percent).

Income replacement for partial-career workers. Estimating replacement rates for full-career workers under the earnings-related pension schemes of the eight study countries is a useful undertaking, because it establishes an upper benchmark for what these systems are promising to deliver. Not everyone works from age 20 to the statutory retirement age, however. Many individuals enter and exit the labor force (often at different ages and for different periods of time) and earn different wages while working (figure 1.5).[11]

To study the adequacy of benefits for partial career workers, we examine three stylized cases. These cases include career type A (someone entering the labor force at age 25 who works continuously for a period of years before leaving the workforce at some point between the ages of 50 and 70 and then claims a benefit); career type B (identical to career type A, except that the worker enters the workforce at age 30 and leaves no earlier than age 55); and career type C (identical to career type A, except that the individual contributes in only three years out of four while in the labor force). In cases where the withdrawal from the formal labor market occurs before the statutory retirement age, the pension is claimed (and the replacement rate calculated) only at the later age. For withdrawals after the statutory retirement age, the ages coincide. Net replacement rates for these stylized, partial-career, middle-income workers are shown in figure 1.5.

Several observations emerge from analysis of figure 1.5:

- Exiting the labor market at an early age exacts a significant cost in terms of net replacement rates. Exiting the labor market at age 45 and then drawing a pension upon reaching the minimum retirement age reduces levels of net income replacement by one-third or more compared to leaving the labor market at age 70 and drawing a pension immediately. Despite this reduction, net replacement rates remain well above country-specific poverty levels, even at one-half of the average earnings.

- Several of the study countries reward workers who elect to remain in the labor market after reaching the standard retirement age (62–65 for men). In these countries, each year of additional contributory service beyond the normal retirement age is rewarded with even more pronounced increases in net replacement rates. In Slovenia, however, net replacement rates are flat at higher retirement ages, which does nothing to encourage older workers to remain in the workforce.

- Entering the labor market later, at age 30 instead of age 25, exacts a significant cost in terms of net replacement rates. For workers retiring

Figure 1.5 Net Replacement Rates for Male Partial-Career Workers in Eight CESE Countries

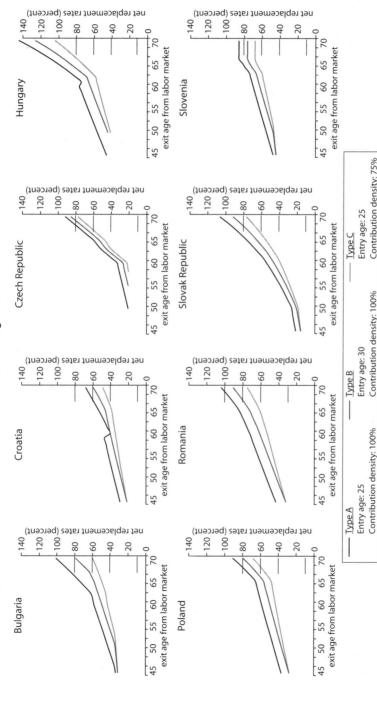

Source: Authors' estimates based on European Commission 2007, national ministries, and national social security institutions. For details, see individual country chapters.

Note: The four dark lines adjacent to the y-axis represent the 80 percent, 60 percent, and 40 percent benchmark; the poverty line is expressed as a percentage of the average wage. See text for description of career types.

at age 65, entering the labor market at age 30 results in levels of net income replacement that are lower by 5–10 percentage points in most countries. The cost of entering the labor market later are compounded for those who also exit the labor market early.

- Working intermittently is costly in terms of net income replacement. Someone who enters the workforce at the same age but who contributes for only three years out of four will receive a net replacement rate 8–20 percentage points lower than someone who contributes continuously.

In most of the study countries, career type A and B workers will attain the lowest of the three benchmarks before reaching retirement age, while career type C workers must work until retirement age. Career type A and B workers can often attain the middle benchmark provided they work beyond retirement age. In many cases, career type C workers will not attain the 80 percent benchmark even if they work until 70.

Benefit indexation. The adequacy of pension benefits is determined not only by the level of an individual's replacement rate at retirement but also by how the benefits are adjusted over retirement in response to changing prices or overall living standards. The debate among pension economists and practitioners continues over whether the optimal path of retirement consumption for a fixed level of pension wealth should rise or fall and, hence, a higher initial replacement rate combined with lower indexation or a lower replacement rate combined with higher indexation. But most would agree that benefits from mandated schemes should at least maintain their real value (that is, be indexed to prices). In a growing economy in which wages are rising faster than inflation, however, price indexation results in a continuous softening of the relative consumption position of retirees over time. The practical consequence of price indexation is that the benefits of two otherwise identical workers will differ as a function of how long they have been retired. In situations in which real annual wage growth is high (say, 2 percent or more), the resulting differences may become substantial. For this reason, a number of countries—in both CESE and around the world—index benefits using the rates of growth of both prices and wages, in varying proportions.

Seven of the eight study countries provide for the indexation of benefits from both the first and (for countries that have them) the second pillar (the exception is Romania, which has yet to establish a policy governing the indexation of second-pillar benefits) (table 1.5). The mechanism by which benefits are indexed, however, varies. The generosity of indexation policies is framed by two countries—Poland and Slovenia—with the latter having only a first-pillar scheme. Poland indexes benefits using 80% price and 20% wage increase, while Slovenia uses wages only. A second country without a second pillar (the Czech Republic) indexes benefits on the basis of prices plus one-third of real wage growth. Countries with both a first and a second pillar typically use Swiss indexation (half prices, half wages) for first-pillar benefits and price indexation for second-pillar benefits.

The effects of indexation policies on replacement rates over retirement are shown in figure 1.6. To facilitate comparisons, replacement rates are normalized to 100 percent for all countries. Underlying modeling

Figure 1.6   Impact of Indexation on Income Replacement (Active Earnings Units) in Eight CESE Countries

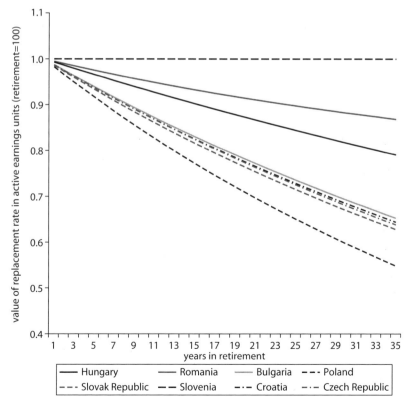

Source: Author estimates.

assumptions—including the assumption that inflation averages 2.5 percent a year and real wage growth averages 2 percent per year—are unchanged. Changes in replacement rates are measured against full wage indexation, which is the functional equivalent of comparing postretirement benefits to the average earnings of current workers (that is, expressing them in active earnings units).[12]

Several observations emerge from analysis of figure 1.6:

- Despite a modest assumption about the growth of real wages, the impact of less than full wage indexation on relative pension benefits in retirement is noticeable in all countries except Slovenia (where benefits are wage indexed).

- In Poland, where benefits are predominantly indexed to prices, the relative income of someone retired for 10 years will be 16 percent lower than that of new retirees with the same relative preretirement wages. After 35 years (that is, for those few people living to almost age 100), relative income will be almost half that of new retirees with the same preretirement wages.

- The use of both prices and wages to index first-pillar benefits in combination with the price indexation of second-pillar benefits—as is done in Croatia and the Slovak Republic—somewhat dampens, but does not eliminate, these changes in relative income position over time.

Financial Sustainability

The sustainability of pay-as-you-go public pension schemes is best evaluated in actuarial terms by estimating the actuarial deficit as the difference between a scheme's liabilities and assets. If the actuarial deficit is positive and large, a scheme is financially unsustainable and will require policy remediation to increase revenues or reduce expenditures. A good proxy for the actuarial deficit is the difference between present value of expected future revenues (that is, contributions and other sources of income) and expected future expenditures (that is, benefit payments, administrative costs, and other expenses) over a long projection period. The difference between the net present value of these two projected cash flows represents an unfunded liability (sometimes referred to as a *financing gap*) on the public-sector balance sheet. Given that the eight individual country studies were also concerned with the path of revenues and expenditures

(and the resulting net cash flow deficit) over a projection period extending to 2050 (figure 1.7), this more pragmatic approach to measuring sustainability has been used. Although the projections discussed as follows
are all based on different sources (and, thus, lack strict comparability), the
methodologies underlying their preparation are reasonably close and,
consequently, provide a reasonable basis for comparison.[13]

Against this benchmark, the pension reforms of all eight study countries made major progress toward addressing underlying issues of sustainability. Progress across the sample is uneven, however, and further
reforms are needed in a number of countries.

Several observations emerge from analysis of figure 1.7:

- The path of projected net cash flows varies widely across the study
  countries. The pension systems of two counties (Croatia before 2050
  and Poland thereafter) are expected to eventually reach fiscal balance
  Other countries (the Czech Republic, the Slovak Republic, and Slovenia)
  start out closer to fiscal balance and show initial improvements before
  deteriorating over the long term. Still others (Bulgaria, Hungary, and
  particularly Romania) show imbalances throughout the projection
  period. Given that all of the study countries are confronting broadly
  similar demographic challenges, differences in cash flow projections
  result primarily from differences in pension system design and (in
  countries with second pillars) varying capacities for financing the transition costs associated with the introduction of funding.

- Countries that introduced systemic reforms (such as Poland and
  Croatia) seem to have been more successful in raising retirement ages
  (to 65 for men and 60 for women) and in lowering levels of gross
  income replacement (to 61 percent and 49 percent, respectively, for
  someone with average earnings) than were countries with less ambitious
  reforms (such as Bulgaria, where retirement ages are 63 for men and 60
  for women and gross replacement rates are 66 percent; Hungary, where
  retirement ages are 62 for both men and women and gross replacement rates are 77 percent; and Romania, where retirement ages are 65
  for men and 60 for women and gross replacement rates are 62 percent). Similar design differences also appear to be driving the projected
  deterioration of fiscal balances in the Slovak Republic (where retirement ages are 62 for men and women and gross replacement rates are
  57 percent) and Slovenia (where retirement ages are 63 for men and
  61 for women and gross replacement rates are 62 percent).

Figure 1.7 Projected Pension System Fiscal Balances after Reform in Eight CESE Countries

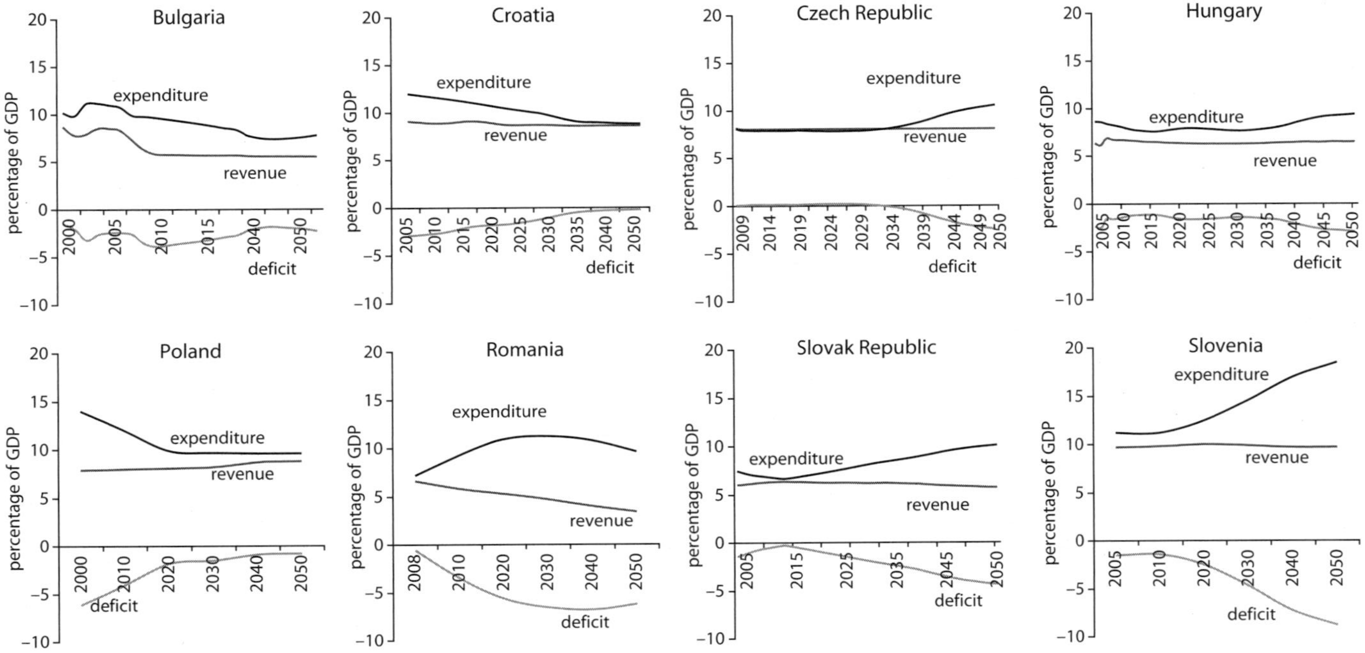

Source: European Commission 2007, national ministries, and national social security institutions. For details, see individual country chapters.

The tools for addressing the sustained pension deficits observed in the projections for some of the study countries are limited. In theory, revenues can be increased and benefits reduced or delayed. In practice, the options available to policy makers are more constrained:

- Pension scheme revenues can be increased by raising contribution rates, but because raising contribution rates can threaten competitiveness—and will likely strengthen incentives for tax evasion, which is already of concern in the region—it is typically not embraced by policy makers. Moreover, it would represent a reversal of policy in most of the study countries.

- For countries in which a large portion of the deficit is attributable to the transition costs of newly introduced funded second pillars, policy makers might consider financing all or part of the transition costs with general revenues. This effectively represents the partial repayment of the implicit debts accrued by their first-pillar pension schemes. Moreover, general revenue financing may be perceived as being more equitable and less distortional.

- Further increasing the retirement age (while concurrently adjusting benefit provisions to fix the level of income replacement awarded at retirement) is an attractive option, because it should improve both revenues and expenditures. Furthermore, raising retirement ages is the most logical and consistent policy for addressing increases in life expectancy. Actually increasing the preponderance of elderly workers in the labor force, however, may require more than simply raising statutory retirement ages and may depend on broader labor and financial market reforms.[14]

- Alternatively—or in addition to, because the options are not mutually exclusive—expenditures can be reduced by cutting benefits. Addressing financial sustainability through benefit cuts has, of course, a direct bearing on benefit adequacy. Achieving fiscal balance by 2050 will require proportionate benefit cuts—evaluated at average earnings—of 20 percent (equivalent to a 10–12 percentage point reduction in net replacement rates) in Bulgaria, the Czech Republic, and Hungary and 35 percent (equivalent to a 25–30 percentage point reduction in net replacement rates) in Romania and Slovenia.

- To offset reductions in first-pillar benefits, in lieu of raising the retirement age, governments could encourage individuals to engage in voluntary savings. To increase income replacement by 1 percentage point, for example, a full-career worker would need to save almost 0.5 percent of his or her earnings from the age of 40 to the current age of retirement.[15] Making up for a 10 percentage point drop in net replacement rates would, therefore, require additional savings of some 5 percentage points of earnings.

Conclusions

All eight of the study countries have made major progress in reforming their pension systems over the past decade. Financial sustainability—a key concern and the dominant driver behind most reforms—has been dramatically improved in most countries. The connection between contributions and benefits has been strengthened, and overall system designs are now better aligned with (and suited for) a market economy given the introduction of voluntary third-pillar schemes in all eight countries and the introduction of mandatory second-pillar schemes in six of them.

A major social policy concern—and a predominant focus of this report and its underlying country studies—has been the (at times, express) concern that reforms may have exacted a high cost in terms of the adequacy of pension benefits of future retirees. In evaluating this concern, the country studies rely on an analytical toolkit that generates estimates for gross and net replacement rates under earnings-related schemes for workers with different earnings levels and lifetime patterns of contributions. These calculations were performed under steady-state assumptions (that is, as if the reforms had been in operation for long enough that current workers had been subjected to the new rules for most of their working lives). A reference year of and mortality projections for 2040 were used to provide a sufficiently long contribution period to approximate steady-state conditions.

Several findings emerge from these calculations:

- Estimated net replacement rates (the relevant welfare indicator for consumption smoothing and the best measure of the degree to which preretirement take-home pay is replaced by disposable income in retirement) suggest that levels of income replacement for full-career workers are generally in line with regional averages and international benchmarks. In five countries (Bulgaria, Croatia, the Czech Republic,

Poland, and the Slovak Republic), net replacement rates evaluated at low and average earnings are between the middle (60 percent) and high (80 percent) benchmarks. In three countries (Romania, Hungary, and Slovenia), net replacement rates exceed 80 percent.

- Estimated net replacement rates for partial-career workers—those who enter the workforce later in life, have intermittent patterns of formal-sector employment, or leave the workforce before reaching the standard retirement age—illustrate the importance of continued formal labor market participation. Although net replacement rates for most partial-career workers are well above the poverty line in most of the study countries, individuals in some countries are not ensured of achieving even the low (40 percent) benchmark. Promoting more continuous and longer labor force participation, however, is a cross-sector labor market challenge that should be addressed with macroeconomic and microeconomic policies that go beyond the use of pension policy to achieve adequate pensions for such workers.

- All of the study countries have introduced voluntary pension schemes to provide a vehicle with which workers can supplement the benefits provided by mandated schemes. Voluntary schemes are particularly important for middle- and high-income earners, because public schemes cannot be expected to provide them with all of their income replacement in retirement.

- All of the study countries have noncontributory, zero-pillar schemes to alleviate poverty among the elderly. In five countries (Croatia, the Czech Republic, Poland, Romania, and the Slovak Republic), the zero pillar is part of a broader scheme of social assistance available to everyone, regardless of age, that is intended to guarantee a minimum income level. Three countries (Bulgaria, Hungary, and Slovenia) provide an age-related social pension specifically for the elderly. Such provisions may gain importance in the future as a way of addressing income gaps and supporting those most seriously affected by the economic transition.

Although progress toward addressing issues of fiscal sustainability has been made in all of the study countries, only a few are fully prepared for the inevitability of population aging. Progress remains uneven. The options available to policy makers are limited: revenues can be increased, benefits can be reduced, or retirement ages can be raised. Increasing revenues by promoting formal-sector employment across all age groups or improving compliance certainly helps improve cash flows in the short-term. Such policies, however, are not a panacea for actuarially unsustainable schemes. On the contrary, an increase of employment in a pension scheme that promises benefits in excess of contributions indexed by the sustainable (implicit) rate of return creates only temporary cash flow surpluses. Because the increase in pension liabilities exceeds the increase in (pay-as-you-go) assets, the sustainability of the scheme actually deteriorates. For this reason, promoting formal-sector employment—an objective that can and should be pursued across the region to increase benefit coverage—is no substitute for pension reforms intended to address underlying design issues of sustainability.

The introduction of second-pillar pension schemes by some study countries increased, rather than reduced, fiscal pressure, because the introduction of funding means that a portion of contributions that were once available for the payment of benefits are diverted to funded accounts. Addressing fiscal imbalances exclusively through benefit cuts threatens benefit adequacy and could undermine political support for reforms. One possible alternative would be to finance transition costs using general revenues, which may have more equitable incidence and be less distortional. CESE countries have been reluctant to use budgetary financing for this purpose given the Maastricht fiscal criteria and their desire to join the euro area. Given that the rules governing the accounts of public pension systems are scheduled to be revised in the European System of National Accounts to reflect the actual debt-reducing nature of transition deficits, CESE countries may have more room in the future to reconsider this option.

Achieving fiscal balance by 2050 for unfunded first-pillar schemes in some of the study countries on the basis of benefit cuts alone would require that average replacement rates be reduced by 35 or more percentage points. In addition to not being politically feasible, such drastic cuts would likely jeopardize the adequacy of pension benefits. An alternative approach (which could be combined with more modest cuts in benefits or implemented on its own) would be to move toward fully price indexing benefits in disbursement. Although the preservation of purchasing power across retirement (for benefits that were adequate in terms of income replacement at retirement) is consistent with adequacy considerations, it would result in a reduction in purchasing power relative to the active population and younger retirees. This may not be politically viable in periods of high real-wage growth. Thus, the introduction of full price indexation may require additional and discretionary increases in benefits conditioned on developments with real wages and budgetary resources.

Given a lack of viable alternative policy options, the challenge of population aging in all countries in the region demands that more decisive steps be taken to encourage and enable extended labor force participation among the elderly. Contribution rates for pensions and other social programs are already very high and may be partly to blame for the existence of sizable informal labor markets in much of the region. Further benefit cuts may unduly undermine benefit adequacy in some countries. Although all of the study countries raised retirement ages as part of their reforms, legal and actual retirement ages are still generally low in comparison to most OECD countries and in comparison to past and future gains in life expectancy at retirement. Moreover, all of the study countries except Hungary continue to allow women to retire substantially earlier than men, despite women's having substantially higher life expectancies.

Although benefit adequacy seems broadly ensured for most workers in all of the study countries—particularly if retirement ages are raised (and equalized) in line with life expectancies and if policy changes regarding the financing of transition costs are enacted—CESE countries may need to think about temporary measures to provide income support for the lost generation that is now emerging from the transition. Many members of this generation suffered from low earnings and patchy formal-sector employment in the years following the end of central planning; they now risk receiving very low pension benefits, if they qualify at all (Augusztinovics and Köllő 2009). Although addressing their needs by making benefits more generous may be tempting (and politically expedient), a longer-term perspective would suggest that targeted transitional measures may be more effective without undermining progress toward fiscal sustainability. Most of the study countries have introduced painful reforms that will bear fruit in the future, weakening, one hopes, some of the incentives driving labor market informality. Permanent changes to meet the special needs of this lost generation would not only undermine sustainability (and adequacy, because unsustainable schemes threaten the adequacy of benefits for future generations of retirees), but also weaken the currently tight linkages between contributions and benefits and encourage continued labor market informality in the future.

Last but not least, the projections for second-pillar pension schemes discussed earlier assumed that the schemes would earn net rates of return 1.5 percentage points higher than earnings growth. Although such returns are in line with historical performance in developed countries and are substantially lower than historical average performance in emerging markets (Musalem and Bebczuk, 2009, forthcoming), there is no assurance that the funded schemes of the study countries will achieve this benchmark. And the current financial crisis has provided a painful reminder that these long-term target rates can be put into jeopardy by exceptional events. But even before the crisis, the performance of pension funds in the region had been highly uneven and often disappointing. Improving their performance calls for a review of pension fund structures and accelerated financial sector reforms if these schemes are to live up to the return expectations of future retirees in light of population aging (Holzmann, 2009).

Notes

1. Although the World Bank undoubtedly influenced the thinking of policy makers through its analytical work, access to information, and capacity-building measures, it has never imposed such an approach to pension reform, as has sometimes been suggested (Orenstein 2008).

2. Benefits from noncontributory schemes are not necessarily tax exempt. Taxing them as ordinary income (as is done in Australia and New Zealand, where benefits are not asset tested) provides a way of clawing back benefits from income-rich retirees.

3. See Tesliuc and others (2008) for a review of the targeting efficiency of social assistance schemes in countries in Europe and Central Asia.

4. See Rudolph and Rocha (2008) for a discussion of the status of and lessons learned from the preparations for the payout phase in Chile.

5. A lower contribution rate for the elderly—or the payment of contributions on their behalf—does not necessarily imply that the elderly are receiving a subsidy. From a life-cycle perspective, what matters is lifetime contributions relative to lifetime benefits. Higher contribution rates for people of working age can compensate for lower contribution rates for when those people are no longer working. The fact that contributions are income related, however, typically effects major redistribution from people who are comparatively wealthier to those who are comparatively poor.

6. In Chile, for instance, 70 percent of retirees from the mandatory public pension system own their home, which is a form of savings (see Valdès-Prieto 2008).

7. These benchmarks approximate the standards developed by the International Labour Organization (ILO) and the Council of Europe (1990). ILO Convention 102 of 1952 sets a minimum benefit equal to 40 percent of the reference wage for married men of pensionable age. This amount was raised

to 45 percent in 1968. The European Code of Security of 1990 sets a minimum standard for members of the Council of Europe equal to 65 percent for married people of a specific age.

8. As a proxy for the poverty line, this study uses 35 percent of the average net wage, which very broadly approximates a US$2.25-a-day poverty line converted into national currency, adjusted for purchasing power parity, expressed relative to the national average net wage, and averaged across the eight study countries.

9. The APEX model was developed by Axia Economics, with funding from the OECD and the World Bank. The model codes detailed eligibility and benefit rules for first- and second-pillar schemes based on available public information that has been verified by country contacts. Because the details of the rules sometimes change on short notice (and limited public disclosure), the calculations presented here should be considered as best approximations only.

10. Gross replacement rates are simulated replacement rates for an unmarried male working a hypothetical career path under the assumption that real wage growth is 2 percent, inflation is 2.5 percent, the rate of return on invested assets is 3.5 percent, and the worker retires at the statutory retirement age. A 1.5 percentage point markup of net returns over the growth rate of average earnings is a conservative assumption in light of historical performance. The observed net rates of return over GDP growth (used as a proxy for earnings growth) in developed countries over the period 1970–1995 was 1.4 percent. For emerging economies (over a more recent period), the observed markup was 2.8 percent (Musalem and Bebczuk, 2009, forthcoming).

11. Only middle-income, partial-career workers are examined, because replacement rates are roughly comparable for workers with lower or higher levels of preretirement income.

12. For Romania, the calculations in figure 1.6 assume that first-pillar benefits are indexed using a combination of wages (with a 70 percent weighting) and prices (with a 30 percent weighting)—as a proxy for endogenous indexation, which depends on changes made to point values—while second pillar benefits are price indexed.

13. The projections for Poland's NDC scheme may refer only to old-age pensions rather than include disability pensions and survivorship benefits as well. As a result, the size and path of the deficit may be understated.

14. See Holzmann, MacKellar, and Repansek (2009) for a discussion of these issues for the countries of southeastern European.

15. This estimate is based on the assumption that real wage growth is 2 percent, the net real rate of return on invested assets is 3.5 percent, and benefits (both from the unfunded and funded pillars) are price indexed.

Bibliography

Augusztinovics, M., and J. Köllő. 2009. "Decreased Employment and Pensions." In *Pension Reform in Southeastern Europe: Linking to Labor and Financial Market Reforms*, ed. R. Holzmann, L. MacKellar, and J. Repansek, pp. 89–104. Washington, DC: World Bank.

Barr, N., and M. Rutkowski. 2004. "Pensions." In *Labor Markets and Social Policy in Central and Eastern Europe: The Accession and Beyond*, ed. Nick Barr, pp. 135–70. Washington, DC: World Bank.

Council of Europe 1990. *European Code of Social Security (Revised)*. Rome.

European Commission. 2007. *Pension Schemes and Projection Models in EU-25 Member Countries*. European Economy Occasional Paper 37, Economic Policy Committee and Directorate General for Economic and Financial Affairs, Brussels.

Gubbels, J., D. Snelbecker, and L. Zezulin. 2007. *The Kosovo Pension Reform: Achievements and Lessons*. Social Protection Discussion Paper 0707, World Bank, Washington, DC.

Hinz, R., A. Zviniene, and A. Vilamovska. 2005. *The New Pensions in Kazakhstan: Challenges in Making the Transition*. Social Protection Discussion Paper 0537, World Bank, Washington, DC.

Holzmann, R. 1997a. *Pension Reform, Financial Market Development, and Economic Growth: Preliminary Evidence from Chile*. International Monetary Fund Staff Paper 44 (June): 149–78.

———. 1997b. "Starting over in Pensions: The Challenges Facing Central and Eastern Europe." *Journal of Public Policy* 17 (3): 195–222.

———, ed. 2009. *Aging Populations, Pension Funds, and Financial Markets: Regional Perspectives and Global Challenges for Central, Eastern, and Southern Europe*. Washington, DC: World Bank and ERSTE Foundation.

Holzmann, R., and R. Hinz. 2005. *Old-Age Income Support in the 21st Century*. Washington, DC: World Bank.

Holzmann, R., L. MacKellar, and J. Repansek, eds. 2009. *Pension Reform in Southeastern Europe: Linking to Labor and Financial Market Reforms*. Washington, DC: World Bank.

Holzmann, R., and E. Palmer, eds. 2006. *Pension Reform: Issues and Prospects for Non-Financial Defined Contribution Schemes*. World Bank: Washington, DC.

ILO (International Labor Organization). 1952. *ILO Convention 102*. Geneva.

———. 1967. *ILO Convention 128*. Geneva.

Musalem, A., and R. Bebczuk. 2009, Forthcoming. "Can the Financial Markets Generate Sustained Returns on a Large Scale?" In *Aging Populations, Pension Funds, and Financial Markets: Regional Perspectives and Global Challenges for*

Central, Eastern, and Southern Europe, ed. R. Holzmann. Washington, DC: World Bank and ERSTE Foundation.

Nickel, J., and C. Almenberg. 2006. "Ageing, Pension Reforms and Capital Market Developments in Transition Countries." Working Paper, European Bank for Reconstruction and Development, London.

OECD (Organisation for Economic Co-operation and Development). 2001. *Ageing and Income: Financial Resources and Retirement in Nine OECD Countries.* Paris: OECD.

Orenstein, M. 2008. *Privatization Pensions: The Transnational Campaign for Social Security Reform.* Princeton, NJ: Princeton University Press.

Rudolph, H., and R. Rocha. 2009, forthcoming. "Population Aging and the Payout of Benefits: Issues and Options." In *Aging Populations, Pension Funds, and Financial Markets: Regional Perspectives and Global Challenges for Central, Eastern, and Southern Europe*, ed. R. Holzmann. Washington, DC: World Bank and ERSTE Foundation.

Schwarz, A. 2007. "Pensions." In *Fiscal Policy and Economic Growth: Lessons for Eastern Europe and Central Asia*, ed. Cheryl Gray, Tracey Lane, and Aristomene Varoudakis, Washington, DC: World Bank.

Tesliuc, E., D. Coady, M. Grosh, and L. Pop. 2008. *Program Implementation Matters for Targeting Performance: Evidence and Lessons from Eastern and Central Europe.* Washington, DC: World Bank.

UN (United Nations). 2007. *World Population Prospects, 2006 Revision.* New York: United Nations.

Valdés-Prieto, S. 2008. *Designs for the First-Pillar Pensions and the 2008 Chilean Reform.* http://editorialexpress.com/cgi-bin/conference/download.cgi?db_name=SECHI2008&paper_id=130.

Whitehouse, E. 1999. *Tax Treatment of Funded Pensions.* Washington, DC: World Bank.

World Bank. 1994. *Averting the Old-Age Crisis.* Washington, DC: World Bank.

———. 2005. *Growth, Poverty, and Inequality: Eastern Europe and the Former Soviet Union.* Washington, DC: World Bank.

———. 2007a. *From Red to Gray: The "Third Transition" of Aging Populations in Eastern Europe and the Former Soviet Union.* Washington, DC: World Bank.

———. 2007b. *Pensions Panorama.* Washington, DC: World Bank.

CHAPTER 2

Bulgaria

Bulgaria inherited a socialist-era defined-benefit pension system financed on a pay-as-you-go basis (meaning that contributions from current workers are used to pay benefits to current beneficiaries). The country's transition from central planning to a market economy affected all sectors of the economy. The change caused living standards for the elderly to decline and increased fiscal pressure on the pension system.

In 1991, the third year of transition, the pension system generated a deficit equivalent to 2.96 percent of gross domestic product (GDP), largely as a result of declining revenues from higher levels of unemployment and growing informality in the labor markets. Between 1991 and 1999, the pension system generated deficits of 0.7–3.1 percent of GDP (except in 1997, when it barely broke even), highlighting the vulnerability of the system to short-term economic changes.

In response to these deficits—and to the fact that the system will face even greater fiscal pressure as a result of the aging of the population—the government launched a comprehensive reform of the pension system in 2000. The reform program included both the redesign of the existing pay-as-you-go scheme and the introduction of a privately managed, fully funded defined-contribution scheme.

Despite these reforms, the pension system is projected to generate deficits reaching 2.3 percent of GDP by 2050. Improving the long-term finances of the pension system will require that benefits be made less generous, that retirement ages be raised, or both. This trade-off between the financial sustainability of the pension system and the benefits it provides will become even more pronounced as life expectancy increases.

Against this backdrop, this chapter evaluates Bulgaria's pension system, focusing on fiscal sustainability and benefit adequacy. Adequacy is evaluated through the lens of statutory net replacement rates for different retirement ages, patterns of contributions, and income levels relative to international benchmarks.

This chapter is organized as follows. The next section discusses the motivation for the reforms. The following section describes the key characteristics of the reformed pension system. The third section assesses the adequacy of pension benefits and the fiscal sustainability of the system. The last section draws conclusions.

Motivation for Reform

Bulgaria inherited a socialist-era pension scheme that suffered from a number of serious design flaws, including relatively high contribution rates, an unequal distribution of the insurance burden, and early retirement (Shopov 1998, 2001). These flaws became increasingly evident in the 1990s, during the country's transition from central planning to a market economy. As a result of declining formal sector employment and increasing informality in the labor markets, pension system revenues fell, resulting in a pension system deficit of 2.96 percent of GDP in 1991 (table 2.1). Between 1991 and 1999, the pension system generated deficits of 0.7–3.1 percent of GDP (except for 1997, when it barely broke even), as a result of large and unpredictable fluctuations of both revenues and expenditures. Over this period, the number of contributors fell 28 percent, while the number of pensioners increased 5 percent.

Projections indicate that, in the absence of reform, the pension scheme would have generated deficits equivalent to 3.4 percent of GDP by 2050 (figure 2.1). The aging of the population is apparent from projections of the country's old-age dependency ratio (the population age 65 and older divided by the population age 20–64), which is projected to increase from 27.5 percent in 2005 to 65.8 percent by 2050 (figure 2.2).

In response to these deficits—and recognizing that the pension system will face greater fiscal pressure as a result of the aging of the Bulgarian

Table 2.1   Fiscal Balance of Bulgaria's Pension System before Reform, 1990–99

(percentage of GDP)

Year	Revenues[a]	Expenditures	Balance
1990	10.98	10.92	0.06
1991	9.03	11.99	−2.96
1992	11.03	12.31	−1.28
1993	10.35	13.48	−3.13
1994	8.90	11.47	−2.57
1995	7.93	9.18	−1.25
1996	7.10	7.81	−0.71
1997	7.53	7.53	0.00
1998	8.66	9.80	−1.14
1999	8.66	10.23	−1.57

Source: National Social Security Institute 2005.
a. Includes contribution revenues only.

Figure 2.1   Projected Fiscal Balance of Bulgaria's Public Pension System before Reform, 2001–50

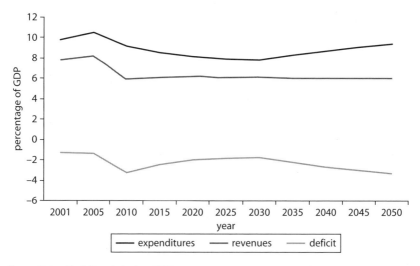

Source: National Social Security Institute 2005.

population—the government launched a comprehensive reform of the system in 2000. This reform included the redesign of the existing pay-as-you-go scheme; the introduction of a privately managed, fully funded defined-contribution scheme; and the shifting of early retirement for workers engaged in hazardous occupations from first-pillar to second-pillar occupational pension schemes sponsored by employers (Hristoskov

Figure 2.2   Projected Old-Age Dependency Ratio in Bulgaria, 2005–50

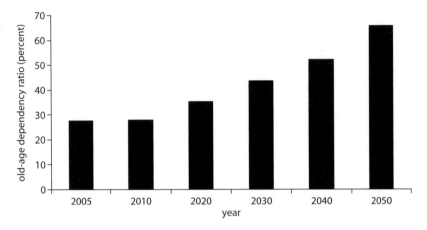

Source: Reiterer 2008.

2000, 2002). This reform moved the pension system from a monopillar design based solely on pay-as-you-go financing to a multipillar design. The new system also includes a voluntary, fully funded defined-contribution scheme, introduced in 1994.

Characteristics of Bulgaria's Pension System

This section describes the main characteristics of Bulgaria's pension system. These include the design of the individual pillars of social insurance; the rules governing pension system taxation, institutional structure, and coverage; and the provisions governing old-age, disability, and survivorship pensions. The design of the pension system is assessed using a conceptual framework developed by the World Bank, which generally recommends including a funded component if conditions are appropriate but increasingly recognizes that a range of choices is available to policy makers to provide effective old-age protection in a manner that is fiscally responsible (see Holzmann and Hinz 2005).

In general, the World Bank supports pension systems composed of some combination of five basic pillars:

• a noncontributory (or zero) pillar (in the form of a demogrant, social pension, or social assistance benefit) intended to provide a minimal level of income protection;

- a first-pillar contributory system linked to earnings, which seeks to replace a portion of preretirement income;
- a mandatory second pillar (essentially, individual savings accounts), which can be designed in various ways;
- a voluntary third pillar, which is flexible and discretionary (this pillar, too, can take a variety of forms); and
- a fourth pillar of informal intrafamily or intergenerational sources of financial and nonfinancial support to the elderly, including access to health care and housing.

Pillar Design

The design of Bulgaria's pension system incorporates all five of the pillars recommended by the World Bank (table 2.2). The publicly managed non-contributory zero pillar, financed with general tax revenues, redistributes income to lower-income groups using means testing, so that eligible beneficiaries receive a benefit sufficient to ensure them a total income equal to the state-defined minimum income guarantee. Both the traditional publicly managed pay-as-you-go first pillar and the privately managed, fully funded second pillar are earnings-related schemes.

First-pillar benefits are computed taking into account the length of an individual's service and the individual's earnings throughout his or her working life. Benefits are adjusted in retirement using a formula based on the average of inflation and wage growth (Swiss indexation), thereby allowing pensions to rise more rapidly than inflation without imposing the heavier fiscal burden of wage indexation.

Second-pillar benefits are determined by an individual's contributions and investment earnings. At retirement, account balances are converted to income streams by the pension fund rather than used to purchase annuities.

Supplementing these earnings-related schemes is a voluntary privately managed third pillar, which is intended to provide individuals with a mechanism for supplementing the benefits provided by the mandatory pillars. The fourth pillar provides health care to the elderly as part of the overall health-care system.

The mandatory first and second pillars are completely tax exempt, a policy that is uncommon. Most countries impose some taxation, at the point at which pension contributions are made, investment income is earned (for funded schemes), or benefits are received (see box 1.1 in chapter 1). The third pillar is subjected to an exempt-exempt-taxed regime, meaning that contributions are partially exempt from taxation, investment income is fully exempt, and benefits are taxed.

Table 2.2 Structure of the Bulgarian Pension System

Scheme type	Coverage	Type	Function	Financing	Generic benefit	Benefit indexation	Taxation		
							Contributions	Investment income/ capital gains	Benefits
Zero pillar (public noncontributory)	Universal	Means tested	Redistribution	Tax revenue	Defined every year by law	Ad hoc decisions by the government	n.a.	n.a.	Exempt
First pillar (public, earnings related)	Mandatory	Defined benefit	Insurance	Percentage of individual earnings	Benefit calculated on the basis of contribution period and individual coefficient	50 percent inflation, 50 percent average insured wage growth over previous year	Exempt	n.a.	Exempt
Second pillar (private, earnings related)	Mandatory	Defined contribution	Insurance	Percentage of individual earnings	Pension from capital accumulation	Income stream from conversion of capital accumulation	Exempt	Exempt	Exempt
Third pillar (private, voluntary)	Voluntary	Defined contribution	Insurance	Voluntary contributions	Pension from capital accumulation	Depends on options chosen	Exempt[a]	Exempt	Taxed
Fourth pillar (public health care)	Mandatory	n.a.	Insurance	Percentage of individual earnings plus tax revenues	Specified basic health service package	n.a.	Exempt	n.a.	n.a.

Sources: European Commission 2007; Shopov 2007.

n.a. = Not applicable.

a. Contributions up to 10 percent of earnings are exempt from taxation; monthly employer contributions of up to lev 60 per worker are exempt from the corporate income tax base.

Noncontributory scheme. Bulgaria provides a noncontributory social pension to people over 70 who are not collecting a pension. Eligibility requires that average income per family member be lower than the guaranteed minimum income for a 12-month period. The government determines the amount of the social pension annually. Since January 2006, the old-age social pension has been roughly 63 leva (Lev) (17.7 percent of the average wage). In 2005, 4,592 people received social pensions (roughly 0.20 percent of the total number of pensioners), a relatively low percentage that reflects the artificial full employment of the socialist era, which qualifies most elderly people for a pension from the first-pillar scheme.

Another noncontributory source of income support comes from the guaranteed minimum income (GMI) program, which provides a means-tested benefit. An important part of the overall social assistance program, the GMI is accessible to the entire population, including the elderly. The amount of GMI was defined in 1992 using an established minimum consumption basket. Since then, it has been increased on the basis of budgetary resources rather than any sort of indexation rule.

In 2005, the GMI was Lev 55 (roughly 37 percent of the minimum wage). The benefits paid under the GMI are adjusted in value such that the beneficiary's total income attains the minimum threshold, which depends on household size, thereby awarding higher benefits to larger households. Retirement benefits are considered when determining the amount of the benefit. In 2005, total expenditures attributable to the GMI were equivalent to 0.26 percent of GDP; 21,600 elderly people (about 10 percent of all GMI beneficiaries) received benefits.

Earnings-related schemes. Both the traditional publicly managed pay-as-you-go first pillar and the privately managed, fully funded second pillar are earnings-related schemes. The first pillar was reformed in 2000; the second pillar was introduced in 2002 (table 2.3). Retirement ages were gradually increased from 60 years to 63 years for men (to be implemented by 2005) and from 55 years to 60 years for women (to be implemented by 2009). Eligibility was made conditional on the accumulation of qualification points, defined as the sum of an individual's age and years of contributions. The income on which benefits are computed was changed from the highest 3 of 15 years of earnings to lifetime earnings (with a grandfather clause for earnings for years before 1997), thereby strengthening the link between contributions and benefits.

The 2000 reforms also introduced two types of fully funded second-pillar pension schemes: occupational schemes, which were launched in

Table 2.3 Parameters of Earnings-Related Schemes in Bulgaria before and after Reform

Scheme type	Period	Vesting period	Contribution rate	Contribution ceiling	Benefit rate	Pension assessment base	Retirement age
First pillar (earnings related, universal)	Prereform	10 years	39 percent (37 percent by employer, 2 percent by employee)	n.a.	55 percent of the wage base (individual coefficient times the average monthly wage for the 3 preceding years)	Highest 3 of last 15 years	60 for men, 55 for women
	Postreform	15 years	23 percent[a] (14.95 percent by employer, 8.05 percent by employee)	Annually fixed in budget law (Lev 1,400 in 2007, roughly 3.5 times average wages)	1 percent per year	Highest 3 of last 15 years before 1997; entire working period after 1997	63 for men, 60 for women
Second pillar (earnings related, universal)	Prereform	n.a.	n.a.	n.a.	n.a.	n.a.	n.a.
	Postreform	n.a.	5 percent (3.25 percent by employer, 1.75 percent by employee)	Annually fixed in the budget law (Lev 1,400 in 2007)	Pension from capital accumulation	Accumulated funds	63 for men, 60 for women (58 for men and 55 for women in case of unemployment)
Second pillar (earnings related, occupational)	Postreform	10 years for Category I, 15 years for Category II	7–12 percent, paid entirely by employer	Annually fixed in budget law (Lev 1,400 in 2007)	Timebound early retirement pension from capital accumulation[b]	Accumulated funds	55 for men and 52 for women for Category I, 60 for men and 57 for women for Category II

Sources: European Commission 2007; Shopov 2007.

n.a. = Not applicable.

a. This figure represents the total contribution for old-age, disability, and survivor pensions in 2007. Individuals participating in only the first pillar pay 23 percent (14.95 percent employer, 8.05 employee). Individuals participating in both the first and the second pillars pay 18 percent (11.70 percent by employer, 6.30 percent by employee) to the first pillar and 5 percent (3.25 percent by employer, 1.75 percent by employee) to the second pillar.

b. This accumulation finances a bridging pension for certain occupations between their low retirement age and the normal retirement age.

2000, and universal (or open) schemes, which were launched in 2002 and are mandatory for people born after December 31, 1959. Second-pillar benefits are a function of an individual's contributions and investment earnings. At retirement, account balances are converted into income streams by the pension fund rather than used to purchase annuities.[1] Both universal earnings-related schemes are financed by contributions from employees and employers; occupational earnings-related schemes are financed by employers only. Before the 2000 reforms, the contribution rate was 39 percent—a comparatively high levy. Because this rate was believed to negatively affect labor competitiveness and create incentives for evasion, the 2000 reforms reduced the rate to reach 23 percent in 2007. Five percentage points of this amount are diverted to the second-pillar universal pension scheme; the remainder is used to finance benefits under the first pillar.

Voluntary scheme. Bulgaria introduced a voluntary privately managed third-pillar pension scheme in 1994 (table 2.4). The scheme is open to everyone 15 and older, with or without an established employer relationship. Contributions must be at least 10 percent of the minimum wage. Actual contributions are determined by a contract with the pension insurance company; they can be set as an absolute amount or as a percentage of the minimum wage or the participant's earnings. When the amount of contributions changes, the contract must be amended. Participants may contribute monthly or at other intervals, depending on the rules of the fund. Lump-sum contributions in larger amounts are also possible. Participation in the scheme is promoted using tax policy. Ten percent of total contributions are fully exempt from taxation. Employers who contribute on behalf of employees may deduct up to Lev 60 per employee per month from their taxable income. Participants are entitled to benefits upon reaching age 58 for men or 55 for women. Participants can collect benefits for five years before reaching retirement age if they are entitled to a benefit from the first-pillar scheme. Disability pensions are provided to people who become incapacitated.

In 2006, eight pension fund management companies operated in the market, two of which managed 71 percent of total assets.[2] In 2005, 549,851 people (10.3 percent of Bulgaria's working-age population) participated in the scheme. At the end of 2006, assets totaled Lev 497.9 million (1.0 percent of GDP).

Health care system. Health care in Bulgaria is provided primarily through mandatory health insurance, although voluntary health insurance is available

Table 2.4   Characteristics of the Voluntary Scheme in Bulgaria

Coverage	Vesting period	Retirement age	Tax advantages to participants	Contributions tax deductible by employers	Lump-sum payments possible in retirement
Open to anyone over age 16	No	58 for men, 55 for women	Yes	Yes	Yes

Source: Shopov 2007.

to supplement the benefits of the mandatory system. The mandatory system covers roughly 92 percent of the population and is managed by the National Health Insurance Fund through contractual relationships with health care providers. The system is financed by contributions from economically active people and from the government on behalf of children under 18 and people receiving social assistance and pensions, among others. In 2007, the contribution rate was 6 percent, evenly split between employers and employees.[3] Contributions paid on behalf of pensioners are based on the amount of their pensions. Pensioners are eligible for the same services as contributors to the health insurance system. The system is also financed by copayments equal to 1 percent of the minimum wage (Lev 180 in 2007) paid upon each visit to a general practitioner or outpatient specialist. Copayments for hospital stays are 2 percent of the minimum wage per day of care, with a ceiling of 10 days a year. Minors, unemployed family members, disabled military personnel, medical staff, prisoners, and people eligible for social assistance (including the elderly receiving social assistance benefits) are not required to make copayments.

In 2005, health expenditures accounted for 7.7 percent of GDP, 60.6 percent of which was public expenditures and 39.4 percent was private expenditure. Of private expenditure, 96.3 percent was attributable to out-of-pocket expenditures (informal payments, direct payments, and copayments) (WHO 2008).

Institutional Structure and Coverage of Earnings-Related Schemes

Bulgaria's mandatory pension schemes cover all salaried employees and self-employed persons, including farmers. The National Social Security Institute (NSSI) administers the first-pillar scheme and various noncontributory pensions through a central office and 28 regional offices. Contributions for the first and second pillars and for health insurance used to be collected by the NSSI. Since January 2006, responsibility for collecting and transferring these contributions has been assumed by the National Revenue Agency, which collects most taxes in Bulgaria.

In 2005, some 2.6 million participants (48.3 percent of the working-age population and 83.5 percent of the labor force) contributed to the first pillar. Of these participants, 2.2 million (84.6 percent of all first-pillar contributors) also participated in the mandatory second pillar and voluntary third pillar.[4] Eight pension fund management companies operate in the mandatory pension fund market, which is overseen by the Financial Supervision Commission. At the end of 2006, assets totaled Lev 1,024.5 million (2.1 percent of GDP), of which 42 percent was managed by the two largest pension fund companies.

Structure of Benefits

The earnings-related pension scheme provides old-age, disability, and survivorship pensions. The provisions governing each of these types of benefits are discussed as follows.[5]

Old-age benefits. Eligibility for an old-age pension in Bulgaria is conditional on the accumulation of qualification points, defined as the sum of an individual's age and years of contributions. Men must accumulate 100 points (37 years of service for men retiring at the normal retirement age), while women must accumulate 94 points (34 years of service for women retiring at the normal retirement age once the age reaches 60 in 2009). The pension assessment base (the wages used in computing benefits) is the product of an individual's coefficient and the average covered earnings over the preceding 12 months.[6] Benefits accrue at the rate of 1 percent of the assessment base per year of contributory service. Starting in January 2007, the accrual rate for each year of service beyond 37 for men and 34 for women was 1.5 percent, an amount that increased to 3 percent in January 2008.

Computing an individual's pension requires multiplying the pension assessment base by the individual's total accrual, which is a function of the individual's length of service. This formula can be presented as follows:

$$\text{old-age pension} = \text{IC} * \text{AMII} \ (12 * \text{CP} * 1 \text{ percent})$$

where IC = the individual coefficient of the pensioner, AMII = the average monthly insurable income over the 12 months before the individual was awarded a pension,[7] and CP = the contribution period (in years).

Early retirement is not permitted, except for certain categories of workers, such as the military and police, who may retire at an earlier age with fewer years of service. Late retirement is available to everyone without restriction.

Subject to eligibility criteria, pensioners may be eligible for benefits under the guaranteed minimum old-age pension, the amount of which is defined in the social security budget each year.[8] People who do not meet these eligibility requirements are eligible for a minimum pension that is 85 percent of the minimum old-age pension, provided they have at least 15 years of credited contributory service and have reached age 65. In 2006, the amount of this pension was Lev 85 (24 percent of the average wage). The maximum pension provided by the first pillar cannot exceed 35 percent of the maximum insurance income for the preceding year. Second-pillar benefits are a function of an individual's contributions, investment earnings, and life expectancy at retirement. Account balances are converted into income streams by the pension fund rather than used to purchase annuities.[9]

Disability benefits. Disability benefits are available to people who elected to remain only in the first-pillar scheme as well as to people who elected to participate in the new two-pillar scheme (table 2.5). Eligibility depends on service, with longer service requirements for older workers. Disability benefits are computed in a manner similar to that used to compute old-age pensions. Service credit is awarded for years lost to disability up to the normal retirement age, with a coefficient applied to these years that reflects the degree of impairment.

For people with more than 90 percent impairment, the coefficient is 0.9; for 71–90 percent impairment, the coefficient is 0.7; for 50–70 percent impairment, the coefficient is 0.5. The minimum disability benefit

Table 2.5   Eligibility Conditions for and Benefits Provided by Disability Pensions under the First Pillar Earnings-Related Scheme in Bulgaria

Vesting period	Contribution rate	Eligibility	Benefit rate	Partial pension
Under age 20: No minimum required Age 20–25: 1 year Age 25–30: 3 years Over age 30: 5 years	No specific contribution rate	At least 50 percent loss of working capacity	1 percent per year	Based on degree of disability

Sources: European Commission 2007; Shopov 2007.

ranges from 85 to 115 percent of the minimum old-age pension, depending on impairment.

Under the second pillar, benefits are paid for life on the basis of the accumulated capital in an individual's account and life expectancy. Benefits are paid directly by the pension fund; annuities are not purchased.

Survivor benefits. Survivor benefits are awarded to the dependents of individuals who, at the time of their death, were receiving (or had met the criteria to receive) an old-age or disability pension (table 2.6). Eligible survivors include widows and widowers who are unable to work or are within five years of the retirement age, orphans up to the age of 18 (26 if attending school), and parents who had been supported by the deceased.

The benefit depends on the number of survivors in the deceased's household. It is 50 percent of the deceased's benefit for one survivor, 75 percent for two survivors, and 100 percent for three or more survivors, divided equally among all survivors. The minimum benefit is 75 percent of the minimum old-age pension (Lev 85 in 2006).

Under the second pillar, survivors of working individuals receive the deceased's account balance paid as a lifetime annuity based on the accumulated capital in the deceased's account and life expectancy. The allocation among survivors is governed by the inheritance law. Benefits are paid directly by the pension fund; annuities are not purchased.

Assessment of the Performance of Bulgaria's Pension System

The World Bank has established four principles for evaluating public pension systems, which together should guide the process of pension reform (see Holzmann and Hinz 2005). Broadly speaking, these include the adequacy and security of benefits, the affordability of contributions, the sustainability of the system over time, and the robustness of the system in the face of demographic changes and macroeconomic shocks. This section focuses primarily on the adequacy of benefits and the financial sustainability of the first- and second-pillar earnings-related pension schemes. The remaining principles are mentioned only briefly. Adequacy is analyzed through the lens of net replacement rates. Financial sustainability is evaluated using projections of pension expenditure and revenues.

Benefit Adequacy

Replacement rates are a useful yardstick for measuring the adequacy of pension benefits, because they express benefits relative to preretirement

Table 2.6 Eligibility Conditions for and Benefits Provided by Survivor Pensions in Bulgaria under the First-Pillar Earnings-Related Scheme

Eligibility	Spouse replacement rate	Benefit duration	Remarriage test	Orphan age limit	Orphan replacement rate	Total family benefit
Eligibility of the deceased for old-age or disability pension	1 survivor: 50 percent of deceased's benefit 2 survivors: 75 percent of deceased's benefit 3 or more survivors: 100 percent of deceased's benefit Alternatively, survivors can receive 20 percent of the pension of the deceased as a supplement to their own pensions.	For life, if spouse is disabled or has reached retirement age	Pension ceases if survivor remarries	18 (26 if orphan is a student)	1 survivor: 50 percent of deceased's benefit 2 survivors: 75 percent of deceased's benefit 3 or more survivors: 100 percent of deceased's benefit	100 percent regardless of number of survivors; if pension is less than minimum pension, minimum pension is paid

Sources: European Commission 2007; Shopov 2007.

earnings, thereby indicating the degree to which income is replaced when workers retire. Two variants are commonly used. Gross replacement rates compute income replacement as the ratio of benefits paid to pretax preretirement earnings. Net replacement rates compute income replacement as the ratio of benefits received (that is, after the payment of taxes and other levies, including contributions for social insurance) to posttax preretirement earnings. In general, net replacement rates are a more useful measure of benefit adequacy, because they capture the degree to which actual take-home pay is replaced when workers retire.

The level of income replacement at retirement is not the only measure of benefit adequacy. To fully assess benefit adequacy, it is also important to determine how postretirement indexation rules will affect replacement rates during retirement. Pension benefits in retirement are expected to be indexed to inflation, so that their real value is maintained. In a growing economy with rising real wages, however, mere price indexation of pensions leads to a deterioration of the relative consumption position of the retirees. For this reason, some countries have introduced mixed indexation of pensions that use varying weights of inflation and wage growth in the indexation formula.

In order to evaluate the effect of indexation on replacement rates in Bulgaria, the replacement rates are normalized to 100 percent, and the assumptions for calculating the replacement rates are maintained (that is, inflation is 2.5 percent a year and real wage growth is 2.0 percent a year). The change in the replacement rate is measured in comparison to full wage indexation or the earnings of an active worker. The results of this analysis indicate that the relative income position of a retiree would deteriorate by 16 percent after 10 years in retirement and by 45 percent after 35 years in retirement. (The evaluation of income replacement that follows considers replacement rates only at retirement; it does not take into account the impact of indexation policies on replacement rates during retirement.)

Replacement rates are a function of the formula governing pension benefits; an individual's contribution history; and, in the case of net replacement rates, the rules of income tax, social security contributions, and other relevant levies. The benefit formula establishes the degree to which the system redistributes income across individuals of different levels of preretirement earnings. Progressive systems provide higher levels of income replacement to people with lower levels of preretirement income. In general, the degree to which a system is redistributive depends on the existence (and value) of flat transfers and minimum pension guarantees, the degree to which benefits are earnings related, and the existence of ceilings on earnings subject to contributions. An individual's contribution history can be characterized by his or her age of entry into the labor force, contribution density, and decisions regarding the timing of retirement. To some degree, these three factors are influenced by the incentives embodied in the pension system. The tax and contribution system influences net replacement rates through the progressiveness of the income tax formula, which taxes (higher) income during a worker's active life more than it taxes (lower) pension benefits in retirement. In addition, social security levies (for pensions; unemployment; health care; and, at times, housing and family benefits) are typically reduced or eliminated altogether in retirement. These benefits are particularly important for low- to middle-income groups.

Benchmarks need to be established for the evaluation of the adequacy of the income replacement provided by the earnings-related pension schemes. Unfortunately, there is no consensus on what constitutes adequacy. According to one widely respected definition, pensions are adequate when they are sufficient to prevent poverty among the elderly and provide the vast majority of the population with a reliable mechanism for smoothing income over a lifetime. Even with a definition, however, establishing benchmarks is problematic, because attitudes vary across countries as a result of social and cultural perceptions. Moreover, benchmarks ignore the other factors that affect the welfare of the elderly—and that also vary across countries—including the existence and generosity of health insurance and long-term care, the cost of housing, the structure of traditional living arrangements, the presence of informal intrafamily or intergenerational sources of financial and nonfinancial support, and the availability and security of other mechanisms for people to save for their own retirement.

One reputable nine-country study (OECD 2001) observes that living standards are roughly comparable for people 10 years older than the normal retirement age and people 15 years younger than the normal retirement age when retirees have disposable income equal to roughly 80 percent of the disposable income of working-age people. In part, this is attributable to the fact that retirees have no work-related expenses (they do not have to commute or buy special clothing or uniforms, for example). This finding, however, does not imply that mandatory first-pillar pension schemes should actually target an 80 percent net replacement rate. To the contrary, in middle- and high-income countries, one can reasonably expect individuals to save for their own retirement—and the empirical evidence suggests that, in practice, they do so.[10] There is also some evidence to suggest that the ratio between pre- and postretirement income is somewhat independent of the income replacement mandate of the public pension system. Put simply, individuals tend to save more in countries with more modest mandates (and vice versa).

Because Bulgaria has access to relatively well-developed financial markets, it would seem reasonable to expect middle- and higher-income workers to save enough to finance at least 25 percent, if not closer to 50 percent, of this 80 percent income replacement target. Given this, three benchmarks are provided: a 40 percent net replacement rate (which implies that individuals would be expected to save enough to finance half of the total income replacement target); a 60 percent net replacement rate (which implies that individuals would be expected to finance a quarter of the target); and an 80 percent net replacement rate (which implies that individuals, most of whom would be low-income earners, would not be expected to contribute anything toward the target).[11] In the following analysis, these benchmarks are used to evaluate the adequacy of benefits in Bulgaria compared with the average net replacement rate observed in 53 countries around the world, the average net replacement rate observed in selected countries in Europe and Central Asia, and the poverty line in Bulgaria.[12]

To estimate gross and net replacement rates, we use the Analysis of Pension Entitlements across Countries (APEX) model to consider two critical dimensions: earnings levels and contribution periods.[13] This model generates estimates for replacement rates under steady-state assumptions (that is, as if the rules of the reformed pension scheme had been in place over the entire active life of the individual). Because life expectancies at retirement are projected to increase over time—which will affect the benefits paid by defined-contribution pension schemes— a reference year must be chosen. For the purpose of this study, 2040 is used, because it provides a sufficiently long contribution period over which to approximate steady-state conditions.

The first critical task is to investigate levels of income replacement across a relevant spectrum of income. Income is represented as a percentage (50–200 percent) of average earnings. The second task is to investigate the impact on income replacement of differences in the duration, timing, and density of an individual's contribution history (where density refers to the percentage of time an individual actually contributes over a given period). To facilitate the presentation of these multidimensional results, replacement rates are computed as a function of the age at which an individual exits the labor market. They are presented separately for full-career and partial-career workers.

Replacement rates for full-career workers. Projected replacement rates for full-career workers are examined first. For the purpose of this analysis, a full career is defined as continuous employment from age 20 to the current normal retirement age of 63 for men. Gross replacement rates clearly show why the earnings-related pension schemes have been described as providing a strong link between benefits and contributions (figure 2.3). Irrespective of income, gross replacement rates are 74.8 percent (55.0 percentage points provided by the first pillar, 19.8 percentage points provided by the second pillar).

The situation does not change significantly when taxes are taken into consideration (figure 2.4). High-income earners receive net replacement rates that are identical to low- and middle income earners.

Examination of replacement rates for full-career workers indicates that these pensions are adequate (figure 2.5), with replacement rates for all levels of preretirement income higher than the high benchmark.[14] This suggests that the pension system is effectively smoothing consumption from work into retirement for all full-career workers and that the objective of poverty alleviation is being met. Levels of income replacement for

Figure 2.3   Sources of Gross Replacement Rates in Bulgaria, by Income Level

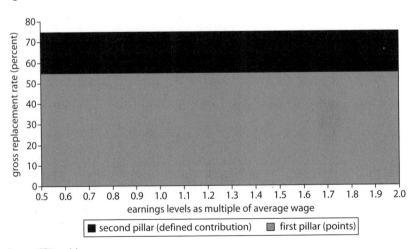

Source: APEX model.

Note: Figure shows projected replacement rate for full-career worker in 2040 as approximation of steady-state conditions.

Figure 2.4   Sources of Net Replacement Rates in Bulgaria, by Income Level

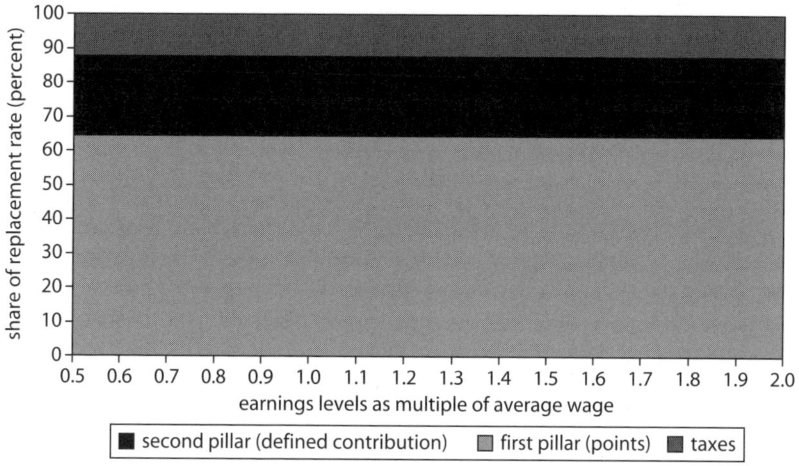

Source: APEX model.

Note: Figure shows projected replacement rate for full-career worker in 2040 as approximation of steady-state conditions.

almost all full-career workers in Bulgaria are higher than regional and world averages. The Bulgarian pension system provides relatively little redistribution from comparatively well-off individuals to those with lower levels of preretirement income.

Replacement rates for partial-career workers. Not everyone works from age 20 to the statutory retirement age. Many individuals enter and exit the labor force (often at different ages and for different periods of time) and earn different wages while working (figure 2.6). To examine the adequacy of benefits for partial-career workers, we consider three stylized cases. These cases include career type A (defined as someone entering the labor force at age 25 who works continuously for a period of years before leaving the workforce at some point between the ages of 50 and 70 and then claims a benefit); career type B (identical to career type A, except that the worker enters the workforce at age 30 and leaves no earlier than age 55); and career type C (identical to career type A, except that the individual contributes in only three years out of four while in the labor force). In cases where the withdrawal from the formal labor market occurs before the statutory retirement age, the pension is claimed (and the replacement rate calculated) only at the later age. For withdrawals after the statutory retirement age, the ages coincide.

Figure 2.5   Net Replacement Rates for Male Full-Career Workers in Bulgaria, Europe and Central Asia, and the World, by Income Level

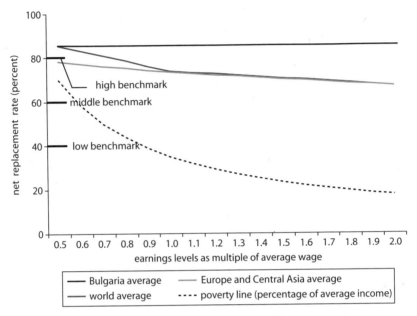

Source: Authors' calculations based on World Bank 2007 and the APEX model.

Note: Figure shows projected replacement rate for full-career worker in 2040 as approximation of steady-state conditions.

Several conclusions can be drawn from figure 2.6. First, leaving the workforce early can be costly. Someone retiring before reaching the retirement age may not receive levels of income replacement higher than even the lowest of the three benchmarks—and those leaving very early may receive levels of income replacement below the poverty line. Second, entering the workforce later in life is costly. Someone entering the workforce at the age of 30 receives a net replacement rate that is 3–21 percentage points lower than someone entering the workforce at age 25. Third, working intermittently is costly. Someone entering the workforce at the same age but who contributes only three years out of four will receive a net replacement rate that is 3–41 percentage points lower than someone who contributes continuously. In all cases, net replacement rates grow faster the longer someone continues to work. This is encouraging, because it indicates that the pension system provides incentives for people to remain in the workforce. Although career type A workers can attain

Figure 2.6   Net Replacement Rates for Male Middle-Income Partial-Career Workers in Bulgaria, by Career Type and Exit Age

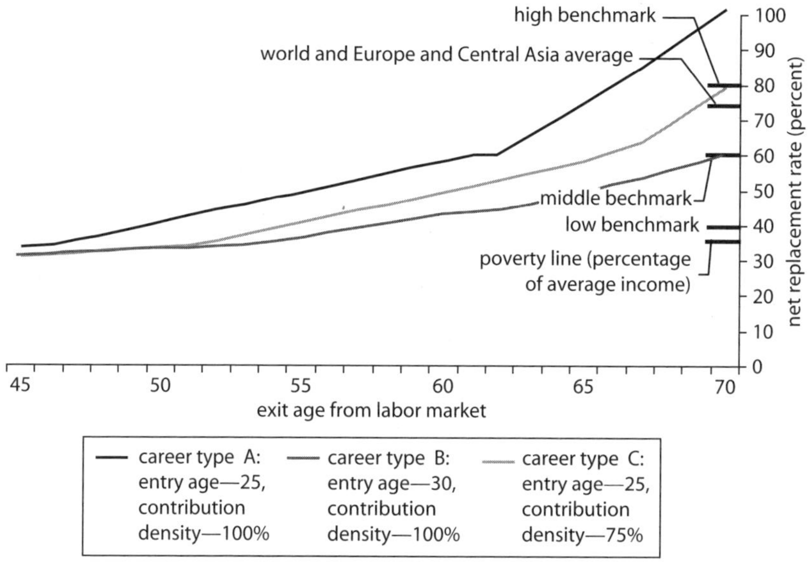

Source: Authors' calculations based on World Bank 2007 and the APEX model.

Note: Figure shows projected replacement rate for partial-career worker in 2040 as approximation of steady-state conditions. (See text for descriptions of career types.)

the 60 percent benchmark before reaching the normal retirement age, career type B and C workers must work three and seven years, respectively, beyond the normal retirement age to attain this benchmark. To replace 80 percent of preretirement earnings, career type A workers must work three years past the normal retirement age. Career type B workers must work until age 70 to attain the 80 percent benchmark. Career type C workers cannot attain the 80 percent benchmark even if they work until age 70.

Fiscal Sustainability

The sustainability of a pay-as-you-go first-pillar pension scheme is best evaluated in actuarial terms by estimating the scheme's actuarial deficit as the difference between its assets and liabilities. If a large actuarial deficit exists, the scheme is financially unsustainable and needs policy actions that increase its assets, reduce its liabilities, or both. A good proxy for the actuarial deficit is the difference between the present value of the scheme's expected future revenues (that is, contributions and other income) and expected future expenditures (that is, benefit payments, administrative costs, and other expenses) over an extended projection period. The difference between these two values represents an unfunded liability (sometimes referred to as a financing gap) on the public sector balance sheet. Because this study is also concerned with the time path of revenues and expenditures (and the resulting balance across the projection period ending in 2050), this more pragmatic approach has been taken. Projections of expenditures, revenues, and deficits are presented on the basis of available postreform fiscal projections.

Despite the improvements attributable to the reforms of 2000, the Bulgarian pension system is expected to generate deficits into the foreseeable future (figure 2.7). Revenues are projected to stabilize at about 8–9 percent of GDP over the period 2001–50, reaching 8.4 percent of GDP by 2050. Expenditures are projected to increase from 9.7 percent of GDP in 2001 to 10.7 percent of GDP by 2050, as first-pillar benefits decline as a share of the total benefits provided by the first two pillars. The net result is a projected deficit of 2.3 percent of GDP in 2050.

What options exist for restoring the system to fiscal balance? Unfortunately, for policy makers, the options are limited. Revenues can be increased by increasing the contribution rate. Alternatively—or in addition, as the options are not mutually exclusive—expenditures can be reduced by cutting benefits, increasing the minimum number of years

Figure 2.7   Projected Fiscal Balance of Bulgaria's Public Pension System after Reform, 2001–50

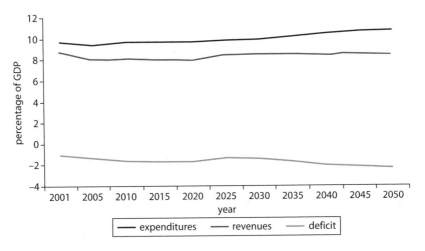

Source: National Social Security Institute 2005.

required to become eligible for benefits, or delaying the payment of benefits by raising the retirement age further. Because raising the contribution rate could threaten competitiveness and will likely strengthen incentives for tax evasion, it is typically not embraced (it would also represent a reversal of policy, because Bulgaria deliberately reduced the contribution rate since 2000 to dampen the adverse impact of high taxes on labor markets). This leaves cutting benefits, tightening eligibility conditions, or raising the retirement age. As a major part of the deficit reflects the transition deficit toward the second pillar, the government may also consider financing part or all of the transition deficit through general revenues. If it does otherwise, restoring sustainability may reduce the adequacy of benefits provided to future beneficiaries. (A back-of-the-envelope analysis suggests that by 2050, retirement ages would have to be increased to at least 69 for men and women in order to bring the system to long-term fiscal balance.[15])

If retirement ages are left unchanged and the current structure of the system is retained, further cuts in benefits—on the order of a 32 percent reduction in the average benefit provided under the first pillar—will be required to make the system sustainable. If benefits are adjusted to maintain a similar fiscal balance in proportion to the overall size of the first-pillar scheme, full-career workers will receive replacement rates roughly 20 percentage points lower in 2040 than they receive today (figure 2.8).

Two conclusions can be drawn from comparison of these new (and lower) net replacement rates against the three benchmarks. First, a 32 percent reduction in benefits results in income replacement broadly at the poverty line for low-income full-career workers. For middle- and high-income full-career workers, replacement rates are significantly higher than the poverty line. This indicates that the pension meets its poverty alleviation objective. Second, the same reduction in benefits will still support the objective of smoothing consumption for middle- and high-income full-career workers, because levels of income replacement are still higher than their 60 percent benchmark.

This last observation is subject to three caveats. First, this analysis considers only full-career workers, while the average worker now contributes for only 27–30 years, substantially less than the 43 years expected of a full career. Contributing to the pension scheme for only 33 years, for example, reduces net income replacement by 30 percentage points for the average worker. Second, if benefit cuts are combined with further increases in the retirement age, benefit cuts will not need to be as steep in order to restore fiscal balance. Third, workers always have the option

Figure 2.8   Net Replacement Rates for Men in Bulgaria before and after Benefit Adjustment

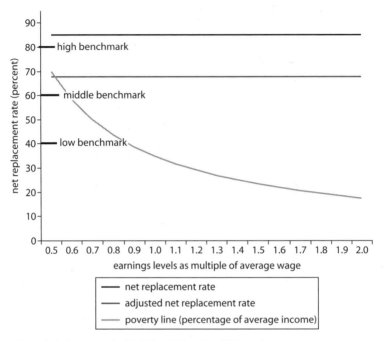

Source: Authors' calculations based on World Bank 2007 and the APEX model.

Note: Figure shows projected replacement rate for full-career worker in 2040 as approximation of steady-state conditions.

of saving outside of the first-pillar pension scheme. To increase income replacement by 1 percentage point, for example, a full-career worker would need to save only about 0.47 percent of his or her earnings from age 40 to the current age of retirement.[16]

Conclusions

In response to deficits in the public pension system—and to the fact that the system will face even greater fiscal pressure as a result of the aging of the population—Bulgaria launched a comprehensive reform of the pension system between 2000 and 2002. The reform program included both the redesign of the existing pay-as-you-go scheme and the introduction of a privately managed, fully funded defined-contribution scheme, which provides workers with a mechanism for diversifying their retirement savings.

Together, these reforms strengthened the link between contributions and benefits and improved incentives for workers to remain in the workforce after reaching the minimum retirement age. The resulting gross and net replacement rates for full-career workers are well above the high benchmark of 80 percent (and higher than regional and international benchmarks [see chapter 1]). As in other countries, workers with less than full careers—because they left the workforce before reaching retirement age, worked intermittently, or have gaps in their employment history—risk receiving income replacement that is closer to—or even below—the lower benchmark of 40 percent.

As a result of reform, the long-term fiscal position of Bulgaria's pension system has improved somewhat, with projected deficits falling from 3.9 percent of GDP in 2008 to 2.3 percent of GDP in 2050. Unless the government is willing and able to finance part or all of the transition deficit resulting from the introduction of the second pillar from general revenues, however, further improvements in the fiscal balance of the first-pillar scheme will require it to increase retirement ages further, to reduce benefits, or both. Increasing the retirement age in step with increases in life expectancy at retirement is a natural choice for both individuals and policy makers, but it requires cross-sectoral policy reforms to enable elderly workers to continue to participate in the labor market.[17]

If retirement ages are left unchanged, average initial replacement rates will have to be reduced by some 20 percentage points to restore the scheme to fiscal balance. Roughly half of these savings can be achieved by moving from Swiss indexation to price indexation of benefits. Following a reduction in benefits, the pension system would still meet its poverty alleviation objective, but it would not be able to adequately smooth income for low-income partial-career workers. Of course, individuals have the option of participating in the voluntary fully funded third-pillar pension scheme, which was introduced to enable workers to save more for retirement than is provided by the mandatory schemes. This option is less relevant for low-income individuals, however, who have lower saving capacity.

Notes

1. There appears to be sufficient political will to enact amendments governing the conversion of accumulated capital from the funded scheme into lifetime annuities, but the mechanism by which those annuities will be provided is still being debated.

2. See the Web site of the Financial Supervision Commission (http://www.fsc.bg). Each company manages three separate pension funds (two that are mandatory and one that is voluntary).

3. The government had planned to increase the contribution rate for health care to 8 percent in 2008, but the increase was postponed until 2009. The ratio of the shares paid by employers and employees has changed and is expected to change further over time. The ratio was 80:20 in 2000, 75:25 in 2002–04, and 70:30 in 2005. Going forward, it will be 60:40 in 2008, 55:45 in 2009, and 50:50 from 2010 onward.

4. Some 66.5 percent of all workers participated in universal (open) funds, 3.8 percent participated in occupational (closed) funds, and 14.3 percent participated in voluntary pension funds in 2005.

5. These rules apply to new entrants; people with accrued rights are subject to transition provisions not addressed in this discussion.

6. An individual's coefficient is determined using the ratio of the individual's average contributory income over three consecutive years (chosen by the individual from the period 1982–96) to the national average salary over the same three-year period) and the ratio of the individual's average contributory income from 1997 onward to the national average monthly salary over the same period (European Commission 2007).

7. The NSSI calculates and publishes this amount every month.

8. The minimum pension is also the basis for the minimum disability pension and the minimum survivor pension.

9. The first old-age beneficiaries are not expected to begin drawing benefits until about 2018. Currently, the rules provide for phased withdrawals, because annuities have not yet been legislated (and only disability pensioners are currently receiving benefits).

10. In Chile, for instance, 70 percent of retirees from the mandatory public pension system own their home, which is a form of savings (see Valdés-Prieto 2008).

11. These benchmarks approximate the standards developed by the International Labour Organization (ILO) and the Council of Europe (1990). ILO Convention 102 of 1952 sets a minimum benefit equal to 40 percent of the reference wage for married men of pensionable age. This amount was raised to 45 percent in 1968. The European Code of Security of 1990 sets a minimum standard for members of the Council of Europe equal to 65 percent for married people of a specific age.

12. As a proxy for the poverty line, this study uses 35 percent of the average net wage, which very broadly approximates a US$2.25-a-day poverty line converted into national currency, adjusted for purchasing power parity, expressed relative to the national average net wage, and averaged across the

nine study countries. Such an approach enables valid comparisons to be made across the sample (see chapter 1).

13. The APEX model was developed by Axia Economics, with funding from the OECD and the World Bank. The model codes detailed eligibility and benefit rules for first- and second-pillar schemes based on available public information that has been verified by country contacts. Because the details of the rules sometimes change on short notice (and limited public disclosure), the calculations presented here should be considered as best approximations only.

14. Replacement rates are simulated for an unmarried male working a hypothetical career path under the assumption that real wage growth is 2 percent, inflation is 2.5 percent, the rate of return on invested assets is 3.5 percent, and the worker retires at the statutory retirement age. Replacement rates shown do not consider the benefits received from occupational schemes.

15. This estimate is based on the World Bank's baseline demographic projections, which assume that everyone over the age of 68 receives a pension, everyone age 20–68 contributes, and all pensioners receive the replacement rate awarded from the first pillar to the median worker.

16. This estimate is based on the assumption that real wage growth is 2 percent, the net real rate of return on invested assets is 3.5 percent, and benefits (both from the unfunded and funded pillars) are price indexed. Country-specific mortality rates are used in this analysis.

17. See Holzmann, MacKellar, and Repansek (2009) for a conference volume that addresses theses issues for the countries of southeastern Europe.

Bibliography

Council of Europe. 1990. *European Code of Social Security (Revised)*. Rome.

Georgieva, L., P. Salchev, R. Dimitrova, A. Dimova, and O. Avdeeva. 2007. *Health Systems in Transition: Bulgaria*. European Observatory on Health Systems and Policies, Copenhagen.

European Commission. 2007. Mutual Information System and Social Protection (MISSOC) database. http://ec.europa.eu/employment_social/.

Financial Supervision Commission. 2005. *Annual Report*. Sofia.

———. 2006. *Annual Activity Report*. Sofia.

GVG (Gesellschaft für Versicherungswissenschaft und -gestaltung) and European Commission. 2003. *Study on the Social Protection Systems in the 13 Applicant Countries: Bulgaria Country Report*. Cologne.

Holzmann, R., and R. Hinz. 2005. *Old Age Income Support in the 21st Century*. Washington, DC: World Bank.

Holzmann, R., L. MacKellar, and J. Repansek, eds. 2009. *Pension Reform in Southeastern Europe: Linking to Labor and Financial Market Reforms*. Washington, DC: World Bank.

Hristoskov, J. 2000. "Mandatory Social Insurance: Changes, Nature, and Content." In *The Bulgarian Pension Model*, USAID Bulgarian Pension Reform Project, Sofia.

———. 2002 "The Relations between the Public and Private Pension Insurance Systems: The Bulgarian and Foreign experience." *Private Pension Series 4*, Organisation for Economic Co-operation and Development, Paris.

ILO (International Labour Organisation). 1952. *ILO Convention 102*. Geneva: ILO.

———. 1967. *ILO Convention 128*. Geneva: ILO.

National Social Security Institute. 2005. *Statistical Yearbook*. Sophia: National Social Security Institute.

OECD (Organisation for Economic Co-operation and Development). 2001. *Ageing and Income: Financial Resources and Retirement in 9 OECD Countries*. Paris: OECD.

Reiterer, A. 2008. *Population Development and Age Structure in Southeastern Europe until 2050*. Social Protection and Labor Unit, World Bank, Washington, DC.

Shopov, G. 1998. "Bulgarie: La reforme du système de retraite." *Chronique Internationale de l'IRES 55*. November.

———. 2001. "Bulgarian Pension System in Restructuring." In *Ten Years of Economic Transformation. Vol. III. Studies in Industrial Engineering and Management 16*. Lappeenranta University of Technology, Finland.

———. 2007. "The Bulgarian Pension System." Background paper prepared for this chapter. Institute of Economics, Bulgarian Academy of Sciences, Sofia.

U.S. Social Security Administration. 2006. *Social Security Systems throughout the World: Europe*. Washington, DC: Social Security Administration.

Valdés-Prieto, S. 2008. *Designs for the First-Pillar Pensions and the 2008 Chilean Reform*. http://editorialexpress.com/cgi-bin/conference/download.cgi?db_name=SECHI2008&paper_id=130.

World Bank. 1999. *Pension Reform Strategy of Bulgaria*. http://www.worldbank.org/pensions.

———. 2007. *Pensions Panorama*. Washington, DC: World Bank.

WHO (World Health Organization). 2008. Database. http://www.who.int/research/en/.

CHAPTER 3

Croatia

Croatia inherited from the former Yugoslavia a traditional defined-benefit pension system financed on a pay-as-you-go basis (meaning that contributions from current workers are used to pay benefits to current beneficiaries). Within a few years of the country's transition to a market economy, pension expenditures began to increase, from a level equivalent to 9.7 percent of gross domestic product (GDP) in 1994 to 12.8 percent of GDP by 2000. Over this period, pension revenues declined from 8.1 percent of GDP to 7.3 percent of GDP, resulting in a pension deficit of 5.5 percent of GDP in 2000.

Recognizing that these deficits were not sustainable and that the system would face even greater challenges in the medium to long term as the population ages, the government began a process of pension reform in 1995 that eventually replaced the traditional scheme with a three-pillar pension system—an approach to reform that was relatively common among transition economies. In 1998, the government replaced the traditional defined-benefit formula with a new formula based on points. In 2002, it introduced a mandatory funded defined-contribution pension scheme and a voluntary scheme to supplement the two mandated schemes. As a result of these reforms, revenues are now projected to remain stable and expenditures to drop gradually, so that the deficit will become progressively smaller by 2040.

Against this backdrop, this chapter evaluates the Croatian pension system, focusing on fiscal sustainability and benefit adequacy. Adequacy is evaluated through the lens of statutory net replacement rates for different retirement ages, patterns of contributions, and income levels, with comparisons to international benchmarks.

The chapter is organized as follows. The next section discusses the motivation for the reforms. The following section describes the key characteristics of the reformed pension system. The third section assesses the adequacy of pension benefits and the fiscal sustainability of the system. The last section draws conclusions.

Motivation for Reform

Upon gaining independence in 1991, Croatia inherited a socialist-era public pension system financed on a pay-as-you-go basis. The system suffered from a number of serious design flaws similar to those observed in other transition economies, including low retirement ages, special privileges for certain occupations, and a high incidence of disability among war veterans. The fiscal balance of the pension system deteriorated steadily throughout the 1990s, with the deficit increasing from 1.6 percent of GDP in 1994 to 5.5 percent of GDP by 2000. The rising deficit was largely the result of steadily rising expenditures (table 3.1), although revenues did fall slightly between 1996 and 2000 as a result of reduced formal sector employment (caused partly by rising unemployment and partly by increasing labor market informality) and enterprise restructuring. The pension system was expected to face even greater challenges in the medium to long term, as the population ages. Croatia's old-age dependency ratio (the population age 65 and older divided by the population age 20–64) is expected

Table 3.1   Projected Fiscal Balance of Croatia's Public Pension System before Reform, 1994–2000

(percentage of GDP)

Year	Revenues	Expenditures	Balance
1994	8.1	9.7	−1.6
1995	8.6	10.8	−2.2
1996	8.7	11.4	−2.7
1997	8.6	12.5	−3.9
1998	7.5	12.0	−4.5
1999	7.4	13.3	−5.9
2000	7.3	12.8	−5.5

Source: Anusic, O'Keefe, and Madzarevic-Sujster 2003.

Figure 3.1   Projected Old-Age Dependency Ratio in Croatia, 2006–50

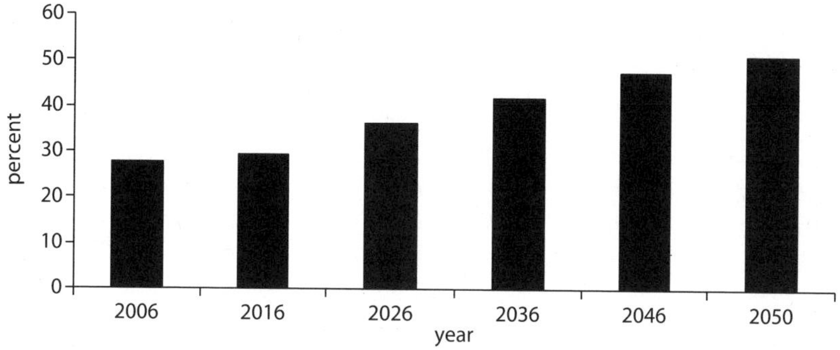

Source: Reiterer 2008.

to increase substantially in the coming decades, from 27.8 percent in 2006 to 51.1 percent by 2050 (figure 3.1).[1]

Recognizing these challenges, the government began a process of pension reform in 1995. In 1998, it eliminated the traditional defined-benefit formula used to calculate pensions in favor of a new formula based on points. In 2002, once a regulatory system was in place for the licensing of pension fund companies and a central clearinghouse had been established, it introduced a mandatory funded defined-contribution pension scheme and a voluntary scheme to supplement the two mandated schemes.

Characteristics of Croatia's Pension System

The main characteristics of the Croatian pension system include the design of the individual pillars of social insurance; the rules governing pension system taxation; and the institutional structure, coverage, and provisions governing old-age, disability, and survivorship pensions. The design of the pension system is assessed using a conceptual framework developed by the World Bank, which generally recommends including a funded component if conditions are appropriate but increasingly recognizes that a range of choices is available to policy makers to provide effective old-age protection in a manner that is fiscally responsible (Holzmann and Hinz 2005).

In general, the World Bank supports pension systems composed of some combination of five basic pillars:

• a noncontributory (or zero) pillar (in the form of a demogrant, social pension, or social assistance benefit) intended to provide a minimal level of income protection

- a first-pillar contributory system linked to earnings, which seeks to replace a portion of preretirement income
- a mandatory second pillar (essentially, individual savings accounts), which can be designed in various ways
- a voluntary third pillar, which is flexible and discretionary (this pillar, too, can take a variety of forms)
- a fourth pillar of informal intrafamily or intergenerational sources of financial and nonfinancial support to the elderly, including access to health care and housing.

Pillar Design

The reformed pension system provides old-age income support to the elderly through all five of these pillars (table 3.2.) The publicly managed noncontributory zero pillar, financed with general tax revenues, redistributes income to lower income groups using means testing such that eligible beneficiaries receive a benefit sufficient to provide them with a minimum state-defined income (which varies by household size). Benefits are adjusted on an ad hoc basis.

Both the traditional publicly managed pay-as-you-go first pillar and the privately managed, fully funded second pillar are earnings-related schemes. Participation in both schemes is mandatory for new entrants and people who were under 40 when the reforms were implemented. First-pillar benefits are computed on the basis of a point system and indexed using a combination of wage and price growth (or Swiss indexation) whereby benefits increase with wages but at a lower rate. Second-pillar benefits are a function of an individual's contributions, investment earnings, and life expectancy at retirement. The third pillar is an optional privately managed, fully funded defined-contribution pension scheme intended to provide individuals with a mechanism for supplementing the benefits paid by the mandatory pillars. The fourth pillar provides health care to the elderly as part of the national health care system.

First-pillar contributions are exempt from taxation, while benefits are taxed. The fully funded second and third pillars are subjected to exempt-exempt-taxed taxation (a classic expenditure tax), meaning that contributions are exempt from taxation and investment income is exempt but benefits are taxed (see box 1.1 in chapter 1). The noncontributory zero pillar (which provides a means-tested benefit for the poor) and the fourth pillar (which provides health care coverage) are completely tax exempt.

Table 3.2 Structure of the Croatian Pension System

Scheme type	Coverage	Type	Function	Financing	Generic benefit	Benefit indexation	Taxation		
							Contributions	Investment income/ capital gains	Benefits
Zero pillar (public, noncontributory)	Universal	Means tested	Redistributive	Tax revenues	Certain percentage of state-defined benefit, depending on household size	Ad hoc	n.a.	n.a.	Exempt
First pillar (public, earnings related)	Mandatory	Point	Insurance	Percentage of individual earnings	Depends on individual wage earned in relation to average wage and length of coverage	50 percent prices, 50 percent wages	Exempt	n.a.	Taxed
Second pillar (private, earnings related)	Mandatory	Defined contribution	Insurance	Percentage of individual earnings	Annuity from capital accumulation	Consumer price index	Exempt	Exempt	Taxed
Third pillar (private, voluntary)	Voluntary	Defined contribution	Insurance	Voluntary contributions	Pension from capital accumulation	Depends on options chosen	Exempt[a]	Exempt	Taxed
Fourth pillar (public health care)	Mandatory	n.a.	Insurance	Percentage of individual earnings plus tax revenues	Specified health service package	n.a.	Exempt	n.a.	n.a.

Sources: Anusic 2007; Anusic, O'Keefe, and Madzarevic-Sujster 2003; INPRS 2003.

n.a. = Not applicable.

a. Contributions of up to 12,000 kunas per year can be deducted from personal income for tax purposes.

93

Noncontributory scheme. A noncontributory social assistance scheme provides financial support to households whose income falls below a minimum threshold. The program is open to anyone, including the elderly. Benefits are means tested. The amount of the benefit is set as a percentage of the state-defined subsistence allowance. The percentage depends on the applicant's age and the size of his or her household. Benefits are adjusted on an ad hoc basis. In 2005, 2.7 percent of the population received a social assistance benefit, at a cost equivalent to 0.22 percent of GDP (World Bank 2007a).

Earnings-related schemes. Both the traditional, publicly managed, pay-as-you-go first pillar and the privately managed, fully funded second pillar are earnings-related schemes. The defined-benefit formula used to calculate pensions under the traditional first-pillar scheme was eliminated in 1998 in favor of a new formula based on points, which are determined by an individual's wages relative to the average wage (table 3.3). The number of years of wages on which benefits are based is gradually increasing, from 10 years to the entirety of an individual's service, thereby tightening the link between the individual's lifetime contributions and the benefits he or she receives in retirement.

The fully funded second-pillar pension scheme was made optional for people age 40–50 but mandatory for everyone under age 40 at the time the scheme was introduced. Because low retirement ages (60 for men and 55 for women) were partly responsible for the fiscal imbalances of the pension system, the reforms raised retirement ages by six months a year, starting in 2000, such that the ages reached 65 for men and 60 for women in 2008. The fact that women can still retire five years earlier than men is problematic, given that women are expected to live eight years longer on average and to collect benefits for more than twice as long as men.[2] To finance the two mandated schemes, employees contribute 20 percent of their wages, 5 percentage points of which go the funded second pillar. For individuals enrolled only in the first-pillar scheme (most of whom are older), all of their contributions go to the first pillar.

Voluntary scheme. The voluntary third-pillar scheme was introduced in 2002, at the same time as the mandatory second-pillar scheme. All adult citizens may participate in the scheme, and employers can make contributions on behalf of participating employees (table 3.4). To encourage participation, the government matches 25 percent of the contributions made

Table 3.3   Parameters of Earnings-Related Schemes in Croatia before and after Reform

Pillar	Stage	Vesting period	Contribution rate	Contribution ceiling	Benefit rate	Pension assessment base	Retirement age
First pillar (earnings related)	Prereform	15 years	25.5 percent		2.2 percent for men and 2.5 percent accrual rate for women	10 best consecutive years' wages	55 for women and 60 for men
	Postreform	15 years	20 percent all from employees[b]	5 times the average wage	0.75 percent a year for an average worker participating in the first pillar only; for second-pillar participant, 0.25 percent of first-pillar benefits plus 0.25 percent of average wage (flat)	Gradually increasing to full-career by 2010	Increasing gradually to 60 for women and 65 for men by 2008
Second pillar (earnings related)	Prereform	n.a.	n.a.	n.a.	n.a.	n.a.	n.a.
	Postreform	15 years	5 percent by employee	5 times the average wage	Life annuity for single people; mandatory joint- and-survivor annuity for married couple. If both spouses (without children) agree, they can take single annuities. People with children under age 18 receive a mandatory annuity with a guarantee period until child reaches age 18.	Accumulated funds	Increasing gradually to 60 for women and 65 for men by 2008

Sources: Anusic, O'Keefe, and Madzarevic-Sujster 2003; consultations with World Bank staff.

n.a. = Not applicable.

a. Until 2009, men are eligible for a pension after completing 40 years of service (for women, the requirement is 35 years) and reaching the retirement ages specified under the prereform scheme.

b. This amount represents the total contribution rate for individuals participating in the first pillar only. Individuals participating in both the first and the second pillars pay 15 percent to the first pillar.

Table 3.4   Characteristics of the Voluntary Scheme in Croatia

Coverage	Vesting period	Retirement age	Tax advantages to participants	Contributions tax deductible by employers	Lump-sum payments possible in retirement
All citizens	No[a]	50	Yes	No	Yes

Source: Anusic 2007.
a. Benefits can be collected once an individual retires from the mandated schemes or upon reaching age 50.

to an individual's account, up to an annual contribution ceiling of 5,000 kunas (HRK). The government further supports the scheme by allowing individuals to deduct contributions up to HRK 12,000 annually from their income for tax purposes. (Surprisingly, the government does not allow employers to deduct contributions made to the third pillar on behalf of employees. Most countries encourage employers to contribute to voluntary schemes by offering some form of tax incentive.) Third-pillar benefits are taxed as regular income under the income tax law. Benefits can be collected once an individual retires from the mandated schemes or upon reaching age 50. They can be received in the form of an annuity, a scheduled withdrawal, or a lump-sum payment (which cannot exceed 30 percent of the account balance). Funds cannot be withdrawn before an individual reaches age 50, except if the individual dies or becomes disabled.

Funds accumulating in the individual accounts of the third-pillar scheme are invested by pension fund management companies. Pension funds can be open (funds that operate with no restrictions on membership) or closed (funds with restrictions on membership, typically open only to the employees of one or more employers). In June 2008, 6 open pension funds were in operation, with 117,478 participants and HRK 727 million (0.3 percent of GDP) in assets, and 13 closed pension funds were in operation, with 15,000 participants and HRK 128 million (0.05 percent of GDP) in assets. Eight percent of the working-age population were enrolled in the scheme. The majority (63.7 percent) of third-pillar assets are invested in Croatian bonds and HRK deposits, despite investment restrictions that are liberal relative to those applied to the funded second pillar.

Health care system. Health care in Croatia is provided mainly through a mandatory insurance scheme administrated by the Croatian Institute for Health Insurance (HZZO), which is responsible for reimbursing covered health care expenditures as defined by law. As the primary purchaser of health care services in Croatia, HZZO also plays a key role in the process of defining and pricing services covered by the scheme.

Health care is financed primarily on the basis of contributions from the economically active population. Employers contribute 15 percent of employee wages to the scheme (employees pay nothing directly), plus an additional 0.5 percent of wages for occupational safety and workers compensation. Active duty military and people who are not economically active—including minors, students, the unemployed, the disabled, veterans, and the elderly—are not required to contribute. Contributions from 1.4 million economically active people covered roughly 80 percent of expenditures in 2002, with the remainder funded from transfers from the government. Given that the scheme provides health insurance coverage to 2.8 million people who do not contribute, the economically active population is subsidizing their coverage (Voncina 2006). Some 20 percent of beneficiaries of the health insurance scheme are required to make copayments for certain health care services and pharmaceuticals. Supplemental insurance is available for those seeking coverage for health care services not covered by the mandatory scheme and (since 2004) to pay for the cost of copayments for services provided under the mandatory scheme. Those elderly persons above the income threshold have subsidized flat premiums for supplementary insurance. In 2004, contributions for the supplemental scheme accounted for 3.5 percent of HZZO's total revenues (Voncina 2006). In 2005, health expenditures accounted for 7.4 percent of GDP, 81.3 percent of which was public expenditure and 18.7 of which was private. Of the private expenditures, 93.6 percent was attributable to out-of-pocket expenditures, in the form of informal payments, direct payments, and copayments (WHO 2008).

Institutional Structure and Coverage of Earnings-Related Schemes

Contributions for the first-pillar pension scheme are collected by the Croatian Tax Administration; the Croatian Pension Insurance Institute administers the scheme and is responsible for paying benefits. Responsibility for collecting all social contributions was transferred to the Croatian Tax Administration, which is responsible for collecting all other taxes, in order to increase administrative efficiency. Contributions for the second-pillar pension scheme are also collected by the Croatian Tax Administration but are administered by the Central Registry of Insured People (REGOS), which also maintains the database of second-pillar contributors and beneficiaries. Employers deposit first-pillar contributions with the Croatian Tax Administration's account and second-pillar contributions with REGOS's account, both of which are maintained by the Croatian Treasury. The Agency for the Supervision of Financial Services is responsible for overseeing REGOS and for licensing, monitoring, and supervising pension funds.

In June 2008, four pension fund management companies were licensed to operate in the mandatory second-pillar pension scheme. They were serving 1.44 million contributors (54 percent of the working-age population and 82 percent of the labor force). Total participants in the scheme represented roughly 90 percent of the total insured population. In June 2008, assets of the scheme represented 8.2 percent of GDP.

Structure of Benefits

The earnings-related pension scheme provides old-age, disability, and survivorship pensions. The provisions governing each of these types of benefits are discussed as follows.

Old-age benefits. To claim an old-age pension, individuals must have at least 15 years of contributory service and have reached retirement age. Retirement ages have been rising at the rate of six months a year such that they will reach 65 for men and 60 for women in 2008. Men with 35 years of contributory service and women with 30 years of service may retire up to five years before reaching their retirement age, subject to a reduction in benefits of 1.8 percent a year of early retirement (before 2008, the reduction was 3.6 percent a year). Benefits for individuals enrolled in both the first- and the second-pillar schemes—everyone under age 40 when the reform was introduced and some older workers who were age 40–50 when the reform was introduced and who elected to join the second-pillar scheme—are paid from both schemes. First-pillar benefits (for those participating in both the first and the second pillars) for years of service realized in the first pillar only are calculated by multiplying the individual's points and the point value. For years of service realized in both of the two mandatory pillars, the basic pension is computed on the basis of two distinct components. The first component is earnings related and points based, with an individual's points determined by his or her wages relative to the average wage.[3] This component is calculated by multiplying total points earned after joining the second pillar by 25 percent of the point value. The point value is indexed on the basis of 50 percent inflation and 50 percent wage growth (Swiss indexation). The second component is a flat benefit computed by multiplying the individual's years of service in the reformed pension system and 0.25 percent of the average gross wage in the previous year.[4] Benefits for individuals who are not participating in the second pillar are paid only from the first pillar and are computed on the basis of the individual's years of contributory service and wages relative to the average wage in each year worked. Total points are calculated by multiplying the average points per year of service by the number of years of service. To calculate the benefit, total points earned are multiplied by the point value. Lifetime lower wage earners are eligible for the minimum pension, which is calculated on the basis of an accrual rate of 0.825 percent applied to the average wage earned in 1998 and indexed on the basis of 50 percent inflation and 50 percent wage growth.[5] Second-pillar benefits are a function of an individual's contributions, investment earnings, and life expectancy at retirement.[6] At the time of retirement, the capital accumulation is converted into life annuities. If workers are married, joint-and-survivor annuities are purchased. If both spouses (without children) agree, they can choose a single annuity.

Disability benefits. Disability benefits are provided mainly by the first pillar of the reformed Croatian pension system. Individuals who lose some or all of their capacity to work are entitled to a disability pension (table 3.5). Depending on the degree of the incapacity, the individual will be entitled to a disability pension caused by either occupational or general incapacity. Occupational incapacity refers to someone with a permanent but partial disability (defined as having lost more than 50 percent of capacity but still capable of working); general incapacity refers to someone who is incapable of working. Disability benefits depend on the degree of an individual's disability, the individual's wages relative to the average wage during the time he or she worked, and the length of contributory service to which service credit is awarded for years lost to disability.

Table 3.5   Eligibility Conditions for and Benefits Provided by Disability Pensions in Croatia

Scheme type	Vesting period	Contribution rate	Eligibility	Benefit rate	Partial pension
First pillar (earnings related)	Minimum coverage of one-third of working life after age 20 (age 26 for individuals with a university degree)	No specific contribution rate for disability benefits	Permanent loss in capacity for a general disability pension; at least 50 percent loss in capacity for a partial disability pension	1 percent per year for an average worker	80 percent

Sources: Anusic, O'Keefe, and Madzarevic-Sujster 2003; U.S. Social Security Administration 2006.

Benefits are paid indefinitely, unless the individual's condition improves. If the total benefits the individual would have received from the first- and second-pillar schemes are lower than the disability pension to which he or she is entitled, the balance in the individual's second-pillar account is transferred to the Croatian Pension Insurance Institute (the administrator of the first-pillar scheme), which pays the individual the higher disability pension.

Survivor benefits. Survivor benefits are awarded to the dependents of individuals who, at the time of their death, were receiving (or had met the criteria to receive) an old-age or disability pension or had at least five years of contributory service (or 10 years of qualifying periods) (table 3.6). If total survivor benefits are higher than the benefits the deceased would have received in total from the first- and second-pillar schemes, the balance in the deceased's second-pillar account is transferred to the Croatian Pension Insurance Institute.

The value of survivor benefits is based on the number of the deceased's survivors and the old-age or disability pension to which the deceased was entitled. Survivor benefits are calculated on the basis of actual and imputed years of service (if the deceased died as a result of an occupational injury or disease) using a formula similar to that used to compute old-age pensions. In no case can the total value of benefits paid to all survivors exceed the benefit to which the deceased would have been entitled.

Eligible survivors include spouses, orphans, parents, and siblings. Spouses who are age 45–49 when they become eligible survivors can begin collecting survivor benefits upon reaching age 50 for women (age 60 for men). Eligible spousal survivors must be caring for children or the disabled or have been fully dependent on the deceased. If a surviving spouse is younger than age 45, the spouse is eligible for only a one-year transition benefit. Orphans are eligible for benefits through age 15 (age 18 if unemployed, age 26 if a full-time student), or indefinitely in cases where the orphan is disabled.

Assessment of the Performance of Croatia's Pension System

The World Bank has established four principles for evaluating public pension systems, which together should guide the process of pension reform (see Holzmann and Hinz 2005). Broadly speaking, these principles include the adequacy and security of benefits, the affordability of contributions, the sustainability of the system over time, and the robustness of the system in the face of demographic changes and macroeconomic

Table 3.6 Eligibility Conditions for and Benefits Provided by Survivor Pensions in Croatia

Scheme type	Eligibility	Spouse replacement rate	Benefit duration	Remarriage test	Orphan age limit	Orphan replacement rate	Total family benefit
First pillar (earnings related)	Eligibility of the deceased for an old-age or a disability pension, a minimum of 5 years of coverage or 10 years of qualifying periods by the deceased	70 percent if the spouse is the only survivor	For life, unless the spouse remarries; also for life upon remarriage if spouse remarries but is older than 50 or disabled	The pension ceases if the spouse remarries and is younger than 50 unless disabled	15 (18 if unemployed, 26 if full-time student)	70 percent if the orphan is the only survivor	70 percent for one survivor; 80 percent for two survivors; 90 percent for three survivors; 100 percent for four or more survivors

Sources: Anusic, O'Keefe, Madzarevic-Sujster 2003; U.S. Social Security Administration 2006.

shocks. This chapter focuses primarily on the adequacy of benefits and the financial sustainability of the earnings-related pension scheme. The remaining principles are mentioned only briefly. Adequacy is analyzed through the lens of net replacement rates. Financial sustainability is evaluated using projections of pension expenditure and revenues.

Benefit Adequacy

Replacement rates are a useful yardstick for measuring the adequacy of pension benefits, because they express benefits relative to preretirement earnings, thereby indicating the degree to which income is replaced when workers retire. Two variants are commonly used. Gross replacement rates compute income replacement as the ratio of benefits paid to pretax preretirement earnings. Net replacement rates compute income replacement as the ratio of benefits received (that is, after the payment of taxes and other levies, including contributions for social insurance) to posttax preretirement earnings. In general, net replacement rates are a more useful measure of benefit adequacy, because they capture the degree to which actual take-home pay is replaced when workers retire.

The level of income replacement at retirement is not the only measure of benefit adequacy. For the full assessment of benefit adequacy, it is also important to determine how postretirement indexation rules will affect replacement rates during retirement. Pension benefits in retirement are expected to be indexed to inflation, so that their real value is maintained. In a growing economy with rising real wages, however, mere price indexation of pensions leads to a deterioration of the relative consumption position of the retirees. Individuals with otherwise identical work histories will receive different pensions depending on when they retire. For this reason, some countries have introduced mixed indexation of pensions that use varying weights of inflation and wage growth in the indexation formula.

For the evaluation of the effect of indexation on replacement rates in Croatia, the replacement rates are normalized to 100 and the assumptions for calculating the replacement rates are maintained (that is, inflation is 2.5 percent a year and real wage growth is 2 percent a year). The change in the replacement rate is measured in comparison to full wage indexation or compared to an active worker (that is, in active earnings units). The results of this analysis indicate that the relative income position of a retiree would deteriorate by 12 percent after 10 years in retirement and by 36 percent after 35 years in retirement. The following evaluation of income replacement considers replacement rates only at retirement and does not take into account the impact of indexation policies on replacement rates during retirement.

Replacement rates are a function of the formula governing pension benefits; an individual's contribution history; and, in the case of net replacement rates, the rules of income tax, social security contributions, and other relevant levies. The benefit formula establishes the degree to which the system redistributes income across individuals of different levels of preretirement earnings. Progressive systems provide higher levels of income replacement to people with lower levels of preretirement income. In general, the degree to which a system is redistributive depends on the existence (and value) of flat transfers and minimum pension guarantees, the degree to which benefits are earnings related, and the existence of ceilings on earnings subject to contributions. An individual's contribution history can be characterized by his or her age of entry into the labor force, contribution density, and decisions regarding the timing of retirement. To some degree, these three factors are influenced by the incentives embodied in the pension system. The tax and contribution system influences net replacement rates through the progressiveness of the income tax formula, which taxes (higher) income during a worker's active life more than it taxes (lower) pension benefits in retirement. In addition, social security levies (for pensions; unemployment; health care; and, at times, housing and family benefits) are typically reduced or eliminated altogether in retirement. These benefits are particularly important for low- to middle-income groups.

Benchmarks need to be established in order to evaluate the adequacy of the income replacement provided by the earnings-related pension schemes. Unfortunately, there is no consensus on what constitutes adequacy. According to one widely respected definition, pensions are adequate when they are sufficient to prevent poverty among the elderly and provide the vast majority of the population with a reliable mechanism for smoothing income over a lifetime. Even with a definition, however, establishing benchmarks is problematic, because attitudes vary across countries as a result of social and cultural perceptions. Moreover, benchmarks ignore the other factors affecting the welfare of the elderly—and varying across countries—including the existence and generosity of health insurance and long-term care, the cost of housing, the structure of traditional living arrangements, the presence of informal intrafamily or intergenerational sources of financial and nonfinancial support, and the availability and security of other mechanisms for people to save for their own retirement.

One reputable nine-country study (OECD 2001) observes that living standards are roughly comparable for people 10 years older than the normal retirement age and people 15 years younger than the normal retirement age when retirees have disposable income equal to roughly 80 percent of the disposable income of working-age people. In part, this is attributable to the fact that retirees have no work-related expenses (they do not have to commute or buy special clothing or uniforms, for example). This finding, however, does not imply that mandatory first-pillar pension schemes should actually target an 80 percent net replacement rate. To the contrary, in middle- and high-income countries, one can reasonably expect individuals to save for their own retirement—and the empirical evidence suggests that, in practice, they do so.[7] There is also some evidence to suggest that the ratio between preretirement and postretirement income is somewhat independent of the income replacement mandate of the public pension system. Put simply, individuals tend to save more in countries with more modest mandates (and vice versa).

Because Croatia has access to relatively well-developed financial markets, it would seem reasonable to expect middle- and higher-income workers to save enough to finance at least 25 percent, if not closer to 50 percent, of this 80 percent income replacement target. Given this, three benchmarks are provided: a 40 percent net replacement rate (which implies that individuals would be expected to save enough to finance half of the total income-replacement target); a 60 percent net replacement rate (which implies that individuals would be expected to finance a quarter of the target); and an 80 percent net replacement rate (which implies that individuals, most of whom would be low-income earners, would not be expected to contribute anything toward the target).[8] In the following analysis, these benchmarks are used to evaluate the adequacy of benefits in Croatia compared with the average net replacement rate observed in 53 countries around the world, the average net replacement rate observed in selected countries in Europe and Central Asia, and the poverty line in Croatia.[9]

To estimate gross and net replacement rates, we use the Analysis of Pension Entitlements across Countries (APEX) model to consider two critical dimensions: earnings levels and contribution periods.[10] This model generates estimates for replacement rates under steady-state assumptions (that is, as if the rules of the reformed pension scheme had been in place over the entire active life of the individual). Because life expectancies at retirement are projected to increase over time—which will affect the benefits paid by defined-contribution pension schemes—a reference year must be chosen. For the purpose of this study, 2040 is used, because it provides a sufficiently long contribution period over which to approximate steady-state conditions.

The first critical task is to investigate levels of income replacement across a relevant spectrum of income. Income is represented as a percentage (50–200 percent) of average earnings. The second task is to investigate the impact on income replacement of differences in the duration, timing, and density of an individual's contribution history (density refers to the percentage of time an individual actually contributes over a given period). For the facilitation of the presentation of these multidimensional results, replacement rates are computed as a function of the age an individual exits the labor market. They are presented separately for full-career and partial-career workers.

Replacement rates for full-career workers. Projected replacement rates for full-career workers in 2040 are examined first. For the purpose of this analysis, a full-career is defined as continuous employment from age 20 to age 65. Gross replacement rates are presented in figure 3.2 as a function of an individual's preretirement income relative to the economywide average wage. This figure reveals the degree to which income is redistributed under the Croatian pension system as a result of the existence of a

Figure 3.2   Sources of Gross Replacement Rates in Croatia, by Income Level

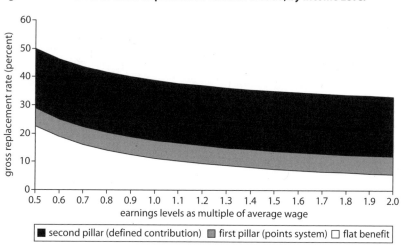

Source: APEX model.

Note: Figure shows projected replacement rate for 2040 as approximation of steady-state conditions.

flat benefit, which contributes less to total benefits as income rises. The shares of income replacement attributable to the points-based first-pillar benefit and to the second pillar are constant across income.

The situation does not change significantly when taxes are taken into consideration (figure 3.3). The effect of taxes and contributions on replacement rates increases as the level of income rises. The tax system does not affect the overall picture of replacement rates. As is the case with gross replacement rates, net replacement rates fall with income.

Net replacement rates by income level are presented in figure 3.4 (in which net replacement rates are represented by the dotted line).[11] Preretirement income is expressed relative to the economywide average wage. The three benchmarks discussed previously are represented by three short horizontal lines abutting the y-axis. The three downward sloping lines represent the world average, the regional average, and the Croatian average,[12] where each of these indicators is expressed relative to the economywide average wage.

The figure suggests that pensions for middle- and high-income full-career workers in Croatia can generally be considered adequate. Replacement rates for middle-income workers are around the 60 percent

Figure 3.3   Sources of Net Replacement Rates in Croatia, by Income Level

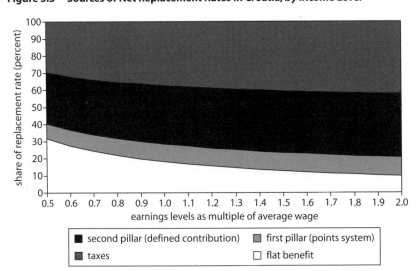

Source: APEX model.

Note: Figure shows projected replacement rate for full-career worker in 2040 as approximation of steady-state conditions.

Figure 3.4   Net Replacement Rates for Male Full-Career Workers in 2040 in Croatia, Europe and Central Asia, and the World

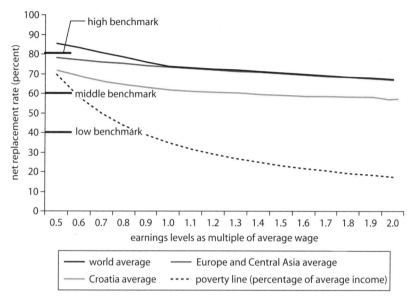

Source: Authors' calculations based on World Bank 2007b and the APEX model.

Note: Figure shows projected replacement rate for 2040 as approximation of steady-state conditions.

benchmark while high-income workers receive replacement rates only slightly below the 60 percent benchmark. This suggests that the pension system is effectively smoothing consumption from work into retirement for these workers. In contrast, replacement rates for low-income workers are about 10–15 percentage points below the 80 percent benchmark despite the existence of a flat benefit component. Given that benefits for all income levels exceed the poverty line, the objective of poverty alleviation is being met. The degree of redistribution in the Croatian pension system is roughly comparable to the regional and world averages (in all cases, net income replacement falls as preretirement income rises), but the levels of income replacement are lower than those provided in some other countries.

Replacement rates for partial-career workers. Not everyone works from age 20 to the statutory retirement age. Many individuals enter and exit the labor force (often at different ages and for different periods of time) and earn different wages while working. To examine the adequacy of benefits

Figure 3.5   Net Replacement Rates for Male Middle-Income Partial-Career Workers in Croatia, by Career Type and Exit Age

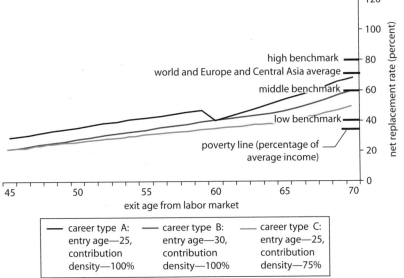

Source: Authors' calculations based on World Bank 2007b and the APEX model.
Note: Figure shows projected replacement rate for 2040 as approximation of steady-state conditions. See text for description of career types.

for partial-career workers, we consider three stylized cases (figure 3.5).[13] These cases include career type A (someone entering the labor force at age 25 who works continuously for a period of years before leaving the workforce at some point between the ages of 50 and 70 and then claims a benefit); career type B (identical to career type A, except that the worker enters the workforce at age 30 and leaves no earlier than age 55); and career type C (identical to career type A, except that the individual contributes in only three years out of four while in the labor force).[14] In cases in which the withdrawal from the formal labor market occurs before the statutory retirement age, the pension is claimed (and the replacement rate calculated) only at the later age. For withdrawals after the statutory retirement age, the ages coincide.

Several conclusions can be drawn from this figure. First, some partial-career workers receive levels of income replacement lower than the poverty line, especially those retiring at very young ages. Second, leaving the workforce very early can be very costly. Someone retiring long before reaching the retirement age may not receive levels of income replacement higher than even the lowest of the three benchmarks.[15] Third, entering the workforce later in life is costly. Someone entering the workforce at age 30 receives a net replacement rate up to nine percentage points lower than someone entering the workforce at age 25. Fourth, working intermittently is costly. Someone who enters the workforce at the same age but who contributes only three years out of four will receive a net replacement rate that is 6–19 percentage points lower than someone who contributes continuously. In all cases, net replacement rates grow the longer someone continues to work. This is encouraging because it demonstrates that the pension system provides incentives for people to remain in the workforce. Career type A and B workers will attain the lowest of the three benchmarks before reaching the retirement age, while career type C workers must work to the retirement age. Similarly, career type A and B workers can attain the middle benchmark, provided that they work three to five years after reaching retirement age, but career type C workers will not be able to attain this benchmark, even if they work until age 70.

Fiscal Sustainability

The sustainability of a pay-as-you-go first-pillar pension scheme is best evaluated in actuarial terms by estimating the scheme's actuarial deficit as the difference between its assets and liabilities. If an actuarial deficit exists and is large, the scheme is financially unsustainable and needs policy actions that positively impact either its assets or liabilities, or both. A good proxy for the actuarial deficit is the difference between the present value of the scheme's expected future revenues (that is, contributions and other income) and expected future expenditures (that is, benefit payments, administrative costs, and other expenses) over an extended projection period. The difference between these two values represents an unfunded liability (sometimes referred to as a financing gap) on the public-sector balance sheet. Because this study is concerned also with the time path of revenues and expenditures (and the resulting balance across the projection period ending in 2040), this more pragmatic approach has been taken, and projections of expenditures, revenues, and deficits are presented on the basis of available postreform fiscal projections.

As a result of the government's reforms, revenues are now projected to remain stable while expenditures will drop gradually, from 12 percent of GDP in 2005 to about 9 percent of GDP by 2040, such that the deficits of the pension scheme will grow progressively smaller by 2040 (figure 3.6).

Figure 3.6   Projected Fiscal Balance of Croatia's Public Pension System after Reform, 2005–40

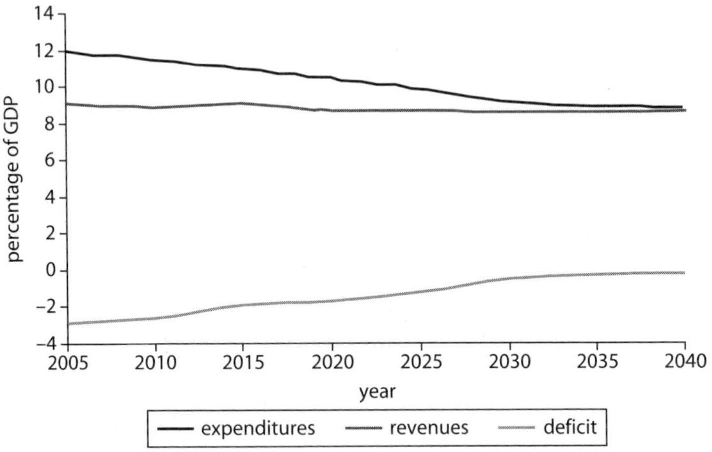

Source: Anusic 2007.

Conclusions

To address growing deficits in the pension system and projections that demonstrated that the aging of the population would place increasing pressure on the finances of the system over time, Croatia began a process of pension reform in the mid-1990s. Three years later, in 1998, it eliminated the traditional defined-benefit formula used to calculate pensions in favor of a new formula based on points and a flat benefit to effect income redistribution and protect low-income workers. In 2002, once a regulatory system was in place for the licensing of pension fund companies and a central clearing house had been established, the government introduced a mandatory funded second-pillar scheme and a voluntary third-pillar scheme to supplement the two mandated schemes. Together, the reforms tightened the link between contributions and benefits and put the pension system on track to eventually becoming financially self-supporting by about 2040.

The resulting projected gross and net replacement rates for full-career workers are roughly in line with regional and world averages, although they tend toward the lower end of the range (see chapter 1). Net replacement rates for full-career workers are projected to be 57–70 percent across the analyzed income spectrum. The stereotypical full-career worker is not, of course, representative of the average worker in Croatia. As is the case in other countries, workers with less than full careers—because they left the workforce before reaching retirement age, worked intermittently, or have gaps in their employment history—risk receiving income replacement that is closer to—or even below—the lower benchmark of 40 percent.[16] Some workers, particularly those who enter the workforce later in life or who have intermittent work histories, may have to remain in the workforce well beyond the normal retirement age to attain sufficient levels of income replacement. Moreover, all workers, including full-career workers, may need to save outside the mandated schemes if they want to replace 80 percent of their preretirement income.

To increase income replacement by one percentage point, a typical full-career worker would need to save about 0.50 percent of his or her earnings from age 40 to the current retirement age.[17] Given that the voluntary third-pillar pension scheme remains small—despite the fact that the government provides matching contributions and exempts contributions from taxable income (both provisions are subject to some restrictions)—an opportunity exists for deepening its reach, possibly by providing incentives for employers to contribute on behalf of their employees. Such incentives do not now exist in Croatia.

Replacement rates have been computed under the assumption that funded pension schemes earn a rate of return of 1.5 percentage points more than wage growth. This earnings differential broadly reflects the performance of pension funds in OECD countries over the past 30 years. The earnings differential in emerging economies is almost twice as large (see Holzmann 2009). The performance of pension funds in Croatia since their inception, however, has been well below this benchmark. If such performance continues, the Croatian pension system will not be capable of delivering the replacement rates projected for 2040. This concern calls for a review of pension fund performance and accelerated progress in financial market development.

Achieving a higher target for income replacement can be accomplished by postponing retirement (either in lieu of, or in combination with, increasing savings through such mechanisms as voluntary pension schemes). Increasing the retirement age in step with increases in life expectancy at retirement is a natural choice, for both individuals and policy makers, but it requires cross-sectoral policy reforms to enable elderly workers to continue to participate in the labor market.[18]

Notes

1. For more information regarding these population projections, see Reiterer (2008).

2. Life expectancy at retirement is currently 73 years for men and 81 years for women, which implies that, on average, men will live 8 years and women 21 years after reaching retirement age (see Anusic 2007).

3. For the length of coverage before 2002, the benefit from the first pillar is calculated on the basis of points earned using the same formula used for individuals participating in the first pillar only (that is, the points earned for years of service before 2002 are multiplied by the point value).

4. The monthly average point value in 2008 is HRK 54.11. In January 2008, the average gross wage was HRK 7,357, and the net wage was HRK 5,019. As a result, the point value is 1.1 percent of net wages and 0.75 percent of gross wages, which translates into accrual rates for an average earner in a traditional benefit formula.

5. Average gross earnings in 1998 were roughly HRK 6,000.

6. Benefits from second- and third-pillar schemes are typically lower than the actuarially neutral benefits presented in these scenarios, because pension funds typically assume life expectancies that are higher than the expectancies derived from general statistics for the entire population in order to protect themselves from adverse selection and other risks.

7. In Chile, for instance, 70 percent of retirees from the mandatory public pension system own their home, which is a form of savings (see Valdés-Prieto 2008).

8. These benchmarks approximate the standards developed by the International Labour Organization (ILO) (1952) and by the Council of Europe (1990). ILO Convention 102 of 1952 sets a minimum benefit equal to 40 percent of the reference wage for married men of pensionable age. This amount was raised to 45 percent in 1968. The European Code of Security of 1990 sets a minimum standard for members of the Council of Europe equal to 65 percent for married people of a specific age.

9. As a proxy for the poverty line, this study uses 35 percent of the average net wage, which very broadly approximates a US$2.25-a-day poverty line converted into national currency, adjusted for purchasing power parity, expressed relative to the national average net wage, and averaged across the nine study countries. Such an approach enables valid comparisons to be made across the sample (see chapter 1).

10. The APEX model was developed by Axia Economics, with funding from the OECD and the World Bank. The model codes detailed eligibility and benefit rules for first- and second-pillar schemes based on available public information that has been verified by country contacts. Because the details of the rules sometimes change on short notice (and limited public disclosure), the calculations presented here should be considered as best approximations only.

11. These are simulated replacement rates for an unmarried male working a hypothetical career path under the assumption that real wage growth is 2 percent,

inflation is 2.5 percent, the rate of return on invested assets is 3.5 percent, and the worker retires at the statutory retirement age.

12. As a proxy for the poverty line, this study uses 35 percent of the average net wage because this percentage very broadly approximates a US$2.25-a-day poverty line converted into national currency, adjusted for purchasing power parity, expressed relative to the national average net wage, and averaged across the nine study countries. Such an approach enables valid comparisons to be made across the sample. See chapter 1.

13. Only middle-income partial-career workers are examined because replacement rates are roughly comparable for workers with lower or higher levels of preretirement income.

14. Only middle-income partial-career workers are examined because replacement rates are roughly comparable for workers with lower or higher levels of preretirement income.

15. The drop in replacement rates for Category Type A workers is attributable to the actuarial reduction for early retirement. Workers with enough years of service (35 years) for early retirement can retire at age 60 if they so choose, but their benefits are subjected to penalties for early retirement. After age 60, replacement rates start increasing because, in addition to receiving more benefits for each year of additional service, early retirement is also penalized less as age retirement increases from age 60 to age 65.

16. The average effective years of service fell from 33 in 1999 to 29 in 2007. For 30 years of service and given the assumptions used in the analysis, the APEX model generates a replacement rate of 45 percent.

17. This estimate is based on the assumption that real wage growth is 2 percent, the net real rate of return on invested assets is 3.5 percent, and benefits (both from the unfunded and the funded pillars) are price indexed.

18. See Holzmann, MacKellar, and Repansek (2009) for a conference volume that addresses theses issues for the countries in southeastern Europe.

Bibliography

Anusic, Z. 2007. "Pension System and Pension Reform in Croatia." Background paper prepared for *Public Finance Review*, World Bank, Washington, DC.

Anusic, Z., P. O'Keefe, and S. Madzarevic-Sujster. 2003. *Pension Reform in Croatia.* Washington, DC: World Bank.

Council of Europe. 1990. *European Code of Social Security (Revised).* Rome.

Holzmann, R., ed. 2009. *Aging Populations, Pension Funds, and Financial Markets: Regional Perspectives and Global Challenges for Central, Eastern, and Southern Europe.* Washington, DC: World Bank.

Holzmann, R., and R. Hinz. 2005. *Old-Age Income Support in the 21st Century.* Washington, DC: World Bank.

Holzmann, R., L. MacKellar, and J. Repansek, eds. 2009. *Pension Reform in Southeastern Europe: Linking to Labor and Financial Market Reforms.* Washington, DC: World Bank.

INPRS (International Network of Pension Regulators and Supervisors). 2003. *Complementary and Private Pensions throughout the World.* Geneva: INPRS.

ILO (International Labour Organization). 1952. *ILO Convention 102.* Geneva: ILO.

———. 1967. *ILO Convention 128.* Geneva: ILO.

OECD (Organisation for Economic Co-operation and Development). 2001. *Ageing and Income: Financial Resources and Retirement in 9 OECD Countries.* Paris: OECD.

Reiterer, A. 2008. "Population Development and Age Structure in Southeastern Europe until 2050." World Bank, Washington, DC.

U.S. Social Security Administration. 2006 *Social Security Systems throughout the World: Europe.* Washington, DC: Social Security Administration.

Valdés-Prieto, S. 2008. *Designs for the First-Pillar Pensions and the 2008 Chilean Reform.* http://editorialexpress.com/cgi-bin/conference/download.cgi?db_name=SECHI2008&paper_id=130.

Voncina, L. 2006. *Health Systems in Transition: Croatia.* Geneva: World Health Organization.

World Bank. 2005. *Growth, Poverty, and Inequality: Eastern Europe and the Former Soviet Union.* Washington, DC: World Bank.

———. 2007a. *Croatia Living Standards Assessment.* Washington, DC: World Bank.

———. 2007b. *Pensions Panorama.* Washington, DC: World Bank.

WHO (World Health Organization). 2008. Database. http://www.who.int/research/en/.

CHAPTER 4

The Czech Republic

The Czech Republic inherited from the former Czechoslovakia a public pension system financed on a pay-as-you-go basis (meaning that contributions from current workers are used to pay benefits to current beneficiaries). Within a few years of the country's transition to a market economy, the fiscal balance of the pension system began to deteriorate. By 1997, the system was generating an annual deficit equivalent to 0.5 percent of gross domestic product (GDP). Pension expenditures continued to increase while revenues remained constant. As a result, by 2000 the deficit had doubled to 0.9 percent of GDP.

Recognizing that these deficits were not sustainable and that the system would face even greater challenges in the medium to long term as the population ages, the government began to undertake a set of parametric reforms starting in the mid-1990s. These reforms—which included gradually increasing the retirement age and changing the benefit formula and indexation rules—improved the fiscal balance of the system.[1] In 1994, the government introduced a voluntary funded pension scheme that benefits from direct government subsidies. In July 2008, parliament approved additional parametric changes.

Despite the parametric reforms of 1995 and 2003, the Czech pension system remains insufficiently prepared for looming demographic change, because it is based predominantly on a single pay-as-you-go, defined-benefit pension scheme. By 2050, the old-age dependency ratio (the population age 65 and older divided by the population age 20–64) is projected to increase to roughly 60 percent, up from 21.7 percent in 2005. Over the same period and before the recently announced reform, pension system revenues were projected to level off at 8.1 percent of GDP while expenditures were projected to rise to 11.7 percent of GPD, resulting in a deficit of 3.4 percent of GDP. The 2008 reform is estimated to reduce expenditures by 1.2 percent of GDP by 2050 and to ensure financial sustainability until 2030, after which a deficit will emerge, eventually reaching 2.5 percent of GDP by 2050. This suggests that further reforms will be required to achieve both adequate and sustainable pensions in the future.

Against this backdrop of demographic change, this chapter evaluates the Czech pension system, focusing on fiscal sustainability and benefit adequacy. Adequacy is evaluated through the lens of statutory net replacement rates for different retirement ages, patterns of contributions, and income levels with comparisons to international benchmarks.

The chapter is organized as follows. The next section discusses the motivation for the reforms. The following section describes the key characteristics of the reformed pension system. The third section assesses the adequacy of pension benefits and the fiscal sustainability of the system. The last section draws conclusions.

Motivation for Reform

The Czech Republic inherited a socialist-era pension system that suffered from a number of serious design flaws. Benefits were comparatively generous, particularly for certain occupations. Lax disability criteria resulted in more disability beneficiaries than were justified on medical grounds. The redistributive benefit formula, augmented by a flat state-compensation benefit introduced in 1990, weakened the link between contributions and benefits. The retirement age was low relative to life expectancy, a problem exacerbated by the generosity of benefits (which increased incentives for early retirement). At the individual level, this increased the value of retirement benefits relative to contributions. For the pension system, this increased the total number of beneficiaries relative to contributors.

The impact of these factors—together with a decline in GDP and increasing unemployment (albeit at levels not nearly as high as in many other countries in the region)—undermined the fiscal health of the pension system. In 1995, two years before the system actually began running

Table 4.1   Fiscal Balance of the Czech Republic's Pension System before Reform, 1994–2000
(percentage of GDP)

Year	Revenues	Expenditures	Balance
1994	8.3	7.1	1.2
1995	8.2	7.5	0.7
1996	8.1	7.8	0.3
1997	8.4	8.8	−0.4
1998	8.3	9.0	−0.7
1999	8.4	9.4	−0.7
2000	8.6	9.5	−0.9

Source: Lasagabaster, Rocha, and Wiese 2002.

deficits (table 4.1), policy makers implemented a set of parametric reforms intended to restore long-term sustainability. These reforms included gradually increasing the retirement age, eliminating special privileges for certain occupations, tightening eligibility conditions for disability benefits, and introducing a benefit formula based on both a flat-rate and an earnings-related benefit. In 2001, penalties for early retirement were increased to levels closer to actuarial neutrality in order to contain the rising number of early retirees.

Characteristics of the Czech Republic's Pension System

This section describes the main characteristics of the Czech Republic's pension system. These characteristics include the design of the individual pillars of social insurance; the rules governing pension system taxation, institutional structure, and coverage; and the provisions governing old-age, disability, and survivorship pensions. The design of the pension system is assessed using a conceptual framework developed by the World Bank, which generally recommends including a funded component if conditions are appropriate but increasingly recognizes that a range of choices is available to policy makers to provide effective old-age protection in a manner that is fiscally responsible (see Holzmann and Hinz 2005).

In general, the World Bank supports pension systems composed of some combination of five basic pillars:

- a noncontributory (or zero) pillar (in the form of a demogrant, social pension, or social assistance benefit) intended to provide a minimal level of income protection;
- a first-pillar contributory system linked to earnings, which seeks to replace a portion of preretirement income;

- a mandatory second pillar (essentially, individual savings accounts), which can be designed in various ways;
- a voluntary third pillar, which is flexible and discretionary (this pillar, too, can take a variety of forms); and
- a fourth pillar of informal intrafamily or intergenerational sources of financial and nonfinancial support to the elderly, including access to health care and housing.

Pillar Design

The design of the Czech Republic's pension system incorporates four of the five pillars recommended by the World Bank (table 4.2). The publicly managed noncontributory zero pillar, financed with general tax revenues, redistributes income to lower income groups using means testing such that eligible beneficiaries receive a benefit sufficient to ensure them a total income equal to the state-defined minimum income guarantee. Benefits are adjusted for inflation, with the objective of ensuring their real value over time. The mandatory first pillar, financed on a pay-as-you-go basis, provides a flat benefit plus an earnings-related benefit. The flat benefit is awarded to all pensioners, irrespective of pre-retirement income or length of service. Because the earnings-related benefit is also progressive, the first pillar is highly redistributive. There is no second pillar (that is, a mandatory funded component). The voluntary third pillar, introduced in 1993 to supplement the benefits of the first pillar, is a defined-contribution scheme in which a participant's benefits depend on his or her contributions and accumulated investment earnings to the point of retirement. The mandatory fourth pillar, financed by a combination of contributions and general tax revenues, provides health insurance to the elderly as part of the national health care system.

The third pillar is subjected to an exempt-exempt-taxed (EET) regime, meaning that contributions are partially exempt from taxation, investment income is fully exempt, and benefits are taxed (see box 1.1 in chapter 1). This is similar to the tax regimes of most of the countries in the Organisation for Economic Co-operation and Development (OECD), which take a more classical EET approach. Benefits paid by the zero pillar are exempt from taxation, contributions to the first pillar are taxed, and benefits are partially exempt from taxation. Contributions to the health care system (the fourth pillar) are taxed.

Table 4.2 Structure of the Czech Republic's Pension System

Scheme type	Coverage	Type	Function	Financing	Generic benefit	Benefit indexation	Taxation Contributions	Taxation Investment income/capital gains	Taxation Benefits
Zero pillar (public noncontributory)	Universal	Means tested	Redistributive	Tax revenues	Difference between minimum defined-benefit level and actual income	Prices	n.a.	n.a.	Exempt
First pillar (private, earnings related)	Mandatory	Defined benefit	Insurance	Percentage of individual earnings	Flat benefit plus earnings-related pension	A minimum inflation rate of plus one-third of real wage growth	Taxed[a]	n.a.	Exempt[b]
Third pillar (private, voluntary)	Voluntary	Defined contribution	Insurance	Voluntary contributions	Pension from capital accumulation	Depends on options chosen	Exempt[c]	Exempt	Taxed
Fourth pillar (public health care)	Mandatory	n.a.	Insurance	Percentage of individual earnings plus tax revenues	Specified health service package	n.a.	Taxed	n.a.	n.a.

Source: Authors' compilation based on data from European Commission 2007a, 2007b; Hemmings and Whitehouse 2006; and Rokosova and Schreyogg 2005.

n.a. = Not applicable.

a. Since January 1, 2008, contributions paid to the first pillar are part of the income tax base, consistent with the tax reform that introduced a flat-rate tax of 15 percent.

b. Pensioners are provided with a large tax allowance on pension income. Pensioners with total taxable income of less than 80 percent of average earnings do not pay income tax, which effectively exempts pensions from taxation for all pensioners except those with substantial income from voluntary pension schemes or other sources. Pensioners who are liable for taxes pay a rate lower than that levied on earnings. As a result, they pay substantially less in taxes than do workers with the same total income (Hemmings and Whitehouse 2006).

c. Contributions of 6,000 koruny–12,000 koruny and employer contributions up to 5 percent of wage are exempt from taxation.

Noncontributory scheme. The elderly in the Czech Republic are eligible for means-tested noncontributory benefits (living minimum) as part of a social assistance scheme intended to guarantee, without any categorical bias, a minimum level of income to the overall population. To be eligible, applicants need to demonstrate that their total income—from gainful activity, revenues from investments, and other regular activity (net of taxes and social insurance contributions)—falls below the state-defined minimum. Eligibility also requires demonstration of a willingness to work (except for those below age 18 or above age 65), strengthening the incentives to seek employment.

The minimum is computed as the sum of two parts.[2] The first part is based on individual income needs (which are determined on the basis of the individual's age). The second part is based on household income needs (which are a function of the number of household members). In 2007 and 2008, a single-person household received a total benefit of 3,126 koruny (CZK). About 4 percent of the households in the Czech Republic are registered beneficiaries of the social assistance system.

Earnings-related scheme. Workers in the Czech Republic are enrolled in a first-pillar earnings-related defined-benefit public pension scheme financed on a pay-as-you-go basis. To address rising fiscal deficits—attributable in part to lax disability eligibility conditions and special privileges awarded to certain groups—and prepare for the aging of the population, the government reformed the parameters of the scheme in 1995, 2003, and 2008 (table 4.3). In January 1996, retirement ages were raised at the rate of two months per year for men and four months per year for women. In January 2004, an additional gradual increase in retirement ages was introduced, equalizing ages for men and childless women at 63 years and setting the age for other women at 59–62 years, based on the number of children. The 2008 reform, which will be implemented starting in 2010, raised the ages further, such that the normal retirement age will—between 2017 and 2030—reach 65 years for men and women with one or no children and 62–64 years for women with more than one child. At the same time, opportunities for early retirement in the future have been increased, albeit with some actuarially inspired reductions (discussed later).

The benefit formula is highly redistributive and includes a flat benefit (applied to all pensioners, regardless of service length or preretirement earnings) and an earnings-related benefit.[3] Individuals with 25 years of service (by 2030, this will rise to 30 years) qualify for a full pension, with

Table 4.3 Parameters of the First-Pillar Earnings-Related Scheme in the Czech Republic before and after Reform

Period	Vesting period	Contribution rate	Contribution ceiling	Benefit rate	Pension assessment base	Retirement age
Prereform	n.a.	n.a.	n.a.	n.a.	Last 10 years' average earnings valorized by wage growth	60 for men, 53–57 for women depending on number of children
Postreform	35 years at normal retirement age by 2019; 20 years for people who retire five or more years after the normal retirement age	28 percent (21.5 percent by employer, 6.5 percent by employee)	None	Flat benefit plus 1.5 percent per year	Gradually increasing to average of last 30 years of earnings by 2016	Gradually increasing to 65 by 2030 for men and for women (with 0–1 children), 64 (for women with two children), 63 (for women with three children), and 62 (for women with four or more children)

Sources: European Commission 2007a, 2007b; information provided by the Ministry of Labor and Social Affairs in July 2008.

n.a. = Not applicable.

1.5 percent of earnings credited for each year of service, not subject to any sort of a ceiling. The computation of the pension assessment base (that is, the wages used in the computation of benefits) is progressive, providing higher income replacement for lower wages with thresholds that are not subject to statutory indexation.[4] The 1995 reforms also introduced changes to the benefit formula, including gradually increasing the number of years used in the pension computation from the past 10 years of wages to 30 years by 2016.[5] Shifting toward the calculation of benefits based on lifetime earnings conforms with international practice and—to some extent—helps tighten the link between contributions and benefits. The degree to which the benefit formula is redistributive dilutes the benefits of this shift, however. Pensions are adjusted such that the average pension rises by at least the sum of inflation plus a third of the growth in real wages. The exact amount, which is set by decree, can be greater than the minimum stipulated under the law. The scheme is financed on a pay-as-you-go basis, with a total levy of 28 percent of earnings, of which 21.5 percentage points are paid by employers and 6.5 percentage points are paid by employees.

Voluntary scheme. The Czech Republic introduced a voluntary pension scheme in 1994 (table 4.4). All citizens of the European Union (EU) age 18 and older who are also participating in either the first-pillar (earnings-related) public pension scheme or the public health-insurance scheme are eligible to enroll in the voluntary pension scheme. To proactively accommodate expected future changes in the first-pillar scheme— changes that will likely reduce benefits—the government is actively encouraging participation in the voluntary scheme through a combination of matching subsidies and tax exemptions. Contributions can be made by workers or their employers. The minimum monthly contribution to the scheme is CZK 100; the minimum monthly state subsidy corresponding to that contribution is CZK 50 (equivalent to 50 percent of the actual contribution). Although the subsidy grows with the amount of the contribution, the ratio between the two gradually falls, such that a maximum subsidy of CZK 150 is provided for contributions of CZK 500 and higher.

Annual contributions that exceed CZK 6,000 a year are deductible from personal income tax, subject to an annual maximum of CZK 12,000. The combination of state subsidies (in the form of matching contributions) and tax exemptions implies that the government supports the first CZK 18,000 of individual voluntary pension savings—equivalent to about

Table 4.4   Characteristics of the Voluntary Scheme in the Czech Republic

Coverage	Vesting period	Retirement age	Tax advantages to participants	Contributions tax deductible by employers	Lump-sum payments possible in retirement
EU citizens age 18 and older enrolled in the public pension or health insurance scheme	Five years	60	Yes	Yes	Yes

Sources: Hemmings and Whitehouse 2006; Iglesias 2003.

8 percent of average earnings. Voluntary pension contributions made by employers are exempt from taxation up to 5 percent of gross earnings. Benefits from the voluntary pension scheme are taxed differently on the basis of whether they originate from employee contributions, state-provided matching contributions, employer contributions, or returns on invested assets. Taxes are levied on investment income at the rate of 15 percent; employer contributions are subjected to standard income tax provisions (Hemmings and White 2006).

Supervision of the voluntary pension scheme is the responsibility of the Czech National Bank; the Ministry of Finance is responsible for overseeing state-provided matching contributions. The assets of the voluntary pension scheme are invested by private management companies. There are currently 11 such companies. Under current law, management companies have some freedom to define the terms of the plans they offer, including options for receiving annuities and lump-sum payments.[6] All plans must offer an old-age pension; disability pensions and survivor benefits are optional. Management companies are required to guarantee a 0 percent nominal rate of return (that is, participants are ensured of getting their money back, albeit without compensation for inflation). Participants may be enrolled in more than one pension plan, but they are restricted to making contributions to one plan at a time.

Given the existence of state-provided matching contributions and preferential tax treatment (Iglesias 2003), participation in the voluntary scheme has expanded rapidly, from 3.5 percent of the labor force in 1994 to 57 percent by 2004.[7] Older workers are more likely to participate than younger workers. Contributions have averaged roughly 2 percent of the average wage since 1999. The accumulated assets of the scheme were equivalent to 3.7 percent of GDP in 2004.

Health care system. Health care in the Czech Republic is provided mainly through a mandatory insurance scheme administrated by nine health insurance funds. In 2005, health expenditures accounted for 7.1 percent of GDP, 88.6 percent of which was public expenditure and the remaining 11.4 was private expenditure. Of private expenditure, 95.3 percent was attributable to out-of-pocket expenditures (informal payments, direct payments, and copayments) (WHO database 2008). Participants have the right to choose their health insurance fund. Of the nine funds, the General Health Insurance Fund is, by far, the largest, covering 68 percent of the overall population in 2002 and the majority of the population for which the Ministry of Finance pays the premiums.

Virtually all medical services are covered. These services include preventive services, diagnostic procedures, ambulatory and hospital curative care, rehabilitation and care for the chronically ill, drugs and medical devices, medical transportation services, and spa therapy (when prescribed by a physician). For all medical services, the least-expensive available treatment is fully covered. Only generic pharmaceuticals are fully covered; patients bear the cost of nongeneric drugs. Nongeneric drugs may be approved for reimbursement if there are no alternatives. A small number of services are excluded (cosmetic surgery for nonmedical reasons and certain services made at a patient's request); a small number require copayments (certain kinds of dental care, including dentures). Prostheses, eyeglasses, and hearing aids may be partially or fully reimbursed. The cost of social care is not covered by the scheme but is, instead, borne directly by patients and the Ministry of Social Affairs. Within the limits established in the benefit package, the scheme provides free health care for all elderly people in all public facilities, irrespective of whether they made insurance premium contributions while they were working.

Under the law, the premium for health insurance is 13.5 percent of pretax wages, subject to a floor of 25 percent of the national average wage and a ceiling of six times the national average wage. One-third of the premium is paid by employees and two-thirds by employers. Self-employed workers pay the same total levy (13.5 percent) but only on 35 percent of their profits, subject to a legally defined minimum contribution (in 2004, this figure was CZK 905; the amount is adjusted periodically for inflation). The 80 percent of the self-employed who declare no profits pay only this minimum. The Ministry of Finance pays health insurance premiums on behalf of the nonactive population, including pensioners and people receiving social assistance, who together represent 56 percent of the total population. Premiums are computed by applying the same

13.5 percent contribution rate to an amount established by a statutory order (CZK 3,458 in 2003).

Voluntary health insurance is also available for those seeking coverage beyond what is provided under the mandatory scheme, although there is virtually no participation. As a result, voluntary insurance accounts for only 0.1 percent of total expenditures on health care.

Institutional Structure and Coverage of Earnings-Related Scheme

Under the supervision of the Ministry of Labor and Social Affairs, the Social Security Administration manages the first-pillar earnings-related pension scheme. The Social Security Administration collects contributions and pays benefits through a central office and 76 district offices located throughout the country. The scheme covers the entire economically active population, including the self-employed. Participation is voluntary for certain categories of individuals, including people employed abroad. In 2006, 4.85 million people were enrolled in the scheme (roughly 66 percent of the total working-age population and 93 percent of the labor force). The same year, 2.68 million people were receiving pensions (roughly 26 percent of the population) (see Czech Social Security Administration 2006 and the World Bank's Statistical Information Management & Analysis database).

Structure of Benefits

The first-pillar earnings-related pension scheme provides old-age, disability, and survivorship pensions. The provisions governing each of these types of benefits are discussed as follows.

Old-age benefits. To be eligible for an old-age pension, applicants must have worked for 25 or more years and have reached the minimum retirement age. Retirement with 15 years of service is allowed at age 65. Old-age pensions are the sum of a flat benefit and an earnings-related benefit based on an individual's earnings history. The earnings-related benefit accrues at a rate of 1.5 percent for each year of service applied to a pension assessment base (that is, the value of wages used in the computation of benefits), which provides higher levels of income replacement for lower levels of wages. Retirement ages have been increasing since 1996 at the rate of two months per year for men and four months per year for women. By 2030, the statutory retirement age will reach 65 for men, childless women, and women with one child; 64 for women with two children; 63 for women with three children; and 62 for women with more than three children.

Early retirement of up to three years is currently allowed for people with 25 or more years of service (by 2018, this will increase to 30 years), subject to the following reduction in benefits. For each 90 days of early retirement, the pension assessment base is reduced by 0.9 percent. The 2008 reform increases that reduction to an (almost) actuarially neutral 1.5 percent if retirement takes place 720 days before the statutory retirement age. All reductions are permanent (that is, they continue even after a pensioner reaches the normal retirement age). After 2020, it will be possible to retire four years before statutory retirement age. After 2030, it will be possible to retire five years before statutory retirement age. People who work beyond the normal retirement age are awarded additional credit equal to 1.5 percent of their pension assessment base for each 90 days they defer their pension.

Disability benefits. Disability benefits are awarded to individuals who suffer impairment that affects their ability to work. Full disability benefits are awarded to people who have lost 66 percent or more of their effective working capacity; partial disability benefits are awarded to people who have lost 33–66 percent of their working capacity. Benefits are subject to vesting requirements (table 4.5). The benefits paid to disabled people are the sum of a flat benefit (which is the same as that provided to old-age pensioners, regardless of whether a person is fully or partially

Table 4.5   Eligibility Conditions for and Benefits Provided by Disability Pensions in the Czech Republic under the First-Pillar Earnings-Related Scheme

Vesting period	Contributions	Eligibility	Benefit rate[a]	Partial pension
Under age 20: Less than 1 year Age 20–22: 1 year Age 22–24: 2 years Age 24–26: 3 years Age 26–28: 4 years Over age 28: 5 years	No specific contribution rate for disability benefits, no ceiling on wages subject to contributions	Full disability: at least 66 percent loss of capacity Partial disability: at least 33 percent loss of capacity	Full disability: flat benefit plus 1.5 percent per year Partial disability: flat benefit plus 0.75 percent per year	Flat benefit plus 0.75 percent per year

Sources: European Commission 2005, 2007a; Czech Social Security Administration Web site (accessed March 2008).
a. The 2008 reform introduced a new classification based on three degrees of invalidity, with reduced benefits for the first degree; details were unavailable in time to be included in this chapter.

disabled) plus an earnings-related benefit. The earnings-related benefit is computed on the basis of a rate of accrual of 1.5 percent (for people who are fully disabled) or 0.75 percent (for people who are partially disabled). Regardless of the results of the benefit computation, disabled people are guaranteed a minimum pension equal to the minimum pension paid to old-age pensioners. In addition, upon reaching the normal retirement age, pensioners are given the choice between receiving their disability pension or their old-age pension, whichever provides them with higher benefits.

Survivor benefits. Survivor benefits are awarded to dependents if the deceased had been receiving (or had met the criteria to receive) an old-age or disability pension. Widows and widowers receive a flat benefit plus 50 percent of the earnings-related component of the deceased's pension (table 4.6). Widows over age 55 and widowers over age 58 are eligible to receive the pension for longer than one year; other widows and widowers receive the pension for only one year. Survivors who are disabled and survivors who are caring for a dependent disabled child or disabled parent are eligible for benefits irrespective of their age. Orphans receive a flat benefit plus 40 percent of the earnings-related component of the deceased's pension for each dependent child under age 26. For disabled survivors, the value of the pension is increased by 50 percent (for fully disabled survivors) or 20 percent (for partially disabled survivors). As a result of these comparatively generous provisions, total survivor benefits can actually exceed the pension to which the deceased was originally entitled.

Assessment of the Performance of the Czech Pension System

The World Bank has established four principles for evaluating public pension systems, which together should guide the process of pension reform (see Holzmann and Hinz 2005). Broadly speaking, these principles include the adequacy and security of benefits, the affordability of contributions, the sustainability of the system over time, and the robustness of the system in the face of demographic changes and macroeconomic shocks. This chapter focuses primarily on the adequacy of benefits and financial sustainability of the first-pillar earnings-related pension scheme. The remaining principles are mentioned only briefly. Adequacy is analyzed through the lens of net replacement rates. Financial sustainability is evaluated using projections of pension expenditures and revenues.

Table 4.6 Eligibility Conditions for and Benefits Provided by Survivor Pensions in the Czech Republic under the First-Pillar Earnings-Related Scheme

Eligibility	Spouse replacement rate	Benefit duration	Remarriage test	Orphan age limit	Orphan replacement rate	Total family benefit
Eligibility of deceased for old-age or disability pension	Flat benefit plus 50 percent of deceased's pension	For life, if spouse is 70 percent disabled, is taking care of a child or a dependent parent, or is age 55 (women) or age 58 (men); otherwise, one year	Pension ceases if survivor remarries	26	Flat benefit plus 40 percent of deceased's pension	No maximum

Sources: European Commission 2005, 2007a; Czech Social Security Administration Web site (accessed March 2008).

Benefit Adequacy

Replacement rates are a useful yardstick for measuring the adequacy of pension benefits because they express benefits relative to preretirement earnings, thereby demonstrating the degree to which income is replaced when workers retire. Two variants are commonly used. Gross replacement rates compute income replacement as the ratio of benefits paid to pretax preretirement earnings. Net replacement rates compute income replacement as the ratio of benefits received (that is, after the payment of taxes and other levies, including contributions for social insurance) to posttax preretirement earnings. In general, net replacement rates are a more useful measure of benefit adequacy because they capture the degree to which actual take-home pay is replaced when workers retire.

Benefit adequacy is determined not only by the level of income replacement at retirement. For a full assessment of benefit adequacy, it is also important to assess how postretirement indexation rules will affect replacement rates during retirement. Pension benefits in retirement are expected to be indexed to inflation so that their real value is maintained. In a growing economy with increasing real wages, mere price indexation of pensions, however, leads to a deterioration of the relative consumption position of the retirees. Individuals with otherwise identical work histories will receive different pensions depending on when they retire. For this reason, some countries have introduced mixed indexation of pensions with varying weights of inflation and wage growth in the indexation formula.

For an evaluation of the effect of indexation on replacement rates in the Czech Republic, the replacement rates are normalized to 100 and the assumptions for calculating the replacement rates are maintained (that is, inflation is 2.5 percent a year and real wage growth is 2 percent a year). The change in the replacement rate is measured in comparison to full wage indexation or compared to an active worker. The results of this analysis indicate that the relative income position of a retiree would deteriorate by 12 percent after 10 years in retirement and by 36 percent after 35 years in retirement. Because benefit indexation in the Czech Republic includes an adjustment amounting to one-third of wage growth over inflation, this deterioration is lower than it is in countries that fully price index benefits. The evaluation of income replacement that follows considers replacement rates only at retirement and does not take into account the impact of indexation policies on replacement rates during retirement.

Replacement rates are a function of the formula governing pension benefits; an individual's contribution history; and, in the case of the net replacement rates, the rules of income tax, social security contributions, and other relevant levies. The benefit formula establishes the degree to which the system redistributes income across individuals of different levels of preretirement earnings. Progressive systems provide higher levels of income replacement to people with lower levels of preretirement income. In general, the degree to which a system is redistributive depends on the existence (and value) of flat transfers and minimum pension guarantees, the degree to which benefits are earnings related, and the existence of ceilings on earnings subject to contributions. An individual's contribution history can be characterized by his or her age of entry into the labor force, contribution density, and decisions regarding the timing of retirement. To some degree, these three factors are influenced by the incentives embodied in the pension system. The tax and contribution system influences net replacement rates through the typical progressiveness of the income tax formula, which taxes higher income during a worker's active life more so than it does lower pension benefits in retirement. In addition—and, even more important, for low to middle-income groups—there are social security levies (for pensions; unemployment; health care; and, at times, housing and family benefits), which are typically reduced (for example, health care) or eliminated altogether in retirement.

The adequacy of income replacement provided by the first-pillar earnings-related pension scheme in the Czech Republic cannot be evaluated without first establishing benchmarks. Unfortunately, there is no consensus on what constitutes adequacy. According to one widely respected definition, pensions are adequate when they are sufficient to prevent poverty among the elderly and provide the vast majority of the population with a reliable mechanism for smoothing income over their lifetime. Even with the benefit of a definition, however, establishing benchmarks is problematic because attitudes vary from one country to another as a function of social and cultural perceptions. Moreover, benchmarks ignore the existence of other factors that affect the welfare of the elderly—and that vary from country to country—including the existence and generosity of health insurance and long-term care, the cost of housing, the structure of traditional living arrangements, the presence of informal intrafamily or intergenerational sources of financial and nonfinancial support, and the availability and security of other mechanisms for people to save for their own retirement.

One reputable nine-country study (OECD 2001) observed that living standards are roughly comparable for people 10 years older than the normal retirement age and people 15 years younger than the normal retirement age when retirees have disposable income equal to roughly

80 percent of the disposable income of working-age people. In part, this is attributable to the fact that retirees have no work-related expenses (that is, they do not have to commute to and from a place of employment or buy special clothing or uniforms, and so forth). This finding, however, does not imply that mandatory first-pillar pension schemes should actually target an 80 percent net replacement rate. To the contrary, in middle- and high-income countries, one can reasonably expect individuals to save for their own retirement—and the empirical evidence suggests that, in practice, this is actually happening.[8] There is also some evidence to suggest that the ratio between preretirement and postretirement income is somewhat independent of the income replacement mandate of the public pension system. Put simply, individuals tend to save more in countries with more modest mandates (and vice versa).

Because the Czech Republic has access to relatively well-developed financial markets, it would seem reasonable to expect middle- and higher-income workers to save enough to finance at least 25 percent, if not closer to 50 percent, of this 80 percent income replacement target. Given this, three benchmarks are provided: a 40 percent net replacement rate (which implies that individuals would be expected to save enough to finance half of the total income replacement target); a 60 percent net replacement rate (which implies that individuals would be expected to finance a quarter of the target); and an 80 percent net replacement rate (which implies that individuals, most of whom would be low-income earners, would not be expected to contribute anything toward the target).[9] In the following analysis, these three benchmarks are used to evaluate the adequacy of benefits in the Czech Republic compared with the average net replacement rate observed in 53 countries around the world, the average net replacement rate observed for selected countries in Europe and Central Asia, and the poverty line in the Czech Republic.

To estimate gross and net replacement rates, we consider two critical dimensions—earnings levels and contribution periods—with the help of the Analysis of Pension Entitlements across Countries (APEX) model.[10] This model generates estimates for replacement rates under steady-state assumptions (that is, as if the rules of the reformed pension scheme had been in place over the entire active life of the individual). Because life expectancies at retirement are projected to increase over time—which will affect the benefits paid by defined-contribution pension schemes—a reference year must be chosen. For this study, 2040 is used, because it provides a sufficiently long contribution period over which to approximate steady-state conditions.

The first critical task is to investigate levels of income replacement across a relevant spectrum of income. Income is represented as a percentage

(50–200 percent) of average earnings. The second task is to investigate the impact on income replacement of differences in the duration, timing, and density of an individual's contribution history (density refers to the percentage of time an individual actually contributes over a given period). To facilitate the presentation of these multidimensional results, replacement rates are computed as a function of the age an individual exits the labor market. They are presented separately for full-career and partial-career workers.

Replacement rates for full-career workers. For the purpose of this analysis, a full career is defined as continuous employment from age 20 to the current normal retirement age of 63. Gross replacement rates clearly show why the Czech Republic's first-pillar earnings-related pension scheme has been described as highly progressive (figure 4.1). The level of gross income replacement provided to someone earning half the average wage is more than twice that provided to someone earning twice the average wage. This is, of course, caused by the presence of the redistributive earnings-related benefit, as well as the flat benefit, which contributes less to total benefits as income rises.

The situation does not change significantly when taxes are taken into consideration. As a result of the impact of taxes and contributions, net replacement rates fall only slightly more than do gross replacement rates when expressed relative to preretirement income (figure 4.2).

Figure 4.1   Sources of Gross Replacement Rates in the Czech Republic, by Income Level

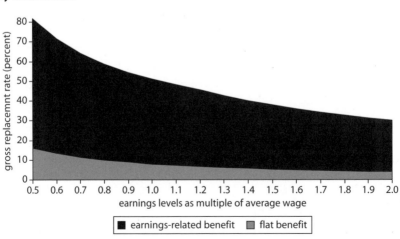

Source: APEX model.
Note: Figure shows projected replacement rate for 2040 as approximation of steady-state conditions.

Figure 4.2   Sources of Net Replacement Rates in the Czech Republic, by Income Level

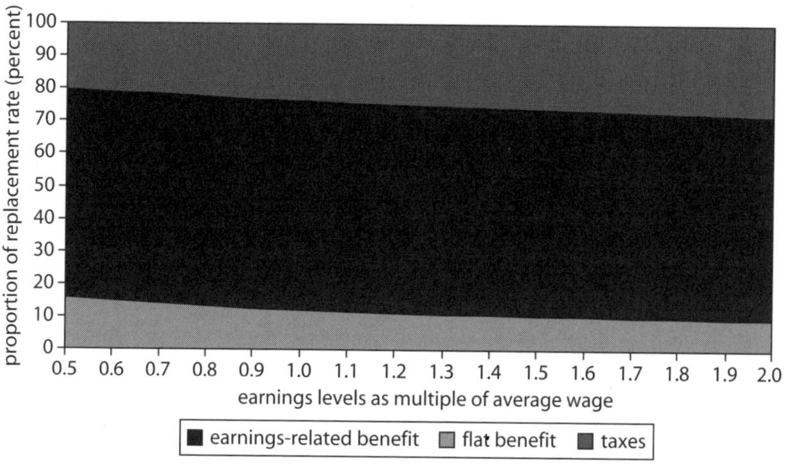

earnings levels as multiple of average wage

■ earnings-related benefit   ■ flat benefit   ■ taxes

Source: APEX model.
Note: Figure shows projected replacement rate for 2040 as approximation of steady-state conditions.

Net replacement rates for full-career workers in the Czech Republic can generally be considered adequate (figure 4.3).[11] Replacement rates are substantially higher than the highest of the three benchmarks for people with low preretirement income, slightly higher than the middle benchmark for people with roughly average preretirement income, and roughly equal to or higher than the lowest benchmark for people with high preretirement income. This finding suggests that the system is effectively smoothing consumption from work to retirement, more so for lower-income workers, who have less capacity to save on their own. Given that benefits for even the lowest full-career workers greatly exceed the poverty line, the objective of poverty alleviation is being met.[12] The pension system in the Czech Republic is more redistributive than the average pension system in the region (or the world), as demonstrated by the fact that it provides higher levels of income replacement for lower-income workers and lower levels of income replacement for higher-income workers, with respect to regional and world averages.

Replacement rates for partial-career workers. Not everyone works from age 20 to the statutory retirement age; many individuals enter and exit the labor force (often at different ages and for different periods of time). To examine the adequacy of benefits for partial-career workers, three stylized cases are considered. These include career type A (someone entering the

Figure 4.3 Net Replacement Rates for Male Full-Career Workers in the Czech Republic, Europe and Central Asia, and the World, by Income Level

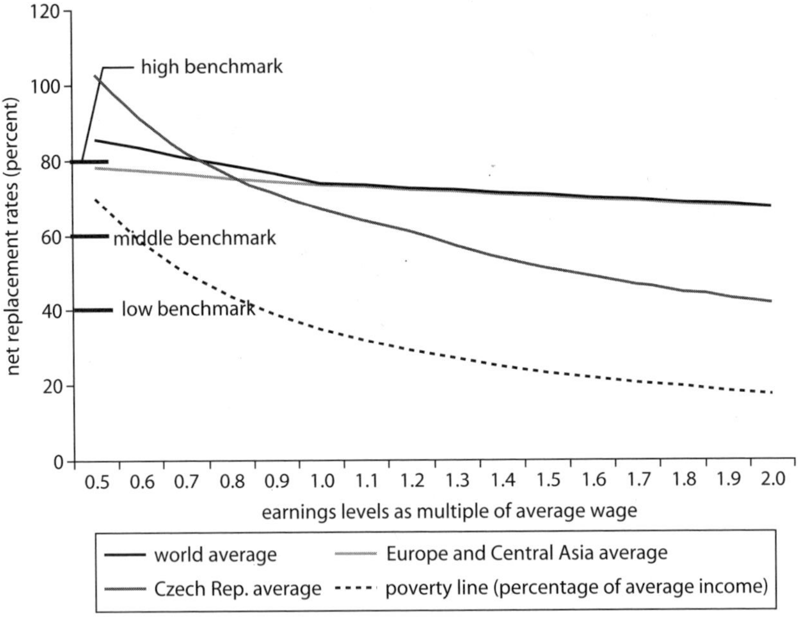

Source: Authors' calculations based on World Bank 2007a and the APEX model.
Note: Figure shows projected replacement rate for 2040 as an approximation of steady-state conditions.

labor force at age 25 who works continuously for a period of years before leaving the workforce at some point between the ages of 50 and 70 and then claims a benefit); career type B (identical to career type A, except that the worker enters the workforce at age 30 and leaves no earlier than age 55); and career type C (identical to career type A, except that the individual contributes in only three years out of four while in the labor force). In cases in which the withdrawal from the formal labor market occurs before the statutory retirement age, the pension is claimed (and the replacement rate calculated) only at the later age. For withdrawals after the statutory retirement age, of course, the ages coincide.

Net replacement rates for low-income partial-career workers are examined first (figure 4.4). Because a minimum of 25 years of contributions are required to become eligible for old-age pension benefits, the age at which these workers can permanently exit the workforce and still claim a benefit can vary (this explains why the lines for each of the three career types start at different ages). The acceleration in the increase in

Figure 4.4   Net Replacement Rates for Male Low-Income Partial-Career Workers in the Czech Republic, by Career Type and Exit Age

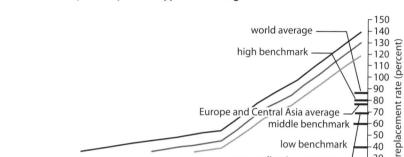

career type A:
entry age—25,
contribution
density—100%

career type B:
entry age—30,
contribution
density—100%

career type C:
entry age—25,
contribution
density—75%

Source: Authors' calculations based on World Bank 2007a and the APEX model.
Note: Figure shows projected replacement rate for 2040 as an approximation of steady-state conditions. See text for descriptions of career types.

replacement rates with years of contributions after age 60 reflects the fact that each extra year's contributions increase benefits both directly and, because retirement is delayed, by a lower actuarial reduction or an actuarial increment.

Two conclusions can be drawn from figure 4.4. First, entering the workforce later in life is costly for low-income workers (someone entering the workforce at age 30 receives a net replacement rate that is some 15 percentage points lower than someone entering the workforce at age 25). Second, working intermittently is costly (someone entering the workforce at the same age but who contributes only three years out of four will receive a net replacement rate that is 9 percentage points lower than someone who contributes continuously). Figure 4.4 also suggests that some low-income partial-career workers—particularly those who exit the labor market long before reaching the statutory retirement age—may not receive acceptable levels of income replacement (their net replacement rates are lower than the lowest of the benchmarks). Some low-income workers (career types A and B) who work until the statutory retirement age (which is likely to include people with limited ability to save on their own, for whom the mandatory system is likely to be their main source of retirement income) receive a net replacement rate of more than 80 percent, while others (career type C) receive a replacement rate of less than 80 percent.

The conclusions about net replacement rates for middle-income partial-career workers are similar, except that the differences in net replacement rates across the three types of workers are smaller, because the contribution of the flat benefit declines as preretirement income increases (figure 4.5). Entering the workforce later in life is still costly for middle-income workers but less so than for low-income workers (the difference between career types A and B is only 6 percentage points). Working intermittently is also costly for middle-income workers but less so than for low-income workers (the difference is only 4–8 percentage points). Some middle-income partial-career workers—including those who exit the labor market long before reaching the statutory retirement age—will not receive acceptable levels of income replacement, because their net replacement rates may be beneath the poverty line. To earn income replacement that is

Figure 4.5   Net Replacement Rates for Male Middle-Income Partial-Career Workers in the Czech Republic, by Career Type and Exit Age

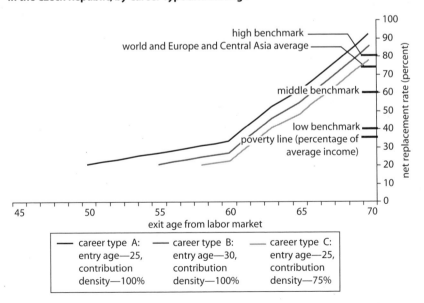

Source: Authors' calculations based on World Bank 2007a and the APEX model.
Note: Figure shows projected replacement rate for 2040 as approximation of steady-state conditions.

higher than the lowest benchmark, for example, middle-income workers must work until age 63, depending on their age of entry into the workforce and their contribution density. To earn income replacement of 60 percent of preretirement income, they must work at least until (and, in some cases, one to two years beyond) the normal retirement age. To achieve income replacement of 80 percent, they must work until at least age 68—five years longer than low-income workers need to work to earn the same level of income replacement.

The results for high-income partial-career workers are similar (figure 4.6). Workers who leave the workforce at earlier ages may receive replacement rates below the poverty line. The Czech pension system still provides high-income partial-career workers with an acceptable level of income replacement, albeit at lower levels than that provided to either middle- or low-income workers, because the benefit formula is progressive.

To earn income replacement that exceeds the lowest benchmark, for example, high-income workers must work until at least age 66 (depending on their age of entry into the workforce and their contribution density). Even if high-income workers continue working until age 70, however, they

Figure 4.6   Net Replacement Rates for Male High-Income Partial-Career Workers in the Czech Republic, by Career Type and Exit Age

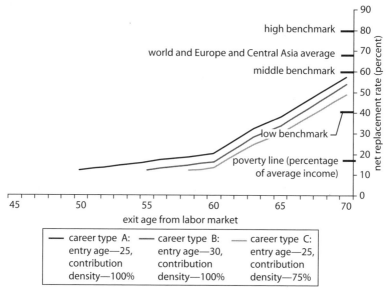

Source: Authors' calculations based on World Bank 2007a and the APEX model.
Note: Figure shows projected replacement rate for 2040 as an approximation of steady-state conditions.

will not earn income replacement of 60 percent of their preretirement income, which implies that these workers must save outside of the pension system in order to preserve their standard of living into retirement.

The key conclusion to be drawn from this analysis is that the Czech pension system generally provides benefits that are adequate to alleviate poverty for all workers but that partial-career workers who leave the workforce before reaching the statutory retirement age and those with intermittent work histories may receive replacement rates that leave them below the poverty line. The Czech pension system provides full-career workers with a reliable means of preserving their standard of living into retirement (that is, lifetime consumption smoothing), but some partial-career workers, particularly those with higher incomes, will need to save outside the pension system in order to accomplish the same objective.

Fiscal Sustainability

The sustainability of a pay-as-you-go first-pillar pension scheme is best evaluated in actuarial terms by estimating the scheme's actuarial deficit as the difference between its assets and liabilities. If an actuarial deficit exists and is large, the scheme is financially unsustainable and needs policy actions that increase assets, reduce its liabilities, or both. A good proxy for the actuarial deficit is the difference between the present value of the scheme's expected future revenues (that is, contributions and other income) and expected future expenditures (that is, benefit payments, administrative costs, and other expenses) over an extended projection period. The difference between these two values represents an unfunded liability (sometimes referred to as a financing gap) on the public-sector balance sheet. Because this study is concerned also with the time path of revenues and expenditures (and the resulting balance across the projection period ending in 2050), this more pragmatic approach has been taken, and projections of expenditures, revenues, and deficits are presented on the basis of available postreform fiscal projections.

The reforms of 1995 and 2003 and those introduced in 2008 are expected to improve the fiscal position of the first-pillar earnings-related pension scheme. They did not, however, ensure the long-term sustainability of the scheme, which is projected to generate a slight surplus until 2032, with revenues and expenditures remaining roughly constant at about 8 percent of GDP (figure 4.7). Starting in 2033, the gap between revenues and expenditures is projected to gradually widen, leading to a deficit equivalent to 2.5 percent of GDP by 2050.[13]

Figure 4.7   Projected Fiscal Balance of the Public Pension System in the Czech Republic after Reform, 2009–50

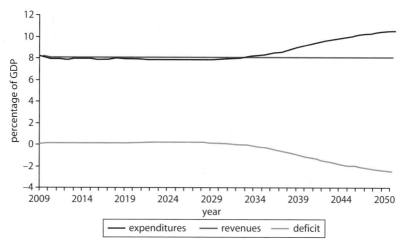

Source: Czech Ministry of Labor and Social Affairs 2008.

Figure 4.8   Projected Old-Age and System Dependency Ratios in the Czech Republic, 2005–50

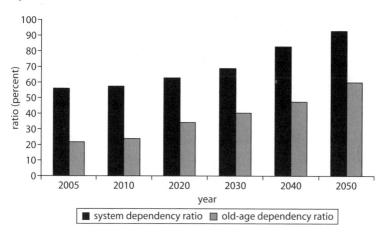

Sources: European Commission 2005; Reiterer 2008.

The aging of the population is largely to blame for these projections. As in other countries in the region—many of which are also facing relatively low rates of fertility in combination with increased life expectancy—the population in the Czech Republic is aging rapidly. Demographic projections indicate that the old-age dependency ratio will rise from 21.7 percent in 2005 to 60.1 percent by 2050 (figure 4.8).[14]

The aging of the population is also driving an increase in the pension scheme's system dependency ratio.[15] Although the system dependency ratio—which is now 2.5 times higher than the old-age dependency ratio—is projected to decline relative to the old-age dependency ratio (as a result of the reforms already undertaken), the aging of the population will eventually drive the pension scheme into insolvency.

What options exist for restoring the system to fiscal balance? Unfortunately, for policy makers, the options are limited. Revenues can be increased by raising the contribution rate. Alternatively (or in addition to—the options are not mutually exclusive), expenditures can be reduced by cutting benefits, increasing the minimum number of years required to become eligible for benefits, or delaying the payment of benefits by raising the retirement age further. Because raising the contribution rate could threaten competitiveness and will likely strengthen incentives for tax evasion, it is typically not embraced by policy makers.

This leaves policy makers with limited options: cutting benefits, tightening eligibility conditions, or raising the retirement age. It also raises the question of whether restoring sustainability will exact a cost in terms of the adequacy of benefits provided to future beneficiaries. A rough analysis indicates that restoring sustainability to the first-pillar earnings-related pension scheme will require either increasing the retirement age to at least 66 by 2050 for both men and women[16] or cutting benefits by an average of 23 percent. A 23 percent reduction in benefits results in a drop in net income replacement of 6–15 percentage points by 2050 (figure 4.9). A comparison of these new (lower) net replacement rates against the three benchmarks suggests that a 23 percent reduction in benefits would not cause income replacement to fall below the poverty line for full-career workers. This indicates that a sustainable first-pillar pension scheme in the Czech Republic will still achieve its poverty alleviation objective. However, the same reduction in benefits would frustrate the objective of smoothing lifetime consumption for full-career workers, because levels of income replacement would be lower than the 80 percent benchmark for low-income workers, lower than the 60 percent benchmark for middle-income workers, and lower than the 40 percent benchmark for high-income workers.

This last observation is subject to three caveats. First, these findings may be unduly pessimistic if coverage is extended (because high rates of coverage will increase the resources available in the medium term for funding benefits, albeit at the cost of higher benefits in the long term) or if retirement ages are also increased (because delaying retirement can

Figure 4.9   Net Replacement Rates for Male Full-Career Workers in the Czech Republic before and after Benefit Adjustment, by Income Level

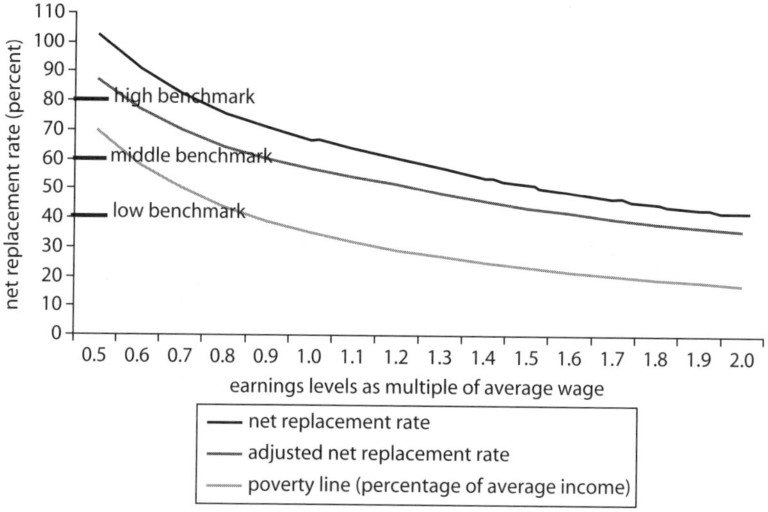

Source: Authors' calculations based on World Bank 2007a and the APEX model.

reduce the rates of return paid on contributions, depending on how a pension scheme is structured). Second, high-income workers always have the option of saving outside of the first-pillar pension scheme. To increase income replacement by 1 percentage point, for example, a full-career worker would need to save only about 0.5 percent of his or her earnings from age 40 to the current age of retirement.[17] Third, this analysis considers only full-career workers, while the average worker now contributes for only about 30 years, substantially less than the 40 years expected over a full career. Contributing to the pension scheme for only 30 years, for example, reduces net income replacement by 18 percentage points (for low-income workers) and 8 percentage points (for high-income workers).

Conclusions

The Czech Republic is one of only a few countries in the region that did not look beyond its first-pillar pay-as-you-go pension scheme when it reformed its pension system in 1995, 2003, and 2008. The reforms enacted to date have been parametric, except for the introduction, in 1994, of a budget-subsidized voluntary third-pillar scheme. These parametric reforms improved the fiscal condition of the scheme, but they did not make the scheme sustainable over the long term, largely because they failed to go far enough to counteract the impact of the aging of the Czech population.

The first-pillar pension scheme is highly progressive, in terms of both its levels of income replacement and the rates of return it provides on contributions. The degree to which the scheme provides more generous income replacement and higher returns to workers with lower levels of preretirement income is attributable to a redistributive earnings-related benefit as well as to the existence of a flat benefit, which contributes less to total benefits as incomes rise.

The resulting gross and net replacement rates for full-career workers at average earnings levels are fully in line with regional and international standards. For workers at lower and higher earnings levels, however, replacement rates deviate substantially from these standards as a result of the redistributive benefit formula (see chapter 1). First-pillar pension benefits are adequate to alleviate poverty for all workers: both full-career and partial-career workers are receiving levels of income replacement well above the poverty line. The scheme is also successfully smoothing lifetime consumption for all full-career workers. Many partial-career workers, however, especially those earning more than the average wage, will have to work beyond even the higher future retirement age of 65 (applicable to men, childless women, and women with one child) or save outside the pension scheme to preserve their standard of living into retirement. Increasing the retirement age in step with increases in life expectancy at retirement is a natural choice for both individuals and policy makers, but it requires cross-sectoral policy reforms to enable elderly workers to continue to participate in the labor market.[18]

In the future, Czech policy makers will have to either allocate funds from the budget to finance deficits in the first-pillar pension scheme or enact further reforms to restore fiscal balance to the scheme. Restoring fiscal balance to the scheme while successfully smoothing lifetime consumption (particularly for middle- and high-income workers) will be difficult to accomplish on the basis of benefit cuts alone. Moreover, unless increases in the statutory retirement age are accompanied by changes in the benefit formula (such as a reduction in the accrual rate, as enacted by the 2003 and 2008 reforms), such increases will only lengthen the average pension contribution period, thereby leading to higher replacement rates and increased expenditures. A complementary option to reducing benefits would be to change to pure price indexation.

The Czech government recognizes that the population is aging. It has been subsidizing the voluntary pension scheme in order to supplement the retirement income provided by the first-pillar scheme. These subsidies explain the comparatively broad coverage enjoyed by the voluntary scheme. However, the low levels of average contributions being made suggest that the scheme will not provide a meaningful benefit (or income replacement) for most participants. Of equal concern is the fact that participation in the voluntary scheme is much lower for younger workers, who are more vulnerable to reforms in the first-pillar scheme that reduce their benefits (but who stand to gain the most by virtue of having longer investment horizons). Clearly, there is scope for the expansion and growth of the voluntary pension scheme in the provision of retirement income. This aspect of the overall pension system in the Czech Republic requires—and deserves—further investigation.

Notes

1. For an overview of the main measures adopted by the Czech Republic since 1990 in the area of social insurance, see Czech Republic Ministry of Labor and Social Affairs (2006).

2. The benefit increases by 2,880 koruny (CZK) for the first additional person in a household and by CZK 2,600 for other additional persons who are not dependent children. It rises by CZK 1,600 for each dependent child under age 6, CZK 1,960 for each dependent child age 6–15, and CZK 2,250 for each dependent child age 15–26 (European Commission 2007a; World Bank 2007a).

3. In 2006 the flat benefit was CZK 1,470, or 7.3 percent of the average wage. The Czech pension system also guarantees a minimum pension equal to the sum of the flat benefit and CZK 770 in 2006.

4. The first CZK 9,100 per month is replaced at 100 percent; earnings of CZK 9,100–CZK 21,800 are replaced at 30 percent; earnings above CZK 21,800 are replaced at 10 percent.

5. This change is being implemented at the rate of one additional year of wages per year (currently, 18 years of wages are used). Historical wages are adjusted (that is, they are valorized by average wage growth).

6. Lump-sum payments accounted for 85 percent of total pension payments in 2004 (Czech National Bank 2004).

7. In 2004, the number of participants was 2,963,730 (Czech National Bank 2004).

8. In Chile, for instance, 70 percent of retirees from the mandatory public pension system own their home, which, of course, is a form of savings (see

Valdés-Prieto 2008). In the Czech Republic, the rate of home ownership among retirees is of similar magnitude.

9. These benchmarks approximate the standards developed by the International Labour Organization (ILO) (1952) and the Council of Europe (1990). ILO Convention 102 of 1952 sets a minimum benefit equal to 40 percent of the reference wage for married men of pensionable age. This amount was raised to 45 percent in 1968. The European Code of Security of 1990 sets a minimum standard for members of the Council of Europe equal to 65 percent for married people of a specific age.

10. The APEX model was developed by Axia Economics, with funding from the OECD and the World Bank. The model codes detailed eligibility and benefit rules for first- and second-pillar schemes based on available public information that has been verified by country contacts. Because the details of the rules sometimes change on short notice (and limited public disclosure), the calculations presented here should be considered as best approximations only.

11. These are simulated replacement rates for unmarried men based on a hypothetical career path and the assumptions that real wage growth is 2 percent, inflation is 2.5 percent, and everyone retires at the statutory retirement age.

12. As a proxy for the poverty line, this study uses 35 percent of the average net wage, because this percentage very broadly approximates a US$2.25-a-day poverty line converted into national currency, adjusted for purchasing power parity, expressed relative to the national average net wage, and averaged across the nine study countries. Such an approach enables valid comparisons to be made across the sample (see chapter 1).

13. These projections by the Ministry of Labor and Social Affairs are based on a somewhat different methodology and assumptions than were those from the Ministry of Finance, which served as an input to the EU Economic Policy Committee—Ageing Working Group (European Commission 2007b). As a result of these differences, these projections estimate the deficits to be lower by about 1 percent of GDP.

14. The old-age dependency ratio is the population age 65 and higher divided by the population age 20–64.

15. The system dependency ratio is the number of people receiving a pension divided by the number of people contributing to the pension scheme.

16. This estimate is based purely on demographic projections. It assumes that everyone age 65 and older receives a pension, everyone age 20–65 contributes, and all pensioners receive the replacement rate awarded to the average worker.

17. This estimate is based on the assumption that real wage growth is 2 percent, the net real rate of return on invested assets is 3.5 percent, and benefits (from both the unfunded and the funded pillars) are price indexed. Country-specific mortality rates are used.

18. See Holzmann, MacKellar, and Repansek (2009) for a conference volume that addresses theses issues for the countries in southeastern Europe.

Bibliography

Council of Europe. 1990. *European Code of Social Security (Revised)*. Rome.

Czech Republic Ministry of Labor and Social Affairs. 2006. *Actuarial Report on Social Insurance*. Prague.

Czech National Bank. 2004. *Annual Report*. Office of the State Supervision in Insurance and Pension Funds, Prague.

Czech Social Security Administration. n.d. http://www.mpsv.cz/cs/.

———. 2006. *Annual Report*. Prague.

European Commission. 2005. *Employment and Social Affairs*. National Strategy Report on Adequate and Sustainable Pensions. Brussels.

———. 2007a. MISSOC (Mutual Information System and Social Protection) database. http://ec.europa.eu/employment_social/.

———. 2007b. *Pension Schemes and Projection Models in EU-25 Member Countries*. European Economy Occasional Paper 37, Economic Policy Committee and Directorate General for Economic and Financial Affairs, Brussels.

GVG (Gesellschaft für Versicherungswissenschaft und –gestaltung) and European Commission. 2003. *Study on the Social Protection Systems in the 13 Applicant Countries: Czech Republic Country Report*. Cologne.

Hemmings, P., and E. Whitehouse. 2006. *Assessing the 2005 Czech Proposal for Pension Reform*. Paris: Organisation for Economic Co-operation and Development.

Holzmann, R., and R. Hinz. 2005. *Old Age Income Support in the 21st Century*. Washington, DC: World Bank.

Holzmann, R., L. MacKellar, and J. Repansek, eds. 2009. *Pension Reform in Southeastern Europe: Linking to Labor and Financial Market Reforms*. Washington, DC: World Bank.

Iglesias, A. 2003. "Strengthening the Private Voluntary Pension Scheme in the Czech Republic." http://www.zavedenieura.cz/cps/rde/xbcr/mfcr/5-SB.pdf.

ILO (International Labour Organization). 1952. *ILO Convention 102*. Geneva: ILO.

———. 1967. *ILO Convention 128*. Geneva: ILO.

Lasagabaster E., R. Rocha, and P. Wiese. 2002. "Czech Pension System: Challenges and Reform Options." Social Protection Discussion Paper 0217, World Bank, Washington, DC.

Laursen, T. 2000. "Pension System Viability and Reform Alternatives in the Czech Republic." Working Paper, International Monetary Fund, Washington, DC.

Lindbeck, A., and M. Persson. 2003. "The Gains from Pension Reform." *Journal of Economic Literature* 41 (March): 74–112.

Natali, David. 2004. "The Reformed Pension System." Observatoire Social Européen.

OECD (Organisation for Economic Co-operation and Development). 2001. *Ageing and Income: Financial Resources and Retirement in 9 OECD Countries.* Paris: OECD.

Reiterer, A. 2008. "Population Development and Age Structure in Southeastern Europe until 2050." World Bank, Washington, DC.

Rokosova, M., and B. Schreyogg. 2005. *Healthcare Systems in Transition: Czech Republic.* World Health Organization, Regional Office for Europe, Copenhagen.

U.S. Social Security Administration. 2006 *Social Security Systems throughout the World: Europe.* Washington, DC: Social Security Administration.

Valdés-Prieto, S. 2008. *Designs for the First-Pillar Pensions and the 2008 Chilean Reform.* http://editorialexpress.com/cgi-bin/conference/download.cgi?db_name=SECHI2008&paper_id=130.

World Bank. 2007a. *Pensions Panorama.* Washington, DC: World Bank.

———. 2007b. *Social Assistance in Central Europe and the Baltic States.* Washington, DC: World Bank.

WHO (World Health Organization). 2008. Database. http://www.who.int/research/en/.

CHAPTER 5

Hungary

Hungary inherited a socialist-era defined-benefit pension system financed on a pay-as-you-go basis (meaning that contributions from current workers are used to pay benefits to current beneficiaries). Within a few years of the country's transition to a market economy, the fiscal balance of the pension system began to deteriorate. The system broke even in 1992 but generated deficits thereafter that were projected to continue to grow. Despite the system's high contribution rate, pension revenues increasingly fell short of expenditures, as a result of declining employment and increasing informality in the labor market. At the same time, disability and old-age pension provisions were used to cushion rising unemployment. Long-term projections showed that the fiscal balance of the system would worsen over time, with deficits reaching 6 percent of gross domestic product (GDP) by 2050, driven by the aging of the Hungarian population.

Recognizing that low retirement ages, lax benefit eligibility conditions, and poor levels of compliance (resulting from high payroll taxes) were imposing short-term pressure on the fiscal balance of the pension system—and aware of the potentially devastating impact of the aging of the population over the long term—Hungarian policy makers launched a comprehensive package of reforms to the pension system in 1997–98. These reforms moved the system from a monopillar design toward a multipillar design that included a mandatory fully funded defined-contribution scheme and introduced parametric changes to the existing pay-as-you-go defined-benefit scheme. Projections at the time of reform suggested that these reforms would improve the long-term fiscal balance of the pension system, with deficits reaching only 3 percent of GDP by 2050 rather than the 6 percent previously projected. Improving the long-term finances of the pension system further will require increasing employment across all ages, making benefits less generous, or raising retirement ages (or some combination thereof).

Against this backdrop, this chapter evaluates the Hungarian pension system, focusing on fiscal sustainability and benefit adequacy. Adequacy is evaluated through the lens of statutory net replacement rates for different retirement ages, patterns of contributions, and income levels relative to international benchmarks.

This chapter is organized as follows. The next section discusses the motivation for the reforms. The following section describes the key characteristics of the reformed pension system. The third section assesses the adequacy of pension benefits and the fiscal sustainability of the system. The last section draws conclusions.

Motivation for Reform

Like other transition economies in the region, Hungary inherited a pension system that suffered from a number of serious design flaws, including low retirement ages, liberal eligibility conditions, and high payroll taxes. By 1993, the combination of these factors resulted in a system deficit equivalent to 0.3 percent of GDP—a deficit that had to be funded using transfers from the central budget (table 5.1). The strongest driver behind the worsening fiscal condition of the pension system was a sharp drop in contribution revenue (from 11 percent of GDP in 1991 to 8.5 percent by 1996) as a result of (a) declining employment in the formal economy;[1] (b) restrictive wage policies introduced by the government in 1995 as part of the stabilization program that led to a fall in real wages (and contributions to the pension scheme) of more than 10 percent that year (Palacios and Rocha 1998); (c) higher student enrollment ratios; (d) high rates of early retirement; and (e) a decline in the number of working pensioners. Average pensions and (consequently) expenditures also fell during this period, albeit not by as much as revenues. Between 1994 and 1996, the pension system experienced deficits of 0.4–1.7 percent of GDP, breaking even again 1997.

Table 5.1   Fiscal Balance of Hungary's Pension System before Reform, 1991–96
(percentage of GDP)

Year	Revenues	Expenditures	Balance
1991	11.0	10.5	0.5
1992	10.4	10.4	0.0
1993	10.1	10.4	−0.3
1994	9.7	11.4	−1.7
1995	8.9	10.5	−1.6
1996	8.7	9.1	−0.4[a]

Source: Palacios and Rocha 1998.
Note: Table includes revenues and expenditures for the entire system, including old-age, disability, and survivor pensions, as well as short-term benefits. Computing the balance of the system was confounded by the fact that health and pension benefits were funded by a common payroll tax. Deficits shown assume a notional contribution rate of 33.6 percent, sufficient to cover all expenditures in 1992 but insufficient to cover subsequent expenditure.
a. Ministry of Finance data.

Projections from 1998 indicate that before the reforms of the mid- to late 1990s, the pension system would have generated increasingly larger deficits, eventually reaching 6 percent of GDP by 2050—a burden that would be unaffordable and difficult to bear given competing demands on the government's resources (figure 5.1). Deficits were projected largely because of aging of the population. As in most other countries in the region, the population in Hungary is projected to age, albeit somewhat less rapidly.[2] The old-age dependency ratio (the population age 65 and older divided by the population age 20–64) is projected to increase from 25 percent in 2005 to 53.3 percent by 2050.[3] The aging of the population is expected to significantly increase the total number of beneficiaries relative to contributors. This is captured by the system dependency ratio (the number of people receiving a pension divided by the number of people contributing to the pension scheme), which was projected to increase from 51 percent in 2005 to 123 percent by 2050 as the number of beneficiaries rises far more rapidly than the number of contributors (figure 5.2).[4]

Growing pension deficits in the pay-as-you-go defined-benefit pension scheme in the mid-1990s prompted policy makers to introduce a multipillar pension system, the primary objective of which was to improve long-term sustainability. The reforms—initiated in 1997 and implemented in 1998—moved the system from a monopillar design toward a multipillar design that included a mandatory, fully funded, defined-contribution scheme and introduced parametric changes to the existing pay-as-you-go defined-benefit scheme. These reforms were considered radical, because Hungary was the first country in the region to attempt to finance a portion of pension benefits on the basis of funded defined-contribution accounts.

Figure 5.1   Projected Fiscal Balance of Hungary's Public Pension System before Reform, 2000–50

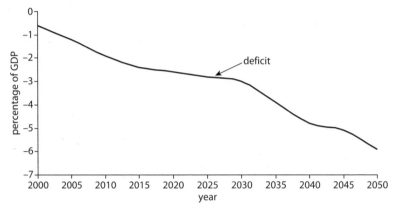

Source: Palacios and Rocha 1998.

Note: The figure includes revenues and expenditures for old-age pensions only.

Figure 5.2   Projected Old-Age and System Dependency Ratios in Hungary, 2005–50

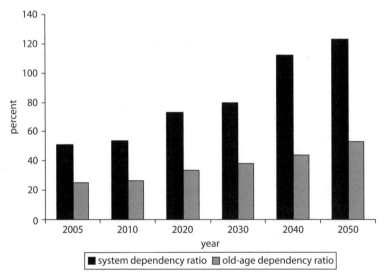

Sources: Palacios and Rocha 1998 (system dependency ratio); Reiterer 2008 (old-age dependency ratio).

Characteristics of Hungary's Pension System

This section describes the main characteristics of Hungary's pension system. These characteristics include the design of the individual pillars of social insurance; the rules governing pension system taxation, institutional structure, and coverage; and the provisions governing old-age, disability, and survivorship pensions. The design of the pension system is compared using a conceptual framework developed by the World Bank, which generally recommends including a funded component if conditions are appropriate but increasingly recognizes that a range of choices is available to policy makers to provide effective old-age protection in a manner that is fiscally responsible (see Holzmann and Hinz 2005).

In general, the World Bank supports pension systems composed of some combination of five basic pillars:

- a noncontributory (or zero) pillar (in the form of a demogrant, social pension, or social assistance benefit) intended to provide a minimal level of income protection;
- a first-pillar contributory system linked to earnings, which seeks to replace a portion of preretirement income;
- a mandatory second pillar (essentially, individual savings accounts), which can be designed in various ways;
- a voluntary third pillar, which is flexible and discretionary (this pillar, too, can take a variety of forms); and
- a fourth pillar of informal intrafamily or intergenerational sources of financial and nonfinancial support to the elderly, including access to health care and housing.

Pillar Design

The design of the Hungarian pension system incorporates all five of these pillars (table 5.2). The publicly managed noncontributory zero pillar, financed with general tax revenues, redistributes income to elderly people whose income would otherwise fall below an established minimum level.

Both the traditional, publicly managed, pay-as-you-go first pillar and the privately managed, fully funded second pillar are earnings-related schemes. First-pillar benefits are adjusted in retirement using a formula based on the average of inflation and wage growth (Swiss indexation), thereby allowing pensions to rise more rapidly than inflation without imposing the heavier fiscal burden of wage indexation.

The second pillar is mandatory. Benefits are a function of an individual's contributions and investment earnings. At retirement, account balances are converted into annuities based on the accumulated capital in an individual's account and the individual's conditional life expectancy. The third pillar is an optional privately managed, fully

Table 5.2 Structure of Hungary's Pension System

Scheme type	Coverage	Type	Function	Financing	Generic benefit	Benefit Indexation	Contributions	Taxation Investment income / capital gains	Benefits
Zero pillar (public non-contributory)	Universal	Means tested	Redistributive	Tax revenues	Supplement to actual income to reach 80 percent of old-age minimum pension	Based on old-age minimum pension	n.a.	n.a.	Exempt
First pillar (public, earnings related)	Mandatory	Defined benefit	Insurance	Percentage of individual earnings	Based on years of service and wage history	50 percent inflation, 50 percent wages	Taxed	n.a.	Exempt[a]

Second pillar (private, earnings related)	Mandatory	Defined contribution	Insurance	Percentage of individual earnings	Pension from conversion of capital accumulation into annuities	50 percent inflation, 50 percent wage-indexed annuity	Taxed	Exempt	Exempt[a]
Third pillar (private, voluntary)	Voluntary	Defined contribution	Insurance	Voluntary contributions	Pension from capital accumulation	Depends on options chosen	Exempt[b]	Exempt	Exempt[c]
Fourth pillar (public health care)	Mandatory	n.a.	Insurance	Percentage of individual earnings plus tax revenues	Specified health service package	n.a.	Exempt	n.a.	n.a.

Source: Authors' compilation based on data from European Commission 2007a, 2007b; OECD 2001; and unpublished information provided by World Bank staff.

n.a. = Not applicable.

a. There is great uncertainty regarding the taxation of benefits after 2013.

b. Thirty percent of contributions are tax deductible up to an annual cap of 100,000 forint.

c. If the pension is taken as a qualified annuity and the accumulation period is 20 (or more) years, than 10–20 years of accumulation are partially taxed.

funded defined-contribution pension scheme intended to provide individuals with a mechanism for supplementing the benefits provided by the mandatory pillars. The fourth pillar provides health care to the elderly as part of the national health care system.

First-pillar contributions are taxed; benefits are tax exempt until 2013, after which they may be taxed, subject to some allowance.[5] Although in 1997 such future taxation policies may have been envisaged by lawmakers, there is no current regulation to this effect. The fully funded second pillar is treated similarly: contributions are fully taxed, while returns on investment and benefits are untaxed (unless this is also changed in 2013). The voluntary third pillar broadly follows an exempt-exempt-exempt regime, meaning that contributions are exempt from taxation (subject to a ceiling), investment income is fully exempt, and benefits are exempt when individuals draw a qualified annuity based on 20 or more years of accumulation (see box 1.1 in chapter 1). The noncontributory zero pillar (which provides a means-tested benefit for the poor) and the fourth pillar (which provides health care coverage) are completely tax exempt.

Noncontributory scheme. Hungary provides a noncontributory old-age allowance as part of its overall social assistance program to ensure a minimum level of income for the elderly. To be eligible, applicants need to be at least age 62 and able to demonstrate that their total income—from gainful activity, revenues from investments, and other sources, net of taxes and social insurance contributions—falls below 80 percent (95 percent for couples) of the minimum old-age pension. The allowance is means tested and adjusted in value such that the beneficiary's total income reaches the minimum threshold. In 2003, this allowance was paid to 6,679 beneficiaries (roughly 0.4 percent of the population age 62 and older), at a cost equivalent to 0.01 percent of GDP (World Bank 2007b).

Earnings-related schemes. Hungary's earnings-related pension scheme consists of two pillars (table 5.3). The first pillar is a traditional defined-benefit pension scheme financed on a pay-as-you-go basis. The second pillar, introduced in 1998, is a fully funded defined-contribution pension scheme.

The reforms of the late 1990s introduced parametric changes to the first pillar. These changes included raising the retirement age (from 60 to 62 for men and from 55 to 62 for women),[6] changing the formula by which pensions are calculated, and changing how pensions are adjusted over time for inflation.

Table 5.3 Parameters of Earnings-Related Schemes in Hungary before and after Reform

Scheme type	Period	Vesting/minimum eligibility period	Contribution rate[a]	Contribution ceiling	Benefit rate	Pension assessment base	Retirement age
First-pillar (earnings related)	Prereform	20 years normally; 15 years at age 62 under special, strict conditions	30 percent (24 percent by employer, 6 percent by employee)	Employee contributions subject to ceiling; no ceiling for employer contributions	33 percent for the first 10 years, 25 percent per year thereafter	Annual wage history since 1988. Since 2008, annual net wages are used; revaluation covers all but last year before retirement	60 for men, 55 for women
	Postreform	20 years normally; 15 years at age 62 under special, strict conditions	25.5 percent (33.5 percent)[a] (24 percent by employer, 1.5 percent [9.5 percent] by employee)	Employee: set annually by the government (at about eight times the minimum wage) Employer: no maximum	Until 2013: 33 percent for the first 10 years, 2 percent for 11–25 years, 1 percent for 26–36 years, 1.5 percent beyond 36 years After 2013: 1.65 percent per year	Average lifetime earnings valorized by wage growth	62 for everyone as of 2009

(continued)

Table 5.3 Parameters of Earnings-Related Schemes in Hungary before and after Reform (*continued*)

Scheme type	Period	Vesting/minimum eligibility period	Contribution rate[a]	Contribution ceiling	Benefit rate	Pension assessment base	Retirement age
Second-pillar (earnings related)	Prereform	n.a.	n.a.	n.a.	n.a.	n.a.	n.a.
	Postreform	No minimum	8 percent (paid by employee)	Employee: set annually by the government (at about eight times the minimum wage) Employer: no maximum	Pension from capital accumulation	Accumulated funds	62 for everyone as of 2009

Source: Authors' compilation based on information from the Ministry of Finance; European Commission 2007a, 2007b; Palmer 2007; and U.S. Social Security Administration 2006.

n.a. = Not applicable.

a. For individuals participating in the first pillar only, employers pay 24.0 percent and employees pay 9.5 percent, for a total of 33.5 percent. For individuals participating in both the first and the second pillars, employers pay 24.0 percent; employees pay 1.5 percent (in 2008) to the first pillar and 8 percent to the second pillar. The first-pillar contribution rates for employers and employees change almost annually. The second-pillar rate paid by employees was raised from 6 percent in 1998 to 7 percent in 2003 and 8 percent in 2008.

The prereform formula suffered from several key design flaws. First, the credit awarded for years of service fell with each additional year of service. Ten years of service provided income replacement of about 33 percent of preretirement wages, whereas 4 times this length of service resulted in a benefit only 2.5 times higher (Palmer 2007). Second, the pension assessment base was computed using only three of the top five years of service (taking into account only wages earned after 1988), which failed to capture an individual's actual wage history. Third, the cap on earnings used to calculate benefits created incentives for the underdeclaration of earnings.[7]

The reforms changed all this. The annual accrual rate was fixed at 1.65 percent of the pension assessment base of service starting in 2013, thereby granting equal weight to all years of service. The pension assessment base is based on average valorized wages earned since 1988, thereby strengthening the link between contributions and benefits. The cap on earnings was substantially increased and is currently about three times average earnings. In 2001, Swiss indexation was introduced, in which pensions are adjusted in retirement using a formula based on the average of inflation and wage growth, thereby allowing pensions to rise more rapidly than inflation but without imposing the heavier fiscal burden of wage indexation.

The reforms of the late 1990s also established a second-pillar pension scheme. The new scheme is mandatory for new entrants and voluntary for those with an established history of contributing to the old pay-as-you-go system. Of the total contribution rate of 33.5 percent in 2008, 25.5 percentage points (24.0 percentage points paid by employers and 1.5 percentage points paid by employees) flow to the first pillar, while 8.0 percentage points (paid entirely by employees) flow to the second pillar. For people enrolled in both pillars, benefits accrue under both pillars so that the accrual rate under the first pillar is reduced from 1.65 percent a year of service to 1.22 percent (this also applies to years before 1998). The reduced first-pillar benefit will be supplemented by the second pillar as a function of both an individual's account balance at retirement and his or her age at retirement.

Voluntary scheme. Hungary introduced a voluntary private pension scheme in 1994 (table 5.4). Benefits are provided after a minimum of 10 years of contributions. Participation is encouraged using tax incentives. Employers are permitted to make contributions on behalf of their employees. The minimum contribution level is established by each individual fund.

Table 5.4   Characteristics of the Voluntary Scheme in Hungary

Coverage	Vesting period	Retirement age	Tax advan-tages to participants	Contributions tax deductible by employers	Lump-sum payments possible in retirement
Every formally and/or legally employed person, including self-employed persons	10 years	Benefit can be withdrawn after 10 years (no set retirement age)	Yes	Yes	Yes

Sources: Leonik 2006; OECD 2001; and consultations with World Bank staff.

Employer contributions to the voluntary scheme are exempted from the social insurance levy up to 50 percent of the minimum wage. Thirty percent of total contributions (including employer contributions) up to an annual cap of 100,000 forint (Ft) are tax deductible, with the amount of the allowance credited to the participant's account (the cap is Ft 130,000 if plan members retire before 2020). Benefits can be collected in the form of a lump-sum payment or as an annuity or be spread over a prespecified period in retirement. In 2006, benefits totaled Ft 29.2 billion. Annuities accounted for a negligible share.

In 2007, 69 private pension funds operated in the market, supervised by the Hungarian Financial Supervisory Authority. In 2005, private pension funds had assets totaling Ft 590.11 billion (2.9 percent of GDP) and were receiving contributions from 1,307,222 participants (31 percent of the labor force and 18.8 percent of the working-age population). In 2006, the bulk of investments were in government bonds (Hungarian Financial Supervisory Authority 2007). Since 1994, the number of participants in the voluntary scheme has increased rapidly, but the value of assets accumulating in the scheme remains relatively small.

Health care system. Health care in Hungary is provided primarily through a mandatory health insurance scheme (the Health Insurance Fund) operated by the National Health Insurance Fund Administration (NHIFA). Health care services are delivered predominantly by public providers owned by local governments through contracts with NHIFA financed by contributions from the covered population. Salaried employees are required to pay a contribution rate of 15 percent (4 percentage points paid by employers and 11 percentage points paid by employees). Self-employed people contribute 15 percent of their declared earnings.

Some people, including pensioners and people with low incomes, are not required to pay contributions. Health care services for such people are financed by the Health Insurance Fund and the government.

Recipients of health care are required to make copayments in order to be eligible for some services, pharmaceuticals, and devices. In 2005, health expenditure accounted for 7.8 percent of GDP, 70.8 percent of which was public expenditure and 29.2 percent of which was private expenditure. Of the private expenditure, 86.8 percent was attributable to out-of-pocket expenditure (informal payments, direct payments, and copayments) (WHO 2008).

Institutional Structure and Coverage of Earnings-Related Schemes

The mandatory pillars of the Hungarian pension system cover salaried employees and self-employed persons. Independent farmers may participate on a voluntary basis. The State Tax Collection Agency collects contributions for the first-pillar pension scheme. The Central Administration of National Pension Insurance administers the scheme. In 2005, 3,881,000 people contributed to the scheme, accounting for 92 percent of the labor force and 56 percent of the working-age population (Hungarian Financial Supervisory Authority 2007).

The Hungarian Financial Supervisory Authority is responsible for regulating private pension fund companies. In 2007, 20 pension funds were operating in the (mandatory) second-pillar pension fund market. Contributions to the second pillar are deducted from salaries by employers and transferred directly to the pension funds. In 2005, 2,509,941 people contributed to the scheme (roughly 65 percent of the number of participants in the first-pillar scheme). In 2005, the assets of the second pillar totaled Ft 1,221 billion (5.6 percent of GDP).

Structure of Benefits

The earnings-related pension scheme provides old-age, disability, and survivorship pensions (from the first pillar only). The provisions governing each of these types of benefits are discussed as follows.

Old-age benefits. Beginning in 2013, the accrual rate under the first-pillar pension scheme will be 1.65 percent per year of service for people not enrolled in the second pillar (mostly older workers) and 1.22 percent for people enrolled in the second pillar (who will also receive benefits from their individual funded accounts). To be eligible for a reduced old-age pension under the first-pillar pension scheme, participants must have

15 years of service. A full pension requires 20 years of service. Both require participants to have reached the statutory retirement age of 62 for men and 61 for women (in 2009, the ages will be equalized at 62). Until 2009, retirement as early as age 57 is allowed without a reduction in benefits provided participants have the required years of service at the time of their retirement. Beginning in 2009, 40 years of service will be required for early retirement, and penalties will be imposed for anyone retiring before age 59. If participants choose to retire early, benefits will be reduced by 1.2 percent per year of early retirement. An accrual rate of 0.5 percent is awarded for each month of service worked after the statutory retirement age.

Under the second pillar, workers who contributed for less than 15 years may opt to receive the accumulated capital as a lump sum; all other workers must accept an annuity. Unisex mortality tables are used to calculate the annuity. Annuities may be provided by the pension fund itself or be purchased from an insurance company. Like first-pillar benefits, annuities are indexed 50 percent to inflation and 50 percent to wage growth.[8]

Disability benefits. Under the first pillar, there are three categories of disability benefits, depending on the degree of incapacitation: 100 percent loss of capacity to work and the need for permanent care (Category I), 100 percent loss of capacity to work and no need for permanent care (Category II), and at least 67 percent loss of capacity to work (Category III) (table 5.5) Eligibility depends on an individual's age and service at the time of disability. Benefits depend on the individual's years of service at the time of disability and the degree of incapacitation; they cannot exceed the individual's average earnings. For people in Category III, benefits are equal to 100 percent of the old-age pension if the individual has at least 25 years of service

Table 5.5   Eligibility Conditions for and Benefits Provided by Disability Pensions in Hungary under the First-Pillar Earnings-Related Scheme

Vesting period	Contributions	Eligibility	Benefit rate	Partial pension
Under age 22: 2 years Age 22–24: 4 years Age 25–29: 6 years Age 30–34: 8 years Age 35–44: 10 years Age 45–54: 15 years Age 55 and over: 20 years	Included in overall pension contribution rate (estimated at about 4 percent)	Loss of at least 67 percent of capacity to work	37.5–100 percent of average individ- ual earnings, depending on level of dis- ability and years of service	37.5–63.0 percent of average indi- vidual earnings

Sources: European Commission 2007a; GVG 2003.

and 37.5–63.0 percent of the individual's average earnings if he or she does not. For Category I, the benefits are 100 percent of the Category III benefits; benefits for Category II are 105 percent of the Category III benefits (European Commission 2007a). The new disability benefit system that came into effect in January 2008 aims to encourage a return to the labor market by new claimants who have been assessed to have remaining work capacities. These individuals have to participate in a rehabilitation plan designed by the employment office. Any suitable job offer received by the individual from the employment authority has to be accepted. For those eligible for the rehabilitation scheme, a transitory rehabilitation benefit is commensurate to the length of the rehabilitation process, albeit capped at three years. The new rehabilitation system involves a focus on training as a way to strengthen the remaining abilities and skills of disabled individuals.

The second pillar provides no disability benefits. In the event of disability, individuals may choose between receiving the accumulated capital in the individual account as a lump sum or having the account balance transferred to the first pillar to improve the disability benefit under that pillar. The benefit under the publicly managed scheme does not depend on the amount transferred (OECD 2001).

Survivor benefits. Survivor benefits are awarded to dependents if the deceased had been receiving (or had met the criteria to receive) an old-age or disability pension (table 5.6). Eligible survivors include a current or former spouse, orphans, parents, domestic partners, sisters, brothers, and grandchildren. Provided that the surviving spouse is not already receiving a pension, the survivor benefit is 60 percent of the deceased's pension. If the spouse is receiving a pension, the survivor benefit is 30 percent of the deceased's pension. The survivor benefit is permanent if the spouse is disabled, raising at least two minor children, or has already reached retirement age. If the spouse was already older than the retirement age when he or she got married, the spouse is entitled to a survivor benefit only if the couple cohabited for at least five years or had a child together. Unmarried couples must have lived together for at least one year if they have a child; otherwise, they must have lived together for at least 10 years. Divorced survivors—or survivors who have been separated for more than one year— are entitled to a benefit only if they were entitled to alimony. Orphans are entitled to 30 percent of the deceased's pension if one parent dies and 60 percent of the higher of the two parents' pensions if both parents die. Orphans may draw a benefit through age 16, unless enrolled full time as a student, in which case eligibility continues through age 25. Disabled

Table 5.6   Eligibility Conditions for and Benefits Provided by Survivor Pensions in Hungary under the First-Pillar Earnings-Related Scheme

Eligibility	Spouse replacement rate	Benefit duration	Remarriage test	Orphan age limit	Orphan replacement rate	Total family benefit
Eligibility of deceased for old-age or disability pension	60 percent of deceased's pension (30 percent if receiving own pension)	For life, if spouse is disabled, is caring for at least two children, or is above retirement age; 12 or 18 months if spouse is caring for a child	Remarriage test before retirement age	25	30 percent of deceased's pension; 60 percent of the higher of the two parents' pensions if child loses both parents	Cannot exceed benefit to which deceased was entitled

Sources: European Commission 2007a; GVG 2003.

orphans may draw a benefit indefinitely. For all categories of survivors, total benefits may not exceed the benefit to which the deceased was originally entitled.

Under the second pillar, participants may designate a beneficiary and elect to receive survivor benefits in a lump sum or in the form of annuity. Benefits are determined by the balance in the deceased's private pension account at the time of his or her death.

Assessment of the Performance of Hungary's Pension System

The World Bank has established four principles for evaluating public pension systems, which together should guide the process of pension reform (see Holzmann and Hinz 2005). Broadly speaking, these principles include the adequacy and security of benefits, the affordability of contributions, the sustainability of the system over time, and the robustness of the system in the face of demographic changes and macroeconomic shocks. This chapter focuses primarily on the adequacy of benefits and the financial sustainability of the earnings-related pension scheme. The remaining principles are mentioned only briefly. Adequacy is analyzed through the lens of net replacement rates. Financial sustainability is evaluated using projections of pension expenditure and revenues.

Benefit Adequacy

Replacement rates are a useful yardstick for measuring the adequacy of pension benefits, because they express benefits relative to preretirement earnings, thereby indicating the degree to which income is replaced when workers retire. Two variants are commonly used. Gross replacement rates compute income replacement as the ratio of benefits paid to pretax preretirement earnings. Net replacement rates compute income replacement as the ratio of benefits received (that is, after the payment of taxes and other levies, including contributions for social insurance) to posttax preretirement earnings. In general, net replacement rates are a more useful measure of benefit adequacy, because they capture the degree to which actual take-home pay is replaced when workers retire.

The level of income replacement at retirement is not the only measure of benefit adequacy. For a full assessment of benefit adequacy, it is also important to determine how postretirement indexation rules will affect replacement rates during retirement. Pension benefits in retirement are expected to be indexed to inflation, so that their real value is maintained. In a growing economy with rising real wages, however, mere price indexation of pensions leads to a deterioration of the relative consumption position of the retirees. For this reason, some countries have introduced mixed indexation of pensions that use varying weights of inflation and wage growth in the indexation formula.

For an evaluation of the effect of indexation on replacement rates in Hungary, the replacement rates are normalized to 100 percent and the assumptions for calculating the replacement rates are maintained (that is, inflation is 2.5 percent a year and real wage growth is 2.0 percent a year). The change in the replacement rate is measured in comparison with full wage indexation or the earnings of an active worker. The results of this analysis indicate that the relative income position of a retiree would deteriorate by 7 percent after 10 years in retirement and by 21 percent after 35 years in retirement as a result of 50 percent inflation and 50 percent wage indexation of benefits in both the first and the second pillars. The evaluation of income replacement that follows considers replacement rates only at retirement; it does not take into account the impact of indexation policies on replacement rates during retirement.

Replacement rates are a function of the formula governing pension benefits; an individual's contribution history; and, in the case of net replacement rates, the rules of income tax, social security contributions, and other relevant levies. The benefit formula establishes the degree to which the system redistributes income across individuals of different levels of preretirement earnings. Progressive systems provide higher levels of income replacement to people with lower levels of preretirement income. In general, the degree to which a system is redistributive depends on the existence (and value) of flat transfers and minimum pension guarantees, the degree to which benefits are earnings related, and the existence of ceilings on earnings subject to contributions. An individual's contribution history can be characterized by his or her age of entry into the labor force, contribution density, and decisions regarding the timing of retirement. To some degree, these three factors are influenced by the incentives embodied in the pension system. The tax and contribution system influences net replacement rates through the progressiveness of the income tax formula, which taxes (higher) income during a worker's active life more so than it does (lower) pension benefits in retirement. In addition, there are social security levies (for pensions; unemployment; health care; and, at times, housing and family benefits), which are typically reduced or eliminated altogether in retirement. These benefits are particularly important for low- to middle-income groups.

Benchmarks need to be established for the evaluation of the adequacy of the income replacement provided by the earnings-related pension schemes. Unfortunately, there is no consensus on what constitutes adequacy. According to one widely respected definition, pensions are adequate when they are sufficient to prevent poverty among the elderly and provide the vast majority of the population with a reliable mechanism for smoothing income over their lifetime. Even with a definition, however, establishing benchmarks is problematic, because attitudes vary across countries as a result of social and cultural perceptions. Moreover, benchmarks ignore the other factors that affect the welfare of the elderly—and that also vary across countries—including the existence and generosity of health insurance and long-term care, the cost of housing, the structure of traditional living arrangements, the presence of informal intrafamily or intergenerational sources of financial and nonfinancial support, and the availability and security of other mechanisms for people to save for their own retirement.

One reputable nine-country study (OECD 2001) observes that living standards are roughly comparable for people 10 years older than the normal retirement age and people 15 years younger than the normal retirement age when retirees have disposable income equal to roughly 80 percent of the disposable income of working-age people. In part, this is attributable to the fact that retirees have no work-related expenses (they do not have to commute or buy special clothing or uniforms, for example). This finding, however, does not imply that mandatory first-pillar pension schemes should actually target an 80 percent net replacement rate. To the contrary, in middle- and high-income countries, one can reasonably expect individuals to save for their own retirement—and the empirical evidence suggests that, in practice, they do so.[9] There is also some evidence to suggest that the ratio between pre- and postretirement income is somewhat independent of the income replacement mandate of the public pension system. Put simply, individuals tend to save more in countries with more modest mandates (and vice versa).

Because Hungary has access to relatively well-developed financial markets, it would seem reasonable to expect middle- and high-income workers to save enough to finance at least 25 percent, if not closer to 50 percent, of this 80 percent income replacement target. Given this, three benchmarks are provided: a 40 percent net replacement rate (which implies that individuals would be expected to save enough to finance half of the total income-replacement target); a 60 percent net replacement rate (which implies that individuals would be expected to finance a quarter of the target); and an 80 percent net replacement rate (which implies that individuals, most of whom would be low-income earners, would not be expected to contribute anything toward the target).[10] In the following analysis, these three benchmarks are used to evaluate the adequacy of benefits in Hungary in conjunction with the average net replacement rate observed in 53 countries, the average net replacement rate observed for selected countries in Europe and Central Asia, and the poverty line in Hungary.

To estimate gross and net replacement rates, we consider two critical dimensions—earnings levels and contribution periods—with the help of the Analysis of Pension Entitlements across Countries (APEX) model.[11] This model generates estimates for replacement rates under steady-state assumptions (that is, as if the rules of the reformed pension scheme had been in place over the entire active life of the individual). Because life expectancies at retirement are projected to increase over time—which will affect the benefits paid by defined-contribution pension schemes—a reference year must be chosen. For the purpose of this study, 2040 is used because it provides a sufficiently long contribution period over which to approximate steady-state conditions.

The first critical task is to investigate levels of income replacement across a relevant spectrum of income. Income is represented as a percentage (50–200 percent) of average earnings. The second task is to investigate the impact on income replacement of differences in the duration, timing, and density of an individual's contribution history (density refers to the percentage of time an individual actually contributes over a given period). To facilitate the presentation of these multidimensional results, we compute replacement rates as a function of the age at which an individual exits the labor market. They are presented separately for full-career and partial-career workers.

Replacement rates for full-career workers. Projected replacement rates for full-career workers in 2040 are examined first. For this analysis, a full career is defined as continuous employment from age 20 to the current normal retirement age of 62.

Gross replacements rates increase as income levels fall (figure 5.3). The share of second-pillar benefits is constant (at 26.2 percentage points) for all income levels, irrespective of income. The amount of first-pillar benefit increases as income levels decline, illuminating the relatively redistributive feature of the first pillar.[12]

The situation changes when taxes are taken into consideration. As a result of the impact of taxes and contributions, middle- and high-income workers receive higher net replacement rates than do low-income workers (figure 5.4).[13] This result reflects the nature of the tax code in Hungary, not the design of the pension system.

Pensions for full-career workers in Hungary are adequate (figure 5.5).[14] Replacement rates for all levels of preretirement income are higher than their respective benchmarks, suggesting that the pension system is

Figure 5.3   Sources of Gross Replacement Rates in Hungary, by Income Level

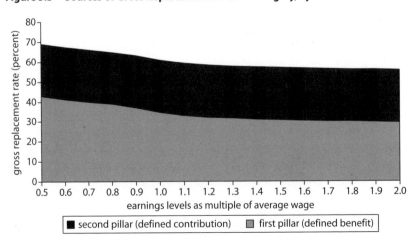

Sources: APEX model.
Note: Figure shows projected replacement rate for 2040 as approximation of steady-state conditions.

Figure 5.4   Sources of Net Replacement Rates in Hungary, by Income Level

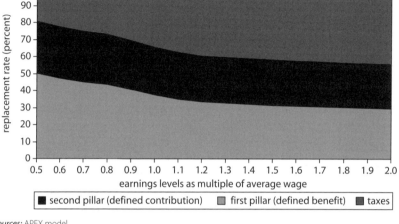

Sources: APEX model.
Note: Figure shows projected replacement rate for 2040 as approximation of steady-state conditions.

Figure 5.5   Net Replacement Rates for Male Full-Career Workers in Hungary, Europe and Central Asia, and the World, by Income Level

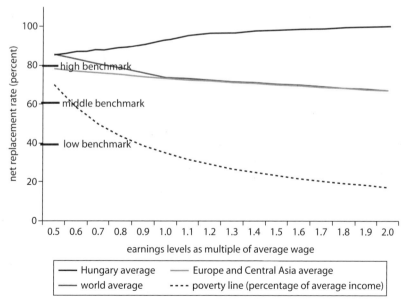

Source: Authors' calculations based on World Bank 2007a and the APEX model.
Note: Figure shows projected replacement rate for 2040 as approximation of steady-state conditions.

effectively smoothing consumption from work into retirement.[15] Indeed, even middle- and high-income individuals are receiving levels of income replacement above the highest of the three benchmarks. The downside of such effective income smoothing is that the system provides little incentive for workers to save outside of the pension system. Given that benefits for even the lowest full-career workers greatly exceed the poverty line, the objective of poverty alleviation is being met. Levels of income replacement in Hungary are higher than the regional and world averages, especially for high-income workers.

Replacement rates for partial-career workers. Not everyone works from age 20 to the statutory retirement age. Many individuals enter and exit the labor force (often at different ages and for different periods of time) and earn different wages while working. To examine the adequacy of benefits for partial-career workers, we consider three stylized cases. These cases include career type A (someone entering the labor force at age 25 who works continuously for a period of years before leaving the workforce at some point between the ages of 50 and 70 and then claims a benefit); career type B (identical to career type A, except that the worker enters the workforce at age 30 and leaves no earlier than age 55); and career type C (identical to career type A, except that the individual contributes in only three years out of four while in the labor force). In cases in which the withdrawal from the formal labor market occurs before the statutory retirement age, the pension is claimed (and the replacement rate calculated) only at the later age. For withdrawals after the statutory retirement age, the ages coincide.

Because a minimum of 20 years of contributions are required for benefit eligibility, the minimum exit ages for the three career types vary (figure 5.6). As a result, the lines for the replacement rates start at different points. The steep rise in replacement rates at age 62 reflects the fact that there is no longer an actuarial reduction in benefits for early retirement; each additional year of contributions contributes directly to higher benefits.

Several conclusions can be drawn from figure 5.6. First, entering the workforce later in life is costly (someone entering the workforce at age 30 receives a net replacement rate 8–19 percentage points lower than someone entering the workforce at age 25). Second, working intermittently is costly (someone who enters the workforce at a given age but who contributes only three years out of four will receive a net replacement rate 15–40 percentage points lower than someone who contributes continuously). Third, the Hungarian pension system provides partial-career

Figure 5.6   Net Replacement Rates for Male Middle-Income Partial-Career Workers in Hungary, by Career Type and Exit Age

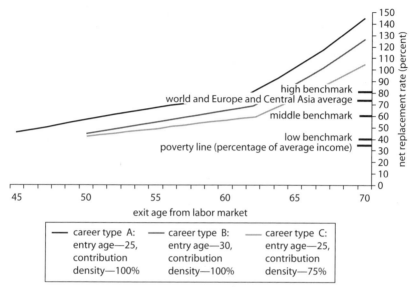

Source: Authors' calculations based on World Bank 2007a and the APEX model.
Note: Figure shows projected replacement rate for 2040 as approximation of steady-state conditions. See text for descriptions of career types.

workers with an acceptable level of income replacement, as evidenced by the fact that even people who exit the labor market long before reaching the statutory retirement age receive a net replacement rate higher than the poverty line. People who work until the statutory retirement age (which is likely to include people with limited ability to save on their own, for whom the mandatory system is likely to be their main source of retirement income) receive a net replacement rate of 60 percent or higher (the middle of the three benchmarks). To receive a replacement rate of 80 percent (the highest of the three benchmarks), career type A workers need to work until retirement age, career type B workers need to work two years beyond retirement age, and career type C workers need to work well beyond the normal retirement age.

Fiscal Sustainability

The sustainability of a pay-as-you-go, first-pillar pension scheme is best evaluated in actuarial terms by estimating the scheme's actuarial deficit as the difference between its assets and liabilities. If a large actuarial deficit exists, the scheme is financially unsustainable and needs policy actions that increase its assets, reduce its liabilities, or both. A good proxy for the actuarial deficit is the difference between the present value of the scheme's expected future revenues (that is, contributions and other income) and the expected future expenditures (that is, benefit payments, administrative costs, and other expenses) over an extended projection period. The difference between these two values represents an unfunded liability (sometimes referred to as a financing gap) on the public-sector balance sheet. Because this study is also concerned with the time path of revenues and expenditures (and the resulting balance across the projection period ending in 2050), this more pragmatic approach has been taken. Projections of expenditures, revenues, and deficits are presented on the basis of available postreform fiscal projections.

The reforms of the late 1990s considerably improved the sustainability of the Hungarian pension system. The revenues of the first pillar are projected to hover at roughly 6.5 percent of GDP between 2005 and 2050, while expenditure is estimated to rise to 9.4 percent of GDP, resulting in a deficit of 2.9 percent of GDP—roughly half what had been projected.[16] Despite this significant improvement, the first-pillar scheme will continue to generate substantial deficits even after the reforms have been fully implemented (figure 5.7). This is partly because of the transition deficit and the diversion of contribution revenue from the first pillar toward the second pillar.[17]

Figure 5.7   Projected Fiscal Balance of Hungary's Public Pension System after Reform, 2005–50

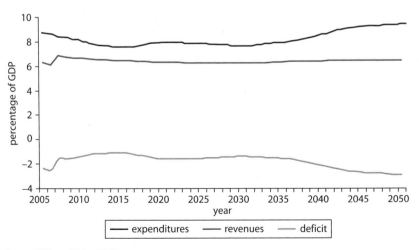

Source: Orbán and Palotai 2005.
Note: Projections were revised in 2007.

What options exist for restoring the system to fiscal balance? Unfortunately, for policy makers, the options are limited. At the level of economic policy, an increase in employment rates across all ages would clearly help, but it would not resolve issues that make the scheme unsustainable. Although higher contribution revenues (resulting from increased employment) will reduce cash deficits, they will also create liabilities that will eventually become due. If an unfunded system is actuarially unsustainable because benefit promises per contributor exceed contribution payments revalued by a sustainable (implicit) rate of return, then greater employment offers a temporary cash respite while actually making the system more unsustainable.

This leaves policy makers with three basic options: increasing contribution rates, reducing benefits, or raising the retirement age. Revenues can be increased by raising the contribution rate (or by transferring funds from general revenue to compensate partly or fully for the transition deficit). Alternatively (or in addition to, because the options are not mutually exclusive), expenditures can be reduced by cutting benefits, increasing the number of years required to become eligible for benefits, or delaying the payment of benefits by raising the retirement age further. Because raising the contribution rate could threaten competitiveness and will likely strengthen incentives for tax evasion, it is typically not embraced (it would also represent a reversal of policy because, until recently, Hungary had been reducing the contribution rate to reduce the adverse impact of high taxes on labor markets). Steps such as raising retirement ages and tightening eligibility criteria have already been taken; additional increases in retirement ages and further tightening of eligibility criteria will be needed to make the pension system sustainable. An informal analysis suggests that retirement ages for men and women would have to be increased to at least 73 by 2050 to restore long-term fiscal balance.[18]

If retirement ages are left unchanged and the current structure of the system is retained, further cuts in benefits—on the order of 41 percent from the public pillar—would be required for the system to become sustainable. Cuts of such a magnitude raise the question of whether restoring sustainability would not exact a cost in terms of the adequacy of benefits provided to future beneficiaries. If benefits are adjusted to maintain a similar fiscal balance in proportion to the overall size of the first-pillar scheme, full-career workers will receive replacement rates roughly 20 percentage points lower in 2050 than they receive today (figure 5.8).

Figure 5.8   Net Replacement Rates for Male Workers in Hungary before and after Benefit Adjustment

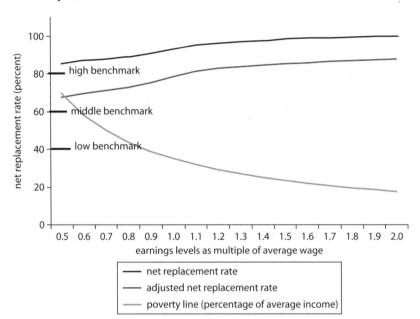

Source: Authors' calculations based on World Bank 2007a and the APEX model.
Note: Figure shows projected replacement rate for 2040 as approximation of steady-state conditions.

Two conclusions emerge from comparing these new (lower) net replacement rates against the three benchmarks. First, a 41 percent reduction in benefits does not cause the income replacement for middle- and high-income full-career workers to fall anywhere near the poverty line. Replacement rates for the lowest-income workers are only slightly below the poverty line. This indicates that a sustainable first-pillar pension scheme in Hungary would still achieve its poverty alleviation objective for almost all workers.

Second, the reduction in benefits will still support the objective of smoothing lifetime consumption for middle- and high-income full-career workers, because levels of income replacement are higher than the 80 percent benchmark. This objective may not be met for low-income workers, however, for whom levels of income replacement are lower than the 80 percent benchmark. This observation is subject to two caveats. One is that this analysis considers only full-career workers, while the average worker now contributes for only about 27–30 years, substantially less than the 40 years expected over a full career. Contributing to the pension scheme for only 30 years, for example, reduces net income replacement by 27 percentage points for middle-income workers. Another caveat is that workers always have the option of saving outside the first-pillar pension scheme. To increase income replacement by 1.0 percentage point, for example, a full-career worker would need to save only about 0.5 percent of his or her earnings from age 40 to the current age of retirement.[19]

Conclusions

In response to emerging deficits in the existing, pay-as-you-go, public pension system (and projections that deficits would grow substantially over the long term as a result of the aging of the population), Hungary launched an ambitious program of reform in the mid-1990s. That program introduced parametric changes to the existing defined-benefit scheme and shifted (in 1998) the system from a monopillar design toward a multipillar design that included a mandatory fully funded defined-contribution scheme (a voluntary third-pillar scheme had been introduced in 1994). These reforms were considered radical, because Hungary was the first country in the region to attempt to finance a portion of pension benefits on the basis of funded defined-contribution accounts.

As a result of these reforms, the long-term fiscal position of Hungary's pension system is projected to improve substantially, with projected deficits in 2050 falling from 6.0 percent of GDP to 2.9 percent of GDP despite the additional burden of the transition deficit through the introduction of the funded second pillar. Some postreform adjustments to the first-pillar scheme, such as the introduction of the 13th monthly payment, have made the system less sustainable; more recent reforms, in particular the move toward a net-income pension base, have moved the system back toward sustainability. Overall, the reforms have broadly strengthened the link between preretirement contributions and postretirement benefits. They are, therefore, expected to create incentives for people to remain in the workforce and contribute for longer periods.

The resulting gross and net replacement rates for full-career workers in Hungary are projected to be well above regional and international averages (see chapter 1). The future net replacement rates for full-career workers are projected to exceed 80 percent (and to approach 100 percent for some workers) for the analyzed income spectrum. As in other countries, partial-career workers—workers who left the workforce before reaching the retirement age, worked intermittently, or have gaps in their employment history—risk receiving a level of income replacement closer to or lower than the 40 percent benchmark. Low contribution density is of substantial concern for benefit adequacy if recent behavior is repeated in the future. Over the period 1997–2006, 43 percent of those employed worked less than eight months a year and 28 percent worked less than six months a year. Improving formal labor force participation and employment rates across all age groups is clearly a key economic policy task for the years come.

High replacement rates that reflect more recent changes may be a reaction to concerns about the "lost generation" emerging from transition. Many members of this generation will approach retirement in the next 10–20 years. These workers have low earnings histories and will receive low benefits if they qualify for pensions at all. Although handling their income needs through changes in the benefit formula may be tempting and politically expedient, a long-term perspective on benefit adequacy in financial sustainability of the reform schemes would suggest tailored and transitory measures. Permanent changes to address the needs of the lost generation will undermine not just adequacy and sustainability but also the contribution–benefit link and will encourage continued informality for the future.

Replacement rates have been computed under the assumption that funded pension schemes earn a rate of return of 1.5 percentage points more than wage growth. This earnings differential broadly reflects the performance of pension funds in Organisation for Economic Co-operation and Development countries over the past 30 years. The earnings differential in emerging economies is almost twice as large (Holzmann 2009). The performance of pension funds in Hungary since their inception, however, has been well below this benchmark. If such performance continues, the Hungarian pension system will not be capable of delivering the replacement rates projected earlier. This concern calls for a review of pension fund performance and accelerated progress in financial market development.

To restore long-term fiscal balance to the pension scheme without changing the benefit design, policy makers need to raise retirement ages, possibly to 73 by 2050. To achieve the full fiscal impact of this measure for the public pillar, they would need to fix the replacement rate at the current retirement age. Increasing the retirement age in step with increases in life expectancy at retirement is a natural choice, both for individuals and for policy makers, but it requires cross-sectoral policy reforms to enable elderly workers to continue to participate in the labor market.[20]

Another option for restoring fiscal balance is to cut benefits at retirement or reduce the generosity of benefit indexation. Rough estimates suggest that, on average, replacement rates at retirement would have to fall by about 20 percentage points to achieve fiscal balance by 2050. Moving to full price indexation would reduce average benefits by some 10 percentage points. Reducing benefits by this amount would not compromise the objective of smoothing lifetime consumption for full-career workers of all income levels when measured against the highest of the three benchmarks employed in this analysis or the objective of alleviating poverty among the elderly because levels of income replacement would still not fall anywhere near the poverty line.

Individuals who wish to defer more of their lifetime consumption into retirement would still have the option of participating in Hungary's voluntary third-pillar pension scheme. Given the low per capita payments into the third-pillar pension scheme, however, this would require some major changes in individual savings behavior (and the capacity to do so) to become effective. Voluntary contributions are currently low, however. Major changes in individual savings behavior (and the capacity to save) will be necessary if the third pillar is to become a significant source of retirement income.

Notes

1. Unemployment rose from 0.3 percent in 1990 to 10 percent in 1995, while employment rates fell from 76 percent to 58 percent. During this period, roughly 30 percent of formal sector jobs were lost (Palmer 2007).

2. The Hungarian population is projected to age less than most other Organisation for Economic Co-operation and Development (OECD) countries, because projected life expectancies for men and women by 2040 are lower than in all OECD countries except Turkey (Kovac 2008).

3. For more information regarding these population projections, see Reiterer (2008).

4. More recent projections of the system dependency ratio, which reflect the impact of the reforms since 1998, suggest a much more optimistic outcome. Projections from the 2008 Pension Round Table indicate that the system dependency ratio will fall below the old-age dependency ratio by 2012 and will remain there until the end of the projection period (2050), at which point the difference between them will reach almost 8 percentage points. Even under these projections, however, the system dependency ratio will increase, from just below 30 percent in 2012 to well over 50 percent by 2050 (conversation with Erzsebet Kovacs).

5. A great deal of uncertainty surrounds taxation policies after 2013.

6. Low retirement ages relative to life expectancy contribute to fiscal imbalance, because they increase the value of lifetime benefits relative to contributions (for individual contributors) and increase the total number of beneficiaries relative to contributors (for the overall pension scheme).

7. As a result of high inflation in 1992–96, the ratio of the cap on earnings used in the calculation of benefits to average gross wages declined from 3.4 to 1.6 (Simonovits 2002).

8. There is an ongoing discussion in Hungary about whether the markets will be able to deliver Swiss indexation as written into the law. Regulations governing annuity provisions are still pending and are expected in late 2008. For a discussion of these issues, see Párniczky (2005).

9. In Chile, for instance, 70 percent of retirees from the mandatory public pension system own their home, which is a form of savings (see Valdés-Prieto 2008).

10. These benchmarks approximate the standards developed by the International Labour Organization (ILO) (1952) and the Council of Europe (1990). ILO Convention 102 of 1952 sets a minimum benefit equal to 40 percent of the reference wage for married men of pensionable age. This amount was raised to 45 percent in 1968. The European Code of Security of 1990 sets a minimum standard for members of the Council of Europe equal to 65 percent for married people of a specific age.

11. The APEX model was developed by Axia Economics, with funding from the Organisation for Economic Co-operation and Development and the World Bank. The model codes detailed eligibility and benefit rules for first- and second-pillar schemes based on available public information that has been verified by country contacts. Because the details of the rules sometimes change on short notice (and limited public disclosure), the calculations presented here should be considered as best approximations only.

12. The pension is calculated on the basis of the net pension assessment base. Because of the progressive tax system, gross replacement rates increase with increases in income. Because the first pillar involves 13 "monthly" pension benefit payments a year, the additional benefit is apportioned to calculate the replacement rates provided under the defined-benefit scheme. This extra monthly benefit was introduced only recently. This benefit represents a departure from the social insurance principle. Effective January 2009, early retirees will not be eligible for this benefit, and a cap will be introduced limiting it to the average wage.

13. Estimates are based on the assumption that real wage growth is 2 percent, the net real rate of return on invested assets is 3.5 percent, and benefits (from the unfunded and funded pillars) are price indexed. As a proxy for the poverty line, a figure of 35 percent of the average net wage is used, because this percentage broadly approximates a US$2.25-a-day poverty

line converted into national currency, adjusted for purchasing power parity, expressed relative to the national average net wage, and averaged across the nine study countries. Such an approach enables valid comparisons to be made across the sample (see chapter 1).

14. Replacement rates are simulated for an unmarried male working a hypothetical career path under the assumption that real wage growth is 2 percent, inflation is 2.5 percent, the rate of return on invested assets is 3.5 percent, and the worker retires at the statutory retirement age. Replacement rates shown do not consider the benefits received from occupational schemes.

15. There is a slight increase in net replacement rates as income levels increase, as a result of the taxation of earnings and pensions. Otherwise, gross replacement rates are equal across income levels.

16. Projections by Orbán and Palotai (2005), covering old-age pensions only, were used for this analysis, because the European Union publishes only those expenditures related to the public pension system. More detailed projections are being developed and are expected to become available in late 2008. These projections are being coordinated by the Pension and Old-Age Round Table, an independent expert body commissioned by Hungary's prime minister. Preliminary results suggest that the long-term deficit may be higher than previously projected.

17. This projected deficit is well below that of the harmonized projection by the Economic Policy Committee–Ageing Working Group (2007). Although projected revenues are roughly similar across the projection period, expenditures for the public scheme are projected to increase to 14.7 percent of GDP, resulting in a deficit of 7.8 percent of GDP by 2050.

18. This estimate is based on the World Bank's baseline demographic projections and assumes that everyone over age 66 receives a pension, everyone age 20–66 contributes, and all pensioners receive the replacement rate awarded to the median worker (40 percent).

19. This estimate is based on the assumption that real wage growth is 2.0 percent, the net real rate of return on invested assets is 3.5 percent, and benefits (from both the unfunded and the funded pillars) are price indexed. Country-specific mortality rates are used for this analysis.

20. See Holzmann, MacKellar, and Repansek (2009) for a conference volume that addresses these issues for the countries of southeastern Europe.

Bibliography

Augusztinovics, M., and J. Köllő. 2009. "Decreased Employment and Pensions." In *Pension Reform in South-Eastern Europe: Linking to Labor and Financial Market Reforms*, ed. R. Holzmann, L. MacKellar, and J. Repansek, 89–104. Washington, DC: World Bank.

Council of Europe. 1990. *European Code of Social Security (Revised)*. Rome.

European Commission. 2006. "The Impact of Ageing on Public Expenditure: Projections for the EU-25 Member States on Pensions, Health Care, Long-Term Care, Education, and Unemployment Transfers (2004–2050)." In *European Economy Special Report 1*, Economic Policy Committee, Brussels.

———. 2007a. Mutual Information System and Social Protection (MISSOC) database. http://ec.europa.eu/employment_social/.

———. 2007b. *Pension Schemes and Projection Models in EU-25 Member Countries*. European Economy Occasional Paper 37, Economic Policy Committee and Directorate General for Economic and Financial Affairs, Brussels.

Gaal, P. 2004. *Health Care Systems in Transition: Hungary*. Geneva: World Health Organization.

GVG (Gesellschaft für Versicherungswissenschaft und -gestaltung) and European Commission. 2003. *Study on the Social Protection Systems in the 13 Applicant Countries: Hungary Country Report*. Cologne.

Holzmann, R., ed. 2009. *Aging Population, Pension Funds, and Financial Market: Regional Perspectives and Global Challenges for Central, Eastern and Southern Europe*. Washington, DC: World Bank.

Holzmann, R., and R. Hinz. 2005. *Old-Age Income Support in the 21st Century*. Washington, DC: World Bank.

Holzmann, R., L. MacKellar, and J. Repansek, eds. 2009. *Pension Reform in South-eastern Europe: Linking to Labor and Financial Market Reforms*. Washington, DC: World Bank.

Hungarian Financial Supervisory Authority. 2007. *Report on the Development of Supervised Sectors in 2006: Achievements and Risks*. Budapest.

ILO (International Labour Organization). n.d. Database. http://laborsta.ilo.org/.

———. 1952. *ILO Convention 102*. Geneva: ILO.

———. 1967. *ILO Convention 128*. Geneva: ILO.

Kovac, E. 2008. "International Comparison of Pension Parameters." *Biztositasi Szemle* 3: 26–37.

Leonik, A. 2006. "*Pension Security System in Poland*." http://www.seminar-burzy.cz/files/leonik03-06.pdf.

OECD (Organisation for Economic Co-operation and Development). 2001. *Insurance and Private Pensions Compendium for Emerging Economies: Private Pensions: Selected Country Profiles*. Working Party on Private Pensions Secretariat, Paris.

———. 2005. *Pensions at a Glance*. Paris: OECD.

———. n.d. *OECD Statistical Extracts*. http://stats.oecd.org/WBOS/.

Orbán, G., and D. Palotai. 2005. *The Sustainability of the Hungarian Pension System: A Reassessment.* Magyar Nemzeti Bank, Budapest.

Palacios, R., and R. Rocha. 1998. "The Hungarian Pension System in Transition." World Bank, Washington, DC.

Palmer, E. 2007. "Pension Reform and the Development of Pension Systems: An Evaluation of World Bank Assistance: Background Paper, Hungary Case Study." World Bank, Washington, DC.

Párniczky, T. 2005. "Financial Sector Assessment Program Update: Hungary." *Technical Note: Pension—Competition and Performance in the Hungarian Second Pillar,* December. World Bank Financial Sector Vice-Presidency, Europe & Central Asia Region Vice-Presidency, and International Monetary Fund, Monetary and Financial Systems Department, Washington, DC.

Reiterer, A. 2008. *Population Development and Age Structure in Southeastern Europe until 2050.* World Bank, Washington, DC.

Simonovits, A. 2002. *Hungarian Pension System: The Permanent Reform.* Institute of Economics, Hungarian Academy of Sciences, Budapest.

U.S. Social Security Administration. 2006. *Social Security Systems throughout the World: Europe.* Washington, DC: Social Security Administration.

Valdés-Prieto, S. 2008. *Designs for the First-Pillar Pensions and the 2008 Chilean Reform.* http://editorialexpress.com/cgi-bin/conference/download.cgi?db_name=SECHI2008&paper_id=130.

Whitehouse, E. 1999. *Tax Treatment of Funded Pensions.* Washington, DC: World Bank.

World Bank. 2005. *Pensions in the Middle East and North Africa.* Washington, DC: World Bank.

———. 2007a. *Pensions Panorama.* Washington, DC: World Bank.

———. 2007b. *Social Assistance in Central Europe and the Baltic States.* Washington, DC: World Bank.

———. 2007c. *Pension System and Reform Discussion Paper.* HDNSP, Washington, DC.

WHO (World Health Organization). 2008. Database. http//:www.who.int/research/en/.

CHAPTER 6

Poland

Poland inherited a public pension system financed on a pay-as-you-go basis (meaning that contributions from current workers are used to pay benefits to current beneficiaries). Like the systems of many of its Eastern European neighbors, Poland's pension system was strained by the country's transition to a market economy, a period characterized by massive economic restructuring and a marked drop in formal sector employment. Pension revenues fell while expenditures remained roughly constant, creating fiscal imbalance in the pension system. By 1992, expenditures had reached the equivalent of 16.3 percent of gross domestic product (GDP), while revenues had fallen to 12.1 percent of GDP, resulting in a deficit of 4.2 percent of GDP. The shortfall had to be financed with general tax revenues. Deficits continued through 1999, although their magnitude varied considerably, partly in response to ad hoc measures taken by the government. Long-term projections suggested that the aging of the population would eventually drive the deficits of the pension system to 6.25 percent of GDP. Among policy makers and social security professionals, consensus emerged regarding the need for reform.

Following a long debate, in 1999 the Polish government introduced a new multipillar pension system.[1] The existing traditional pay-as-you-go public pension scheme was replaced with a mandatory notional defined-contribution (NDC) scheme,[2] a mandatory, privately managed, defined-contribution scheme, and a voluntary, fully funded, defined-contribution scheme intended to provide workers with a mechanism for saving outside of the mandated schemes. Together, these reforms considerably improved the fiscal position of the pension system to the point where the system is expected to generate a surplus of about 1 percent of GDP in the long term.

Against this backdrop, this chapter evaluates the Polish pension system, focusing on fiscal sustainability and benefit adequacy. Adequacy is evaluated through the lens of statutory net replacement rates for different retirement ages, patterns of contributions, and income levels relative to international benchmarks.

This chapter is organized as follows. The next section discusses the motivation for the reforms. The following section describes the key characteristics of the reformed pension system. The third section assesses the adequacy of pension benefits and the fiscal sustainability of the system. The last section draws conclusions.

Motivation for Reform

During Poland's transition from a centrally planned economy to a market economy, the pension system began to experience difficulties meeting its benefit obligations on the basis of the contributions it collected from current workers. Revenues declined as formal sector employment fell; expenditure rose as a result of low retirement ages, liberal provisions that permitted workers in many sectors to retire early, and relatively generous benefits.[3] In 1992, expenditures reached an amount equivalent to 16.1 percent of GDP while revenues fell to 12.1 percent of GDP, resulting in a deficit of 4.2 percent of GDP, which had to be funded from the general budget. The next few years saw some improvement in the fiscal condition of the pension system as a result of ad hoc measures undertaken by the government. By 1999, the fiscal deficit was 2.2 percent of GDP (table 6.1).

As a result of these ad hoc measures, the fiscal condition of the pension system was expected to improve to the point where the system would run a slight surplus by the early 2000s. Over the long term, however, as the impact of these measures diminishes and the population ages, the deficits were expected to return, reaching an amount equivalent to 6.25 percent of GDP by 2050 (figure 6.1).

These long-term projections are driven primarily by the aging of the Polish population, reflected in old-age dependency ratios (defined as the population age 65 and older divided by the population age 20–64),

Table 6.1   Fiscal Balance of Poland's Pension System before Reform, 1992–99

Year	Revenues	Expenditures	Balance
1992	12.1	16.3	−4.2
1993	11.8	15.8	−4.0
1994	12.2	16.1	−3.9
1995	11.6	12.5	−0.9
1996	11.9	13.0	−1.1
1997	11.7	13.7	−2.0
1998	11.3	12.8	−1.5
1999	10.4	12.6	−2.2

Source: Authors' compilation based on information provided by the Ministry of Social Policy.

Figure 6.1   Projected Fiscal Balance of Poland's Public Pension System before Reform, 2000–50

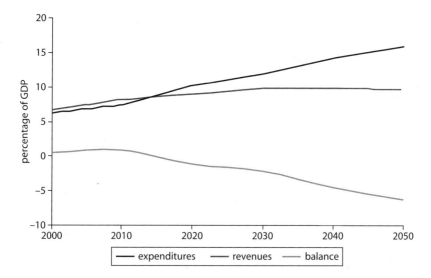

Source: Authors' compilation based on information provided by the Ministry of Social Policy.
Note: Projections cover revenues and expenses associated with old-age pensions only.

which are projected to rise from 21.0 percent in 2005 to 55.3 percent by 2050. The system dependency ratio (defined as the number of people receiving pensions divided by the number of people contributing to the pension scheme) was projected to rise from 29.2 percent in 2000 to 71.6 percent by 2050, in the absence of reform (figure 6.2).[4]

To address these problems, in 1999 the Polish government introduced a multipillar pension system consisting of a mandatory NDC pension

Figure 6.2   Projected Old-Age and System Dependency Ratios in Poland, 2005–50

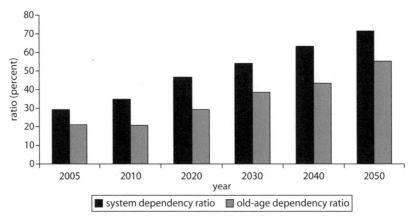

Source: Reiterer 2008.

scheme; a mandatory, privately managed, defined-contribution scheme; and a voluntary, privately managed, defined-contribution scheme. This multipillar design was intended to improve old-age income security by diversifying retirement savings. Productivity growth in the Polish labor market and rates of return on invested capital now play equally important roles, with productivity growth driving returns from the pay-as-you-go first pillar and rates of return driving returns from the funded second and third pillars. Together, these reforms are intended to restore fiscal sustainability to a pension system that would otherwise have continued to require transfers from the state budget (see Chlon, Gora, and Rutkowski 1999).

Characteristics of Poland's Pension System

This section describes the main characteristics of Poland's pension system. These characteristics include the design of the individual pillars of social insurance; the rules governing pension system taxation, institutional structure, and coverage; and the provisions governing old-age, disability, and survivorship pensions. The design of the pension system is assessed using a conceptual framework developed by the World Bank, which generally recommends including a funded component if conditions are appropriate but increasingly recognizes that a range of choices is available to policy makers to provide effective old-age protection in a manner that is fiscally responsible (see Holzmann and Hinz 2005).

In general, the World Bank supports pension systems composed of some combination of five basic pillars:

- a noncontributory (or zero) pillar (in the form of a demogrant, social pension, or social assistance benefit) intended to provide a minimal level of income protection;
- a first-pillar contributory system linked to earnings, which seeks to replace a portion of preretirement income;
- a mandatory second pillar (essentially, individual savings accounts), which can be designed in various ways;
- a voluntary third pillar, which is flexible and discretionary (this pillar, too, can take a variety of forms); and
- a fourth pillar of informal intrafamily or intergenerational sources of financial and nonfinancial support to the elderly, including access to health care and housing.

Pillar Design

The reformed Polish pension system provides old-age income support to the elderly through all five of these pillars (table 6.2). The publicly managed, noncontributory zero pillar (social assistance benefit), which is financed with general tax revenues, redistributes income to lower-income groups using means testing. Both the traditional, publicly managed, pay-as-you-go first pillar and the privately managed, fully funded second pillar are earnings-related schemes for which participation is mandatory. The first pillar is an NDC scheme financed by mandatory contributions (paid by employees and employers in equal shares). The total contribution rate is 19.52 percent of wages, with 12.22 percentage points going to the NDC scheme and 7.30 percentage points going to the funded second pillar. The second pillar is a privately managed, fully funded defined-contribution scheme. Benefits from both schemes are payable in the form of annuities, the values of which are computed on the basis of contributions; credited investment earnings (which, in the case of the NDC scheme, are notional and based on the rate of growth in covered wages); and life expectancy at retirement. Supplementing the benefits of the first and second pillars is a voluntary third-pillar defined-contribution scheme. The mandatory fourth pillar is financed by a combination of contributions and general tax revenues and provides health insurance to the general population, including the elderly (table 6.3).

Contributions to the first-pillar scheme are exempt from taxes while benefits are taxed. The second pillar is subjected to classical

Table 6.2 Structure of Poland's Pension System

| | | | | | | | Taxation | | |
| | | | | | | | | Investment income/ capital | |
Scheme type	Coverage	Type	Function	Financing	Generic benefit	Benefit indexation	Contributions	gains	Benefits
Zero pillar (public noncontributory)[a]	Universal	Means tested	Redistributive	Tax revenues	Difference between minimum threshold and actual income	Regular increases based on social assistance legislation	n.a.	n.a.	Exempt
First pillar (public, earnings related)	Mandatory	Notional defined-contribution	Insurance	Percentage of individual earnings	Pensions from conversion notional capital accumulation into annuities	Indexed to inflation plus 20 percent of the growth in wages	Exempt	n.a.	Taxed
Second pillar (private, earnings related)	Mandatory	Defined contribution	Insurance	Percentage of individual earnings	Pensions from conversion capital accumulation into annuities	Annuity increased with 90 percent of return from investment from annuity reserves[b]	Exempt	Exempt	Taxed

Third pillar (private, voluntary)	Voluntary	Defined contribution	Insurance	Voluntary contributions	Pension from capital accumulation	Depends on options chosen	Taxed[c]	Exempt[d]	Exempt
Fourth Pillar (public health care)	Mandatory	n.a.	Insurance	Percentage of individual earnings plus tax revenues	Specified health service package	n.a.	Exempt	n.a.	n.a

Sources: Chłon, Gora, and Rutkowski 1999; European Commission 2007a, 2007b; OECD 2001; and data provided by the Ministry of Labour and Social Affairs.

n.a. = Not applicable.

a. There is also a minimum pension guarantee under the old-age pension system. For pensioners who contributed for at least 25 years (men) and 20 years (women) whose total pension falls below a certain threshold, the difference is topped up from the state budget. The guaranteed minimum benefit is currently 636 zlotys per month. Minimum pensions are taxed according to the general personal income tax rules.

b. This increase is scheduled according to the draft law submitted by the government to the Parliament in 2008.

c. Employer contributions to the third pillar are deductible from the employer's taxable income.

d. Employees are granted tax relief up to 150 percent of average wage, above which they must pay taxes for capital gains and retirement savings.

expenditure taxation (exempt-exempt-taxed), meaning that contributions are exempt from taxation and investment income is exempt from taxation while benefits are taxed (see box 1.1 in chapter 1). The voluntary third pillar is subjected to taxed-exempt-exempt taxation, meaning that contributions and investment income are partially taxed while benefits are not taxed. The noncontributory zero pillar and the fourth pillar are not taxed.

Noncontributory scheme. Like many of its neighbors, Poland has a non-contributory social assistance program that provides financial support to households in which income falls below a minimum threshold. In 2006, the threshold was about 14 percent of the average wage. Eligibility for social assistance benefits is not dependent on age. The elderly (including those collecting pensions) are not treated specially. For qualifying households, the scheme provides two types of benefits: permanent benefits, payable to individuals incapable of working because of age or disability; and temporary benefits, payable to individuals incapable of working because of long-term illnesses, temporary disability, unemployment, or ineligibility for benefits from other social protection programs. Permanent benefits are means tested and adjusted to ensure that the household receives the minimum income threshold. Since October 2006, the maximum permanent benefit has been 444 zlotys (Zl) per month (18 percent of the average wage, which was Zl 2,477 per month in 2006). Temporary benefits are also means tested and adjusted for household income, but the benefit is equal to only 50 percent of the difference between household income and the minimum income threshold.

Earnings-related schemes. Rather than changing the parameters of the existing, defined-benefit, pension scheme, Poland closed the scheme to younger workers (those born after 1948) and enrolled them in a new first-pillar scheme based on NDCs. Their pensionable rights that accrued under the old system until 1998 were converted into initial capital, which was credited to their individual accounts.[5]

Under the new scheme, benefits are computed using a defined-contribution formula, but the scheme's underlying financing remains on a pay-as-you-go basis. Individual account balances and investment earnings are purely notional (that is, they are an administrative record of contributions and credited interest without any underlying funds). Total old-age contributions are evenly split between employers and employees at the rate of 19.52 percent levied on wages up to 2.5 times the national

Table 6.3 Parameters of Earnings-Related Schemes in Poland before and after Reform

Scheme type	Period	Vesting period	Contribution rate	Contribution ceiling	Benefit rate	Pension assessment base	Retirement age
First pillar (earnings related)	Prereform	20 years for women, 25 years for men	45 percent paid by employer, not divided into specific risk categories	No ceiling on contributions; ceiling of 2.5 times national average wage on benefit level	Flat component (24 percent of reference wage) plus 1.3 percent for each year of contribution and 0.07 percent for each year of noncontribution[a]	Best 3 consecutive years from the last 12 years since 1993, increasing gradually to best 10 consecutive years from last 20 years	65 for men, 60 for women (with many exemptions, actual retirement age is about 59 for men and 55 for women)
	Postreform	No minimum period required; women are eligible for minimum guarantee after 20 years, men after 25 years	27.97 percent[b] (old-age: 19.52 percent[c]; disability and survivor: 6 percent; sickness and maternity: 2.45 percent)	2.5 times national average wage	Pension from capital accumulation	Notional capital accumulation	65 for men, 60 for women
	Prereform	n.a.	n.a.	n.a.	n.a.	n.a.	n.a.

(continued)

Table 6.3 Parameters of Earnings-Related Schemes in Poland before and after Reform (*Continued*)

Scheme type	Period	Vesting period	Contribution rate	Contribution ceiling	Benefit rate	Pension assessment base	Retirement age
Second pillar (earnings related)	Postreform	None; women are eligible for minimum guarantee after 20 years, men after 25 years	7.3 percent	2.5 times national average wage	Pension from capital accumulation	Accumulated funds	65 for men, 60 for women

Sources: European Commission 2007a, 2007b; consultations with World Bank staff.

n.a. = Not applicable.

a. As specified in the law, periods of university education, mandatory army service, maternity and child care leave, and unemployment are recognized.

b. Individuals participating only in the first pillar pay 19.52 percent to the first pillar for old-age pensions (split equally between employers and employees). Individuals participating in both the first and the second pillars pay 12.22 percent to the first pillar (9.76 percent paid by employers and 2.46 percent paid by employees) and 7.3 percent to the second pillar (paid entirely by employees). Employers also pay contributions for work injury. The rate varies by industry.

c. In 1999, all wages were increased by the contribution rate paid by employees in order to guarantee the same level of net income. This means that the rates of contributions are calculated on different bases and are therefore not directly comparable.

average wage; 12.22 percent of wages is credited to the NDC pillar. The rate of credited "interest" is the rate of growth in covered wages in the system. At retirement, an individual's account balance is used to compute the amount of his or her benefit as a function of life expectancy. Actual benefits are paid from the contributions of current workers.

The advantage of NDCs is that they improve incentives (by more tightly linking contributions with benefits and by making lifetime benefits conditional on lifetime wages rather than on a few best years of wages, as had been the case) and are fiscally self-balancing (inasmuch as accrued rights grow in proportion to the tax base used to fund them). Given the rapid aging of the Polish population, this aspect of NDCs is particularly important.

Younger workers are also enrolled in a mandatory second-pillar scheme of funded individual accounts for which the contribution rate is 7.3 percent of wages. Benefits from both schemes are paid in the form of lifetime annuities. A minimum pension guarantee is awarded to men with 25 years of service and to women with 20 years of service.

Voluntary scheme. The voluntary, defined-contribution, third-pillar scheme includes both employee pension funds and individual retirement accounts (table 6.4). Employee pension funds are registered and supervised by the Insurance and Pension Funds Supervisory Commission. The state encourages employee pension plans by deducting the 7 percent contributed to the voluntary pillar from the wage base for the payment of social security contributions to the first pillar. Employees can make their own contributions, which are deducted directly from their wages and transferred to their accounts. Benefit eligibility begins at age 60. Benefits can be claimed as a lump sum or as a lifetime benefit. Employee pension plans are based on agreements with investment funds, insurance companies, or individual pension funds.

As of April 2008, about 1,179 plans had been registered with the Financial Supervision Commission, 1,040 of which were active. Plans can be sponsored by one employer or by multiple employers with a minimum of five employees each. Employees must be 18 years old and have worked for the employer for at least three months to be eligible to participate. Employees with more than one employer may participate in multiple plans simultaneously.

Individual retirement accounts were established in 2005. They can be held with open-ended investments funds, brokerage houses, banks, and insurance companies. Participants must contribute for at least five years

Table 6.4   Characteristics of the Voluntary Scheme in Poland

Coverage	Vesting period	Retirement age	Tax advantages to participants[a]	Contributions tax deductible by employers[a]	Lump-sum payments possible in retirement
Workers age 18 and older	5 Years	60	Yes	Yes	Yes

Sources: European Commission 2007a; Leonik 2006.
a. Participants are provided with tax relief up to 150 percent of average wage, above which they have to pay taxes for capital gains on retirement savings. As of January 2009, the ceiling will be increased to 300 percent of average wage. Employers are exempt from paying social security contributions to the first pillar for the 7 percent contribution they pay to the voluntary pillar.

and cannot withdraw benefits until age 60 (the same age applied to employee pension plans). Participants are provided with tax relief up to 150 percent of the national average wage, above which they pay taxes on capital gains on their retirement savings. By the end of 2007, more than 915,000 individuals (about 4 percent of the working-age population in Poland) had individual retirement accounts.

Health care system. Health care in Poland is provided primarily through a mandatory health insurance system administered by the National Health Fund. Services are financed primarily by contributions from the covered population, at the rate of 9 percent of income, the definition for which varies by group.[6] People receiving social insurance benefits—which include pensioners and recipients of social welfare allowances—pay contributions based on their gross benefits.

Recipients of health care are required to make copayments for some health care services, pharmaceuticals, and medical devices (Kuszewski and Gericke 2005). In 2005, health expenditure accounted for 6.2 percent of GDP, 69.3 percent of which was public expenditure and 30.7 percent was private expenditure. Of the private expenditure, 85.1 percent was attributable to out-of-pocket expenditure (informal payments, direct payments, and copayments) (WHO 2008).

Institutional Structure and Coverage of Earnings-Related Schemes

The mandatory first- and second-pillar schemes cover all salaried employees and the self-employed (roughly 87 percent of the labor force in 2005). There are special systems for farmers, the police, and members of the military. The farmers' pension fund is administered by the Agricultural Social Insurance Fund. The Social Insurance Institution (ZUS) administers the first-pillar scheme through regional branches and local offices located throughout the country. The second pillar is administered by private pension-fund management companies. Contributions for both pillars are collected by ZUS, which transfers second-pillar contributions to the management company of the participant's choice within five days.

The Financial Supervision Commission is responsible for licensing and supervising open pension funds and pension-fund management companies. In 2007, there were 15 open pension funds and pension-fund management companies operating. The industry is concentrated, with the three largest companies controlling 64 percent of the market. Open pension funds have become some of the largest institutional investors in Poland, with total assets equivalent to 12 percent of GDP at the end of 2007. This percentage compares favorably with other countries that have introduced multipillar reforms (Rocha and Rudolph 2007).

Structure of Benefits

Poland's pension system provides old-age, disability, and survivorship pensions. The provisions governing each of these types of benefits are discussed as follows.

Old-age benefits. There is no work experience requirement to become eligible for an old-age pension; reaching the retirement age is sufficient. However, to become eligible for the minimum old-age pension guarantee from the mandatory system, men must have at least 25 years of service (women require 20 years) and have reached the retirement age of 65 (women can retire at age 60). Early retirement is not allowed. Delayed retirement is allowed without restriction. Workers who defer their pension may continue to contribute to their notional and open pension-fund accounts in order to increase the amount of their pension.

Upon a person's retirement, both first- and second-pillar accounts are converted into pensions. The time of conversion is the same for both pillars. Under the first-pillar NDC scheme, an individual's account balance is simply an administrative record of contributions and notionally credited interest (based on the growth of economywide covered wages). At retirement, the account balance is used as the basis for computing the value of the individual's annuity based on life expectancy. Benefits are paid using the contributions of current workers. Benefits from the second pillar are also paid in the form of annuities but are funded using the accumulated capital in the individual's investment account. Annuities are calculated using unisex mortality tables and are increased by 90 percent of the interest earned by annuity companies on their annuity reserves, according to the draft law submitted by the government to Parliament in

June 2008. Men who have contributed for 25 years and women who have contributed for 20 years are eligible for a minimum pension in cases where their combined first- and second-pillar benefits would otherwise fall below the minimum pension (equal to 23 percent of the average wage in 2004).[7] Minimum pensions are taxed according to the general personal income tax rules.

Disability benefits. Disability benefits are determined on the basis of an individual's inability to work. They are provided to workers with at least 5 years of service credit over the 10 years before becoming disabled (for workers below age 30, the requirement is 1–4 years, depending on age), subject to the additional restriction that the noncontributory periods do not exceed one-third of the years of total contribution (table 6.5).

Benefits for people who are totally disabled are calculated using the same rules used to compute old-age pensions. Benefits for people who are partially disabled are 75 percent of the amount awarded for total disability. Benefits are converted into an old-age pension upon reaching retirement.

In 2008, the government proposed significant changes to the benefit formula to link disability pensions to old-age pensions based on the NDC

Table 6.5   Eligibility Conditions for and Benefits Provided by Disability Pensions in Poland under the First-Pillar Earnings-Related Scheme

Vesting period	Contribution rate	Contribution ceiling	Eligibility	Benefit rate	Partial pension
Under age 20: 1 year Age 20–22: 2 years Age 22–25: 3 years Age 25–30: 4 years Over age 30: 5 years	6 percent (4.5 percent by employer, 1.5 percent by employee)[a]	250 percent of average wage	Total or partial incapacity to work[b]	Flat component (24 percent of reference wage) plus 1.3 percent for each year of contributions and 0.07 percent for each noncontribu- tory year or years required to top up the total to 25 years	75 percent of total disability pension

Source: European Commission 2007a.

a. This rate also covers survivor pension contributions. In 1999, the contribution rate for disability and survivor benefits was set at 13 percent, split equally between employees and employers. This was reduced in 2007 and 2008 to reach the current 6 percent level.

b. Not defined in percentages.

formula, with a view to making the system consistent across all of its component programs. The new formula will apply to pensions awarded from 2009 onward.

Survivor benefits. Survivor benefits are awarded to dependents if the deceased had been receiving (or had met the criteria to receive) an old-age or disability pension. (table 6.6).

Survivors who are contributing to the second pillar are entitled to the accumulated capital in the deceased's account, with 50 percent of the account balance going to the survivor's spouse and the remainder going to one or two other people named in the participant's contract with an open pension fund. For participants who do not name a beneficiary, the remainder is divided among the deceased's closest relatives (spouses and orphans are primary beneficiaries, parents and grandchildren are secondary beneficiaries). The accumulated capital can be distributed as a lump sum or as installments over a two-year period, as specified by the beneficiary. For survivors of workers who had already been receiving an annuity from the second pillar, benefit eligibility (and the amount of the benefit) depends on the type of annuity that was purchased.

Assessment of the Performance of Poland's Pension System

The World Bank has established four principles for evaluating public pension systems, which together should guide the process of pension reform (see Holzmann and Hinz 2005). Broadly speaking, these principles include the adequacy and security of benefits, the affordability of contributions, the sustainability of the system over time, and the robustness of the system in the face of demographic changes and macroeconomic shocks. This chapter focuses primarily on the adequacy of benefits and the financial sustainability of the earnings-related pension scheme. The remaining principles are mentioned only briefly. Adequacy is analyzed through the lens of net replacement rates. Financial sustainability is evaluated using projections of pension expenditure and revenues.

Benefit Adequacy

Replacement rates are a useful yardstick for measuring the adequacy of pension benefits, because they express benefits relative to preretirement earnings, thereby indicating the degree to which income is replaced when workers retire. Two variants are commonly used. Gross replacement rates compute income replacement as the ratio of benefits paid to

Table 6.6 Eligibility Conditions for and Benefits Provided by Survivor Pensions in Poland under the First-Pillar Earnings-Related Scheme

Eligibility	Spouse replacement rate	Benefit duration	Remarriage test	Orphan age limit	Orphan replacement rate	Total family benefit
Eligibility of the deceased for an old-age or a disability pension	85 percent of deceased's pension if sole surviving relative	For life, if spouse is disabled, is taking care of a child (until the child finishes school), or is above age 50; otherwise, one year	Benefits paid even if surviving spouse remarries	18 (25 for university students)	85 percent of deceased's pension if sole surviving relative	90 percent of deceased's pension for two survivors, 95 percent regardless of number of survivors

Sources: European Commission 2007a, 2007b.

Note: An earnings test is conducted for survivor pensions. The amount of the benefit is reduced if a survivor is younger than the statutory retirement age or has an income of 70–130 percent of average national earnings. The benefit is suspended if the survivor's income exceeds 130 percent of average national monthly earnings. No income test is conducted once a survivor reaches the statutory retirement age (U.S. Social Security Administration 2006).

pretax preretirement earnings. Net replacement rates compute income replacement as the ratio of benefits received (that is, after the payment of taxes and other levies, including contributions for social insurance) to posttax preretirement earnings. In general, net replacement rates are a more useful measure of benefit adequacy, because they capture the degree to which actual take-home pay is replaced when workers retire.

The level of income replacement at retirement is not the only measure of benefit adequacy. For a full assessment of benefit adequacy, it is also important to determine how postretirement indexation rules will affect replacement rates during retirement. Pension benefits in retirement are expected to be indexed to inflation, so that their real value is maintained. In a growing economy with rising real wages, however, mere price indexation of pensions leads to a deterioration of the relative consumption position of the retirees. For this reason, some countries have introduced mixed indexation of pensions that use varying weights of inflation and wage growth in the indexation formula.

For an evaluation of the effect of indexation on replacement rates in Poland, the replacement rates are normalized to 100 percent and the assumptions for calculating the replacement rates are maintained (that is, inflation is 2.5 percent a year and real wage growth is 2.0 percent a year). The change in the replacement rate is measured in comparison with full wage indexation or the earnings of an active worker. The results of this analysis indicate that the relative income position of a retiree would deteriorate by 16 percent after 10 years in retirement and by 45 percent after 35 years in retirement. The evaluation of income replacement that follows considers replacement rates only at retirement; it does not take into account the impact of indexation policies on replacement rates during retirement.

Replacement rates are a function of the formula governing pension benefits; an individual's contribution history; and, in the case of net replacement rates, the rules of income tax, social security contributions, and other relevant levies. The benefit formula establishes the degree to which the system redistributes income across individuals of different levels of preretirement earnings. Progressive systems provide higher levels of income replacement to people with lower levels of preretirement income. In general, the degree to which a system is redistributive depends on the existence (and value) of flat transfers and minimum pension guarantees, the degree to which benefits are earnings related, and the existence of ceilings on earnings subject to contributions. An individual's contribution history can be characterized by his or her age of entry into the labor force, contribution density, and decisions regarding the timing of retirement. To some degree, these three factors are influenced by the incentives embodied in the pension system. The tax and contribution system influences net replacement rates through the progressiveness of the income tax formula, which taxes (higher) income during a worker's active life more so than it does (lower) pension benefits in retirement. In addition, there are are social security levies (for pensions; unemployment; health care; and, at times, housing and family benefits), which are typically reduced or eliminated altogether in retirement. These benefits are particularly important for low- to middle-income groups.

Benchmarks need to be established for an evaluation of the adequacy of the income replacement provided by the earnings-related pension schemes. Unfortunately, there is no consensus on what constitutes adequacy. According to one widely respected definition, pensions are adequate when they are sufficient to prevent poverty among the elderly and provide the vast majority of the population with a reliable mechanism for smoothing income over their lifetime. Even with a definition, however, establishing benchmarks is problematic, because attitudes vary across countries as a result of social and cultural perceptions. Moreover, benchmarks ignore the other factors that affect the welfare of the elderly—and that also vary across countries—including the existence and generosity of health insurance and long-term care, the cost of housing, the structure of traditional living arrangements, the presence of informal intrafamily or intergenerational sources of financial and nonfinancial support, and the availability and security of other mechanisms for people to save for their own retirement.

One reputable nine-country study (OECD 2001) observes that living standards are roughly comparable for people 10 years older than the normal retirement age and people 15 years younger than the normal retirement age when retirees have disposable income equal to roughly 80 percent of the disposable income of working-age people. In part, this is attributable to the fact that retirees have no work-related expenses (they do not have to commute or buy special clothing or uniforms, for example). This finding, however, does not imply that mandatory first-pillar pension schemes should actually target an 80 percent net replacement rate. To the contrary, in middle- and high-income countries, one can reasonably expect individuals to save for their own retirement—and the empirical evidence suggests that, in practice, they do so.[8] There is also some evidence to suggest that the ratio between preretirement and postretirement income is somewhat independent of the income replacement mandate of the public pension system. Put simply, individuals tend to save more in countries with more modest mandates (and vice versa).

Because Poland has access to relatively well-developed financial markets, it would seem reasonable to expect middle- and higher-income workers to save enough to finance at least 25 percent, if not closer to 50 percent, of this 80 percent income replacement target. Given this, three benchmarks are provided: a 40 percent net replacement rate (which implies that individuals would be expected to save enough to finance half of the total income replacement target); a 60 percent net replacement rate (which implies that individuals would be expected to finance a quarter of the target); and an 80 percent net replacement rate (which implies that individuals, most of whom would be low-income earners, would not be expected to contribute anything toward the target).[9] In the following analysis, these three benchmarks are used to evaluate the adequacy of benefits in Poland compared with the average net replacement rate observed in 53 countries around the world, the average net replacement rate observed for selected countries in Europe and Central Asia, and the poverty line in Poland.

To estimate gross and net replacement rates, we use the Analysis of Pension Entitlements across Countries (APEX) model to consider two critical dimensions: earnings levels and contribution periods.[10] This model generates estimates for replacement rates under steady-state assumptions (that is, as if the rules of the reformed pension scheme had been in place over the entire active life of the individual). Because life expectancies at retirement are projected to increase over time—which will affect the benefits paid by defined-contribution pension schemes—a reference year must be chosen. The year 2040 is used, because it provides a sufficiently long contribution period to approximate steady-state conditions.

The first critical task is to investigate levels of income replacement across a relevant spectrum of income. Income is represented as a percentage (50–200 percent) of average earnings. The second task is to investigate the impact on income replacement of differences in the duration, timing, and density of an individual's contribution history (density refers to the percentage of time an individual actually contributes over a given period). To facilitate the presentation of these multidimensional results, we compute replacement rates as a function of the age at which an individual exits the labor market. They are presented separately for full-career and partial-career workers.

Replacement rates for full-career workers. Full-career workers are examined first. For the purpose of this analysis, a full career is defined as continuous employment from age 20 to the current normal retirement age of 65 for men. Two earnings-related pension schemes contribute to gross replacement rates (figure 6.3).[11] The two schemes directly connect the benefits an individual receives in retirement to the contributions he or she made while working. Regardless of income, gross replacement rates are 62.1 percent, 30.0 percentage points of which comes from the first pillar and 31.2 percentage points of which comes from the second. The situation does not change significantly when taxes are taken into consideration (figure 6.4).

Pensions for most full-career workers in Poland can be considered adequate (figure 6.5). Replacement rates for workers of all levels of preretirement income are substantially higher than the middle benchmark, which implies that the pension system is effectively smoothing consumption from work to retirement, especially for middle- and high-income workers.[12] Replacement rates for low-income workers are 5 percentage points lower than the 80 percent benchmark. Given that benefits for even the lowest-income full-career workers greatly exceed the poverty line, the objective of poverty alleviation is being

Figure 6.3   Sources of Gross Replacement Rates in Poland, by Income Level

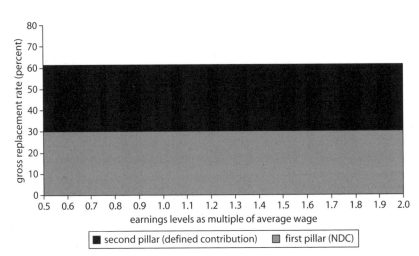

Source: APEX model.
Note: Figure shows projected replacement rate for 2040 as approximation of steady-state conditions.

Figure 6.4   Sources of Net Replacement Rates in Poland, by Income Level

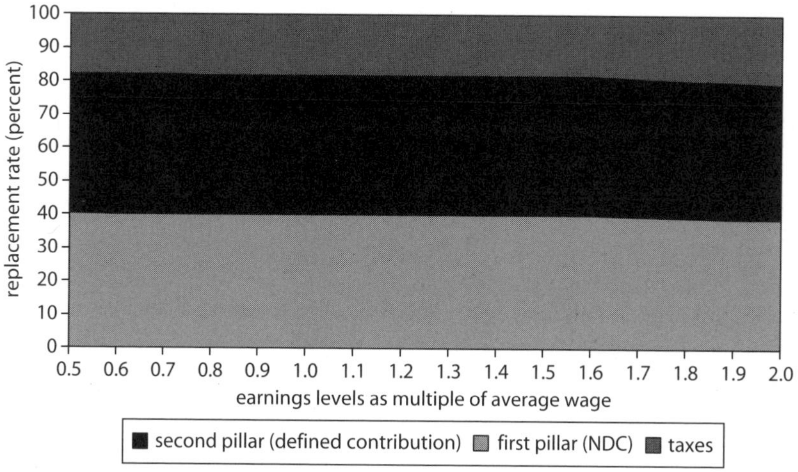

Source: APEX model.
Note: Figure shows projected replacement rate for full-career worker in 2040 as approximation of steady-state conditions.

met.[13] Levels of income replacement are higher than the world and regional averages for high-income workers but lower than both averages for low-income workers. This finding indicates that the strong link between contributions and benefits found in the Polish pension system also results in the system affecting comparatively little redistribution from workers with high preretirement income to those with lower preretirement income.

Replacement rates for partial-career workers. Not everyone works from age 20 to the statutory retirement age. Many individuals enter and exit the labor force (often at different ages and for different periods of time) and earn different wages while working (figure 6.6). To examine the adequacy of benefits for partial-career workers, we consider three stylized cases. These cases include career type A (someone entering the labor force at age 25 who works continuously for a period of years before leaving the workforce at some point between the ages of 50 and 70 and then claims a benefit); career type B (identical to career type A, except that the worker enters the workforce at age 30 and leaves no earlier than age 55); and career type C (identical to career type A, except that the individual contributes in only three years out of four while in the labor force). For

Figure 6.5   Net Replacement Rates for Male Full-Career Workers in Poland, Europe and Central Asia, and the World, by Income Level

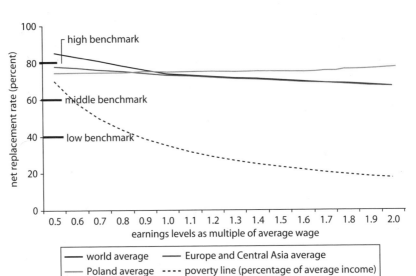

Source: Authors' calculations based on World Bank 2007a and the APEX model.
Note: Figure shows projected replacement rate for 2040 as approximation of steady-state conditions.

cases in which the withdrawal from the formal labor market occurs before the statutory retirement age, the pension is claimed (and the replacement rate calculated) only at the later age. For withdrawals after the statutory retirement age, the ages coincide.

Four conclusions can be drawn from examination of net replacement rates for partial-career middle-income workers (only middle-income partial-career workers are examined because replacement rates are comparable for workers with lower and higher levels of preretirement income). First, all three types of workers receive levels of income replacement that exceed the poverty line. Second, leaving the workforce very early can be very costly. Third, entering the workforce later in life is costly, because a worker who enters the workforce at age 30 receives a net replacement rate 9–12 percentage points lower than a worker who enters at age 25. Fourth, working intermittently is costly, because contributing three years out of every four results in a net replacement rate that is 9–23 percentage points lower than when contributing continuously.

In all cases, net replacement rates grow faster the longer an individual works. This is encouraging, because it provides incentives for individuals to

Figure 6.6   Net Replacement Rates for Male Middle-Income Partial-Career Workers in Poland, by Career Type and Exit Age

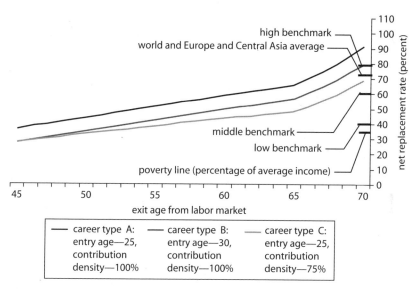

Source: Authors' calculations based on World Bank 2007a and the APEX model.
Note: Figure shows projected replacement rate for 2040 as approximation of steady-state conditions. See text for descriptions of career types.

defer retirement. Although career type A workers can attain the 60 percent benchmark before reaching the normal retirement age, career type B workers must work one year beyond the normal retirement age and career type C workers must work four additional years to reach this benchmark. To replace 80 percent of preretirement earnings, career type A workers must work for up to three years past the normal retirement age, while career type B workers must work until age 70. Career type C workers cannot attain the 80 percent benchmark even if they work until age 70.

Fiscal Sustainability

The sustainability of a pay-as-you-go first-pillar pension scheme is best evaluated in actuarial terms by estimating the scheme's actuarial deficit as the difference between its assets and liabilities. If a large actuarial deficit exists, the scheme is financially unsustainable and needs policy actions that increase its assets, reduce its liabilities, or both. A good proxy for the actuarial deficit is the difference between the present value of the scheme's expected future revenues (that is, contributions and other

Figure 6.7   Projected Fiscal Balance of Poland's Public Pension Scheme, 2004–50

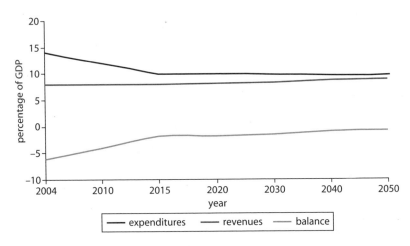

Source: European Commission 2007b.
Note: Projections 1998 and cover old-age pensions only.

income) and expected future expenditures (that is, benefit payments, administrative costs, and other expenses) over an extended projection period. The difference between these two values represents an unfunded liability (sometimes referred to as a financing gap) on the public-sector balance sheet. Because this study is also concerned with the time path of revenues and expenditures (and the resulting balance across the projection period ending in 2050), this more pragmatic approach has been taken. Projections of expenditures, revenues, and deficits are presented on the basis of available postreform fiscal projections.

The reforms of 1999 eliminated the pension system's unfunded liability. As a result, the system will eventually come very close to fiscal balance (figure 6.7). Over time, projected revenues will increase slightly, to about 8.8 percent of GDP by 2050. Expenditures are expected to fall more substantially, eventually reaching an amount equivalent to 9.6 percent of GDP, down from about 14.0 percent of GDP in 2004. As a result, the pension system is expected to generate a deficit of about 0.8 percent of GDP in the long term, down from about 6.1 percent in 2004.

Conclusions

To address lingering deficits in the pension system and projections that show that the aging of the population will put increasing pressure on the finances of the system over time, Poland introduced a multipillar pension system in 1999. The existing traditional pay-as-you-go public pension scheme was replaced with a mandatory, NDC first-pillar scheme; a mandatory, privately managed, defined-contribution second-pillar scheme; and a voluntary, fully funded, defined-contribution third-pillar scheme, intended to provide workers with a mechanism for saving outside of the mandated schemes. The mandated schemes directly connect benefits received in retirement to an individual's contributions made while working, thereby improving incentives to participate and to remain in the workforce (albeit at the cost of affecting comparatively little redistribution from high-income workers to lower-income workers).

Poland's approach to pension reform was more radical than the approaches taken by its neighbors, many of which elected only to change the parameters of their existing defined-benefit schemes. Poland's program of reform was named "Security through Diversity," because its multipillar approach effectively diversified retirement savings by enabling benefits to be paid both from a pay-as-you-go scheme (which, over time, will become much smaller than it is currently) and from a funded scheme (the returns of which are not perfectly correlated). Together, Poland's reforms improved the fiscal position of the pension system.

The improvement in the fiscal balance of the pension system results from higher standard retirement ages than are found in most countries in the region (65 for men and 60 for women) and from automatic reductions in replacement rates in step with increases in life expectancy. This incentive structure of both the first- and the second-pillar schemes should motivate individuals to postpone their retirement in line with increases in their life expectancy at retirement and should increase labor force participation across all ages (see Chlon-Dominczak 2009). Enabling elderly workers to continue to participate in the labor market, however, will require the introduction of cross-sectoral policy reforms.[14]

These improvements in the fiscal balance of the scheme notwithstanding, the resulting gross and net replacement rates for full-career workers are fully in line with regional and world averages (see chapter 1). The projected net replacement rates are close to the high benchmark of 80 percent. As in other countries, workers with less than full careers—because they leave the workforce before reaching retirement age, work intermittently, or have gaps in their employment history—risk receiving a level of income replacement that is closer to—or even below—the lower benchmark of 40 percent.

All workers have the option of saving outside of the two mandated schemes by participating in the voluntary third-pillar pension scheme. To increase income replacement by 1 percentage point, full-career workers would need to save only about 0.5 percent of their wages between age 40 and the retirement age. Given that participation in the third-pillar scheme remains low, an opportunity exists for broadening its reach.

Notes

1. The reform was named "Security through Diversity," because the multipillar approach effectively diversified retirement savings by enabling benefits to be paid from both a pay-as-you-go pillar and a funded pillar, the returns of which are not perfectly correlated (see Chlon, Gora, and Rutkowski 1999).

2. An NDC pension scheme is financed on a pay-as-you-go basis, but its benefits are computed using a defined-contribution formula. Under an NDC scheme, an individual's account "balance" and investment "earnings" are purely notional (that is, an administrative record of contributions and credited interest without any underlying funds). The rate of credited "interest" is often based on some economic proxy, such as the rate of growth in average wages. At retirement, an individual's account balance is used to compute the amount of his or her benefit, as a function of life expectancy. Actual benefits are paid from the contributions of current workers, as in all pay-as-you-go pension schemes. The advantage of NDCs is that they improve incentives (by more tightly linking contributions with benefits) and, to some degree, are fiscally self-balancing, inasmuch as accrued rights grow more in line with the resources required to fund them (see Holzmann and Palmer 2006).

3. Most occupations permitted workers to retire up to five years before reaching the legal retirement age. Some offered even more liberal provisions. Miners, for example, could retire after 25 years of service and teachers after 30 years, regardless of age; ballet dancers could retire at age 38 (see Chlon, Gora, and Rutkowski 1999).

4. For more information regarding these population projections, see Reiterer (2008).

5. Individuals covered by the new system who accrued rights under the old system by the end of 2008 can retire under the old rules. The 2008 cutoff was initially proposed to end in 2006; on the basis of decisions by the Parliament in 2005 and 2007, it was extended for two more years to address the lack of regulations related to the conversion of some early retirement options into so-called "bridging pensions."

6. Salaried employees make contributions based on their total income (that is, there is no ceiling on income for contribution purposes). The self-employed make contributions on the amount of their declared income or on 75 percent of the average wage, whichever is higher. The basis for calculating health insurance contributions for farmers is the price of 0.5 quintals of rye per standard hectare of the farm.

7. The difference between the minimum pension and the benefit the individual would have received is financed from general tax revenues. The minimum pension is indexed according to general indexation rules.

8. In Chile, for instance, 70 percent of retirees from the mandatory public pension system own their home, which is a form of savings (Valdés-Prieto 2008).

9. These benchmarks approximate the standards developed by the International Labour Organization (ILO) (1952) and the Council of Europe (1990). ILO Convention 102 of 1952 sets a minimum benefit equal to 40 percent of the reference wage for married men of pensionable age. This amount was raised to 45 percent in 1968. The European Code of Security of 1990 sets a minimum standard for members of the Council of Europe equal to 65 percent for married people of a specific age.

10. The APEX model was developed by Axia Economics, with funding from the Organisation for Economic Co-operation and Development and the World Bank. The model codes detailed eligibility and benefit rules for first- and second-pillar schemes based on available public information that has been verified by country contacts. Because the details of the rules sometimes change on short notice (and limited public disclosure), the calculations presented here should be considered as best approximations only.

11. Replacement rates are simulated for an unmarried man working a hypothetical career path under the assumption that real wage growth is 2 percent, inflation is 2.5 percent, the rate of return on invested assets is 3.5 percent, and the worker retires at the statutory retirement age.

12. Estimates are based on the assumption that real wage growth is 2 percent, the net real rate of return on invested assets is 3.5 percent, and benefits (from the unfunded and funded pillars) are price indexed.

13. As a proxy for the poverty line, a figure of 35 percent of the average net wage is used, because this percentage broadly approximates a US$2.25-a-day poverty line converted into national currency, adjusted for purchasing power parity, expressed relative to the national average net wage, and averaged across the eight study countries. Such an approach enables valid comparisons to be made across the sample (see chapter 1).

14. See Holzmann, MacKellar, and Repansek (2009) for a conference volume that addresses theses issues for the countries of southeastern Europe.

Bibliography

Chlon A., M. Gora, and M. Rutkowski. 1999. *Shaping Pension Reform in Poland: Security through Diversity.* Washington, DC: World Bank.

Chlon-Dominczak, A. 2009. "Pension System and Employment of Older Workers: How to Change the Incentive Structure? The Polish Experience." In *Pension*

Reform in Southeastern Europe: Linking to Labor and Financial Market Reforms, ed. R. Holzmann, L. MacKellar, and J. Repansek, 163–76. Washington, DC: World Bank.

Council of Europe. 1990. *European Code of Social Security (Revised)*. Rome.

European Commission. 2006. "The Impact of Ageing on Public Expenditure: Projections for the EU-25 Member States on Pensions, Health Care, Long-Term Care, Education, and Unemployment Transfers (2004–2050)." In *European Economy Special Report 1*, Economic Policy Committee, Brussels.

———. 2007a. Mutual Information System and Social Protection (MISSOC) database. http://ec.europa.eu/employment_social/.

———. 2007b. "Pension Schemes and Projection Models in EU-25 Member Countries." European Economy Occasional Paper 37, Economic Policy Committee and Directorate General for Economic and Financial Affairs, Brussels.

GVG (Gesellschaft für Versicherungswissenschaft und -gestaltung) and European Commission. 2003. *Study on the Social Protection Systems in the 13 Applicant Countries: Poland Country Report*. Cologne.

Gora, M., and M. Rutkowski. 2000. *The Quest for Pension Reform: Poland's Security through Diversity*. Working Paper No. 286, University of Michigan.

Holzmann, R., and R. Hinz. 2005. *Old-Age Income Support in the 21st Century*. Washington, DC: World Bank.

Holzmann, R., and E. Palmer, eds. 2006. *Pension Reform: Issues and Prospects for Non-Financial Defined Contribution Schemes*. Washington, DC: World Bank.

Holzmann, R., L. MacKellar, and J. Repansek, ed. 2009. *Pension Reform in Southeastern Europe: Linking to Labor and Financial Market Reforms*. Washington, DC: Word Bank.

INPRS (International Network of Pension Regulators and Supervisors). 2003. *Complementary and Private Pensions throughout the World*. Geneva: INPRS.

ILO (International Labour Organization). 1952. *ILO Convention 102*. Geneva: ILO.

———. 1967. *ILO Convention 128*. Geneva: ILO.

Kuszewski, K., and C. Gericke. 2005. *Health Care Systems in Transition: Poland*. World Health Organization Regional Office for Europe, Copenhagen.

Leonik, A. 2006. "Pension Security System in Poland." http://www.seminar-burzy.cz/files/leonik03-06.pdf.

OECD (Organisation for Economic Co-operation and Development). 2001. *Ageing and Income: Financial Resources and Retirement in 9 OECD Countries*. Paris: OECD.

Putelbergier, B. 2000. "Changes in the Financing of the Pension System in the Face of Aging: The New Pension System in Poland and Its Adaptation to Other

Countries' Systems." Paper presented at the International Social Security Association Conference on Social Security, Helsinki, September 25–27.

Reiterer, A. 2008. *Population Development and Age Structure in Southeastern Europe until 2050*. World Bank, Washington, DC.

Rocha, R., and H. Rudolph. 2007. "Competition and Performance in the Polish Second Pillar." Working Paper 107, World Bank, Washington, DC.

ZUS (Social Insurance Institution). 2006. *Social Insurance in Poland: Information, Facts*. Warsaw.

U.S. Social Security Administration. 2006 *Social Security Systems throughout the World: Europe*. Washington, DC: Social Security Administration.

Valdés-Prieto, S. 2008. *Designs for the First Pillar Pensions and the 2008 Chilean Reform*. http://editorialexpress.com/cgi-bin/conference/download.cgi?db_name=SECHI2008&paper_id=130.

Whitehouse, E. 1999. *Tax Treatment of Funded Pensions*. Washington, DC: World Bank.

World Bank. 2005. *Growth, Poverty and Inequality: Eastern Europe and the Former Soviet Union*. Washington, DC: World Bank.

———. 2007a. *Pensions Panorama*. Washington, DC: World Bank.

———. 2007b. *Social Assistance in Central Europe and the Baltic States*. Washington, DC: World Bank.

WHO (World Health Organization). 2008. Database. http://www.who.int/research/en/.

CHAPTER 7

Romania

Romania inherited a socialist-era public pension system financed on a pay-as-you-go basis (meaning that contributions from current workers are used to pay benefits to current beneficiaries). As a result of increased informality in labor markets following its transition from a centrally planned economy to a market economy, pension system revenues fell from the equivalent of 9.3 percent of gross domestic product (GDP) in 1992 to 6.3 percent of GDP by 1998—despite an increase in contribution rates—while expenditure fluctuated at about 7 percent of GDP. As a result, net cash flow fell from a surplus of 1.9 percent of GDP to a deficit of 0.8 percent of GDP.

Recognizing that a pension system that offered comparatively generous benefits, low retirement ages, and lax benefit eligibility conditions would not be sustainable over the long term as the population ages, the government introduced substantial reforms to the pension system in 2000. These reforms raised retirement ages, extended the service period required to become eligible for a full pension, imposed new conditions on early retirement, and replaced the traditional defined-benefit formula with a new formula based on points. In 2006, the government passed legislation to introduce a mandatory, fully funded, defined-contribution scheme, which became operational in 2008.

Against this backdrop, this chapter evaluates Romania's pension system, focusing on fiscal sustainability and benefit adequacy. Adequacy is evaluated through the lens of statutory net replacement rates for different retirement ages, patterns of contributions, and income levels relative to international benchmarks.

This chapter is organized as follows. The next section discusses the motivation for the reforms. The following section describes the key characteristics of the reformed pension system. The third section assesses the adequacy of pension benefits and the fiscal sustainability of the system. The last section draws conclusions.

Motivation for Reform

The pension system that Romania inherited suffered from a number of serious design flaws similar to those observed in other transition economies. These included (a) low retirement ages, which allowed pensioners to receive benefits for very long periods; (b) generous benefits, which created incentives for early retirement, further increasing the period over which benefits were paid; (c) the computation of benefits based on an individual's last five years of wages rather than his or her lifetime wages, which weakened the link between contributions and benefits and created incentives for workers to underreport income or to migrate from the formal to informal sectors; and (d) lax eligibility conditions governing the award of disability pensions, which resulted in more beneficiaries than could be justified on the basis of impairment. The pension system was also fragmented and provided special privileges for particular occupations.

In the early years of the transition to a market economy, pension system revenues in Romania fell, as a result of increasing informality in labor markets and the restructuring of state enterprises, which contributed to rising informal-sector employment. As a result, the number of individuals contributing to the pension system fell from about 8 million in 1990 to 5 million by 1999. To ease the impact of enterprise restructuring, the government granted many workers early retirement. As a result, the number of beneficiaries rose from 2.2 million to 4.0 million over the same period. To cope with these changes, the government increased the contribution rate from 14 percent in 1990 to 28 percent in 1992 (World Bank 2004). Despite the change, revenues still fell short of expenditures, and by 1995, the scheme generated a deficit of 0.2 percent of GDP (table 7.1).

The deficits of the pension system in the late 1990s were not huge and could probably have been afforded were it not for the fact that they were

Table 7.1 Fiscal Balance of Romania's Pension System before Reform, 1992–98
(percentage of GDP)

Year	Revenues	Expenditure	Balance
1992	9.3	7.4	1.9
1993	8.1	6.7	1.4
1994	7.1	6.7	0.4
1995	6.8	7.0	−0.2
1996	6.7	6.9	−0.2
1997	6.5	6.5	−0.0
1998	6.3	7.1	−0.8

Source: World Bank 2004.

expected to grow substantially over the medium and long terms as a result of the aging of the population.[1] The aging of Romania's population is captured in the old-age dependency ratio (the population age 65 and older divided by the population age 20–64), which is projected to rise from 23.6 percent in 2005 to 56.6 percent by 2050.[2]

Recognizing these challenges, the government introduced substantial reforms to the pension system in 2000. These changes included raising retirement ages, extending service periods for eligibility for full pensions, imposing new conditions for early retirement, and replacing the traditional defined-benefit formula with a new formula based on points. These measures managed—at least in the short run—to balance revenues and expenditures and to achieve a fragile surplus equivalent to 0.3 percent of GDP in 2006 and 0.2 percent in 2007. In 2006, the government passed legislation to introduce a mandatory fully funded defined-contribution scheme, which became operational in May 2008.

Characteristics of Romania's Pension System

This section describes the main characteristics of Romania's pension system. They include the design of the individual pillars of social insurance; the rules governing pension system taxation, institutional structure, and coverage; and the provisions governing old-age, disability, and survivorship pensions.

The design of the pension system is assessed using a conceptual framework developed by the World Bank, which generally recommends including a funded component if conditions are appropriate but increasingly recognizes that a range of choices is available to policy makers to provide effective old-age protection in a manner that is fiscally responsible (see Holzmann and Hinz 2005).

In general, the World Bank supports pension systems composed of some combination of five basic pillars:

- a noncontributory (or zero) pillar (in the form of a demogrant, social pension, or social assistance benefit) intended to provide a minimal level of income protection;
- a first-pillar contributory system linked to earnings, which seeks to replace a portion of preretirement income;
- a mandatory second pillar (essentially, individual savings accounts), which can be designed in various ways;
- a voluntary third pillar, which is flexible and discretionary (this pillar, too, can take a variety of forms); and
- a fourth pillar of informal intrafamily or intergenerational sources of financial and nonfinancial support to the elderly, including access to health care and housing.

Pillar Design

The design of Romania's pension system incorporates all five of the pillars recommended by the World Bank (table 7.2). The publicly managed noncontributory zero pillar, financed with general tax revenues, redistributes income to lower-income groups using means testing that considers both income and assets. The amount of the noncontributory benefit is based on the state-defined minimum income guarantee, which is adjusted by the government on the basis of inflation.

Both the publicly managed, pay-as-you-go first pillar and the newly introduced, privately managed, fully funded second pillar are earnings-related schemes. Benefits under the first pillar are calculated from an individual's accumulated points, which are determined by his or her wages relative to the average wage. Second-pillar benefits are a function of an individual's contributions and investment earnings; the procedures governing the payout of benefits are yet to be established. Contributions for the second pillar started in May 2008. The third pillar is an optional privately managed, fully funded, defined-contribution pension scheme, which is intended to provide individuals with a mechanism for supplementing the benefits paid by the mandatory pillars. The fourth pillar provides health care to the elderly as part of the national health care system.

First-pillar contributions are exempt from taxation while benefits are taxed. The fully funded second and third pillars will be subjected

Table 7.2 Structure of Romania's Pension System

Scheme type	Coverage	Type	Function	Financing	Generic benefit	Benefit indexation	Taxation		
							Contributions	Investment income/ capital gains	Benefits
Zero pillar (public noncontributory)	Universal	Means tested	Redistributive	Tax revenues	Difference between minimum income guarantee and actual income	Government decision based on changes in consumer price index	n.a.	n.a.	Exempt
First pillar (public, earnings related)	Mandatory	Points	Insurance	Percentage of individual earnings	Benefit calculated on the basis of the number of points earned	Adjusted on the basis of changes in point value[a]	Exempt	n.a.	Taxed
Second pillar (private, earnings related)	Mandatory	Defined contribution	Insurance	Percentage of individual earnings	Pension from capital accumulation	Regulation on benefits does not exist yet	Exempt	Exempt	Taxed
Third pillar (private, voluntary)	Voluntary	Defined contribution	Insurance	Voluntary contributions	Pension from capital accumulation	Regulation on benefits does not exist yet	Exempt[b]	Exempt	Taxed
Fourth pillar (public health care)	Mandatory	n.a.	Insurance	Percentage of individual earnings plus tax revenues	Specified health service package	n.a.	Exempt	n.a.	n.a.

Sources: European Commission 2007; OECD n.d.

n.a. = Not applicable.

a. The point value cannot fall below 45 percent of the gross average wage. The percentage is adjusted based on ad hoc decisions by the government.

b. An amount up to 200 euros per year per participant is tax exempt.

to exempt-exempt-taxed taxation (that is, classic expenditure tax), meaning that contributions are exempt from taxation (partially for the third pillar) and investment income is exempt but benefits are taxed (see box 1.1 in chapter 1). The zero and fourth pillars are completely tax exempt.

Noncontributory scheme. Romania does not have a noncontributory social protection scheme specifically for the elderly, but the elderly are eligible for the minimum-income guarantee program, which provides financial support to households whose income falls below a minimum threshold. The threshold is a function of household size and income; the amount of the benefit is adjusted to make up the difference between the minimum income threshold and actual household income (World Bank 2003). In 2006, the monthly benefit was leu 92 (about 9 percent of the average wage) for a one-person household and leu 166 (15 percent of the average wage) for a two-person household. Benefits for large households rise in diminishing amounts. In 2005, 834,000 beneficiaries received minimum-income guarantee benefits, at a cost of leu 472 million, equivalent to 0.2 percent of GDP (World Bank 2007b).

Earnings-related schemes. Both the publicly managed, pay-as-you-go first pillar and the newly introduced privately managed, fully funded second-pillar are earnings-related schemes (table 7.3). In 2000, the defined-benefit formula used to calculate pensions under the traditional first-pillar scheme was eliminated in favor of a new formula based on points. Under this formula, an individual's points are determined by his or her wages relative to the average wage. Benefits are based on total accumulated points at retirement.[3] The number of years of wages on which benefits are based is gradually increasing, from the best five years to the entirety of an individual's service, thereby improving transparency and tightening the link between lifetime contributions and the benefits received in retirement. Under the law, the point value cannot fall below 45 percent of the gross average wage—the exact value of which is set by the government on an ad hoc basis. Pensions paid to existing beneficiaries are also adjusted on the basis of changes made to the point value.[4]

Retirement ages are gradually being raised from 62 to 65 for men and from 57 to 60 for women, a change that is being implemented so slowly that it will not be fully implemented until 2015. Moreover, although the new retirement age for men is consistent with international norms, the age for women remains low by international standards. By 2050, Romanian women will collect benefits for 50 percent longer than men.[5]

Table 7.3 Parameters of Earnings-Related Schemes in Romania before and after Reform

Scheme type	Period	Vesting period	Contribution rate	Contribution ceiling	Benefit rate	Pension assessment base	Retirement age
First pillar (earnings related)	Prereform	10 years	25.5 percent (employee-employer breakdown not available)	5 times the average wage	2.5 percent accrual rate for men for the first 30 years and 1 percent for each year thereafter; 3 percent accrual rate for women for the first 25 years and 1 percent for each year thereafter	5 best consecutive years in last 10 years	62 for men, 57 for women
	Postreform	15 years	29.5 percent[a] (20.0 percent by employer, 9.5 percent by employee)	None	Benefit calculated on the basis of the number of points earned	Lifetime average indexed to nominal wage growth	65 for men, 60 for women
Second pillar (earnings related)	Prereform	n.a.	n.a.	n.a.	n.a.	n.a.	n.a.
	Postreform	Not yet established by law	2 percent increasing to 6 percent (over a period of 8 years)	None	Pensions from capital accumulation	Accumulated funds	65 for men, 60 for women

Sources: European Commission 2007; World Bank 1998, 2004.

n.a. = Not applicable.

a. The total contribution rate for old-age, disability, and survivor pensions is 29.75 percent. Individuals participating only in the first pillar pay 29.5 percent. Individuals participating in both the first and the second pillars pay 27.5 percent to the first pillar (18.0 percent by employer, 9.5 percent by employee) and 2 percent rising to 6 percent to the second pillar (paid entirely by the employer). In 2009, the contribution rate will be reduced to 28 percent (18.5 percent by employer, 9.5 percent by employees).

Eligibility for a full pension now requires 35 years of service for men and 30 years for women, up from 30 years and 25 years, respectively, under the old system. The reform reduces costs and creates incentives for individuals to remain in the workforce longer (retiring with higher benefits). The minimum contribution period required to become eligible for benefits (the vesting period) was raised from 10 to 15 years, a change that will not be fully implemented until 2015.

In 2006, the government passed legislation to introduce the fully funded, defined-contribution, second-pillar pension scheme. This scheme is mandatory for everyone up to age 35 and voluntary for people age 36–45. Contributions will be diverted from the first pillar, starting at 2 percent in 2008 and increasing by half a percentage point each year until the rate reaches 6 percent in 2016.[6]

Voluntary scheme. A voluntary, privately managed, fully funded third-pillar pension scheme was introduced as part of the government's reform program to provide individuals with a mechanism for supplementing the benefits paid by the mandatory pillars (table 7.4). Benefits payable under the third-pillar scheme will be a function of an individual's contributions and investment earnings at retirement. The mechanism by which benefits will be paid under the scheme will be discussed in 2009. Total contributions are limited to 15 percent of gross monthly salary (total of employer and employee). Contributions can be made by employees or employers on the basis of agreements between the parties or existing labor contracts. Contributions are deductible (for both employees and employers), up to 200 euros per year. Benefit eligibility requires that participants reach age 60, have contributed for at least 90 months, and have accumulated capital sufficient to meet a minimum threshold. In the event of disability before retirement, a

Table 7.4   Characteristics of Romania's Voluntary Scheme

Coverage	Vesting period	Retirement age	Tax advantages to participants	Contributions tax deductible by employers	Lump-sum payments possible in retirement
Employees and the self-employed	90 months	60	Yes	Yes	Regulation on benefits does not exist yet

Source: OECD n.d.

participant is entitled to receive the funds in his or her account. In the event that the participant dies before reaching retirement, account funds will be distributed to the participant's surviving dependents.

Seven pension fund management companies are currently sponsoring voluntary pension funds. The largest three manage 73 percent of the assets in the scheme (Romania Private Pension Supervisory Commission Web site [http://w4.csspp.ro/en/]). At the end of 2007, 50,887 individuals (0.5 percent of the labor force) were participating in the scheme, and assets totaled leu 14.3 million (less than half of one percent of GDP). The scheme appears to be growing quickly. By March 2008, the number of participants had increased to 75,423, and total assets had reached leu 24.8 million.

Health care system. Health care in Romania is provided primarily through mandatory health insurance. Voluntary health insurance is available, but it is purchased mainly for travel abroad to countries in which services are not covered by Romania's mandatory scheme. The mandatory scheme is administered by district health insurance funds, which are responsible for collecting contributions and reimbursing claims from providers for health care services in their respective districts. The funds are regulated by the National Health Insurance Fund.

The system is financed primarily by contributions from the covered population. The contribution rate for employed people is 14 percent of payroll, split equally between employers and employees. The contribution rate for self-employed people, farmers, and pensioners is 7 percent. Children, people with disabilities, war veterans with no income, and the dependants of insured people do not pay for coverage. Recipients of health care services are required to make copayments for some medical services and pharmaceuticals (WHO 2000).

In 2005, health expenditure accounted for 5.5 percent of GDP, 70.3 percent of which was public expenditure and 29.7 percent was private expenditure. Of the private expenditure, 85.0 percent was attributable to out-of-pocket expenditure (informal payments, direct payments, and copayments) (WHO 2008).

Institutional Structure and Coverage of Earnings-Related Schemes

The first-pillar pension scheme covers employees with individual labor contracts, civil servants, judges, cooperative members, and recipients of unemployment benefits. There are special schemes for some professions, including lawyers and members of the military. In 2005, 5.9 million individuals (39.1 percent of the working-age population and 57.6 percent of the labor force) contributed to the scheme.

The National House of Pensions is responsible for collecting contributions and paying benefits. It will also be tasked with collecting second-pillar contributions and transferring them to the appropriate private pension fund management company. The Romanian Private Pension System Supervision Commission is responsible for licensing and regulating the activities of the private pension companies. As of October 2007, six companies had applied for licenses to operate second-pillar schemes.

Structure of Benefits

The first-pillar earnings-related pension scheme provides old-age, disability, and survivorship pensions.[7] The provisions governing each of these types of benefits are discussed below.

Old-age benefits. Eligibility for a reduced old-age pension under the first-pillar scheme currently requires individuals to have at least 11 years and 2 months of contributory service. This requirement is gradually being increased to 15 years by 2015. Eligibility for a full pension requires 30 years and 9 months of service for men and 25 years and 9 months of service for women. This requirement is gradually being increased to 35 years for men and 30 years for women by 2015. The retirement age is 62 years and 9 months for men and 57 years and 9 months for women. Retirement ages are gradually being increased to 65 for men and 60 for women by 2015. Individuals may retire up to five years before reaching their retirement age, subject to a reduction in benefits, provided they have contributed for 10 years more than the number of years of contributory service required to earn a full pension (European Commission 2007). Old-age benefits are based on a point system. Points are awarded each year on the basis of an individual's wages divided by the average wage. At retirement, an individual's total accumulated points are divided by his or her total years of service. This value is then multiplied by the pension point value to determine the individual's benefit. Under the law, the point value must not fall below 45 percent of the gross average wage, the exact value of which is set by the government on an ad hoc basis.

Disability benefits. Disability pensions are awarded to individuals who have lost at least 50 percent of their capacity to work. Participants who achieved the contributory period identified are entitled to a disability pension (table 7.5). Participants entitled to a disability pension are granted a potential contributory period representing the difference between the full contributory period and the actual period of contribution at the time of disability.

There are three categories of disability depending on the degree of incapacity. The first, second, and third categories are awarded 0.75, 0.60, and 0.40 points per year, respectively. Upon reaching retirement age, recipients of disability benefits can continue to receive their benefits or elect to receive an old-age pension instead. Under the second-pillar scheme, participants who become disabled will be entitled to a lump-sum payment or periodic payments for up to five years if their account is insufficient for a minimum payment. Otherwise, participants can collect the pension they are entitled to from the second pillar.

Survivor benefits. Survivor benefits are awarded to spouses and orphans of individuals who, at the time of their death, were receiving (or had met the criteria to receive) an old-age or disability pension (table 7.6). Upon reaching the retirement age, spouses are entitled to 50 percent of the deceased's pension if the spouse had been married for at least 15 years. Spouses married for 10–15 years are entitled to reduced benefits. Benefits are reduced by 0.5 percent a month for each month short of 15 years of marriage. Disabled spouses are entitled to survivor benefits regardless of age, provided the spouse was married for at least one year. If the deceased died as a result of a work-related accident, occupational disease, or tuberculosis, spouses are entitled to survivor benefits, regardless of age or the number of years of marriage, provided that the spouse's earnings are subject to mandatory insurance coverage and represent less than 25 percent of the average gross wage.

Table 7.5   Eligibility Conditions for and Benefits Provided by Disability Pensions in Romania under the First-Pillar Earnings-Related Scheme

Vesting period	Contribution rate	Eligibility	Benefit rate	Partial pension
Under age 25: 5 years Age 25–31: 8 years Age 31–37: 11 years Age 37–43: 14 years Age 43–49: 18 years Age 49–55: 22 years Over age 55: 25 years	No specific contribution rate for disability benefits	At least 50 percent loss in capacity to work	Calculated on the basis of number of points	Depending on degree of disability, pensioners receive 0.75, 0.60, or 0.40 points per year

Source: European Commission 2007.

Table 7.6 Eligibility Conditions for and Benefits Provided by Survivor Pensions under Romania's First-Pillar Earnings-Related Scheme

Eligibility	Spouse replacement rate	Benefit duration	Remarriage test	Orphan age limit	Orphan replacement rate	Total family benefit
Eligibility of deceased for an old-age or a disability pension	50 percent of deceased's pension if married for 15 years; 0.5 percent for each month less than 15 years up to a minimum of 10 years; 50 percent of deceased's pension if spouse is disabled and married for at least one year; 50 percent if spouse has children under age 7	For life, if spouse meets one of the first three spouse replacement rate conditions; until youngest child turns 7; or 6 months if none of spouse replacement rate conditions is met	No	16 (26 if orphan is student; for duration of disability if orphan becomes disabled while receiving survivor benefit)	50 percent if sole survivor	75 percent for two survivors; 100 percent for three or more survivors

Source: European Commission 2007.

For spouses who meet none of the three eligibility conditions specified in table 7.6, benefits are paid for six months or until the spouse's youngest child turns seven. Spouses who are eligible for a pension of their own may choose to receive their own pension or a survivor pension.

Orphans are entitled to survivor benefits until age 16 (26 if orphan is enrolled in school) or for the duration of their disability in cases in which the orphan becomes disabled while receiving a survivor benefit. The benefit replacement rate for orphans who have lost both parents is 75 percent.

Under the second pillar, if a participant dies before becoming eligible for a pension, his or her beneficiaries are entitled to the balance of his or her account. Beneficiaries who are not participating in a private pension fund can elect to receive a lump-sum payment or periodic payments for up to five years. Beneficiaries who are participating in a private pension fund can elect to have the deceased's account merged with their own.

Assessment of the Performance of Romania's Pension System

The World Bank has established four principles for evaluating public pension systems, which together should guide the process of pension reform (see Holzmann and Hinz 2005). Broadly speaking, these principles include the adequacy and security of benefits, the affordability of contributions, the sustainability of the system over time, and the robustness of the system in the face of demographic changes and macroeconomic shocks. This chapter focuses primarily on the adequacy of benefits and financial sustainability of the first-pillar earnings-related pension scheme. The remaining principles are mentioned only briefly. Adequacy is analyzed through the lens of net replacement rates. Financial sustainability is evaluated using projections of pension expenditure and revenues.

Benefit Adequacy

Replacement rates are a useful yardstick for measuring the adequacy of pension benefits, because they express benefits relative to preretirement earnings, thereby indicating the degree to which income is replaced when workers retire. Two variants are commonly used. Gross replacement rates compute income replacement as the ratio of benefits paid to pretax preretirement earnings. Net replacement rates compute income replacement as the ratio of benefits received (that is, after the payment of taxes and other levies, including contributions for social insurance) to posttax preretirement earnings. In general, net replacement rates are a more useful measure of benefit adequacy, because they capture the degree to which actual take-home pay is replaced when workers retire.

The level of income replacement at retirement is not the only measure of benefit adequacy. For a full assessment of benefit adequacy, it is also important to determine how postretirement indexation rules will affect replacement rates during retirement. Pension benefits in retirement are expected to be indexed to inflation, so that their real value is maintained. In a growing economy with rising real wages, however, mere price indexation of pensions leads to a deterioration of the relative consumption position of the retirees. For this reason, some countries have introduced mixed indexation of pensions that use varying weights of inflation and wage growth in the indexation formula.

For an evaluation of the effect of indexation on replacement rates in Romania, the replacement rates are normalized to 100 and the assumptions for calculating the replacement rates are maintained (that is, inflation is 2.5 percent a year and real wage growth is 2 percent a year). The change in the replacement rate is measured in comparison with full wage indexation or the earnings of an active worker.

The results of this analysis indicate that the relative income position of a retiree would deteriorate by 5 percent after 10 years in retirement and by 13 percent after 35 years in retirement. This deterioration is much more modest than that of countries that use price indexation for adjusting retirement befits. This is because Romania revalues existing pensions from the first pillar on the basis of changes in the point value, which maintains the value of pensions relative to the average wage. The evaluation of income replacement that follows considers replacement rates only at retirement; it does not take into account the impact of indexation policies on replacement rates during retirement.

Replacement rates are a function of the formula governing pension benefits; an individual's contribution history; and, in the case of net replacement rates, the rules of income tax, social security contributions, and other relevant levies. The benefit formula establishes the degree to which the system redistributes income across individuals of different levels of preretirement earnings. Progressive systems provide higher levels of income replacement to people with lower levels of preretirement income. In general, the degree to which a system is redistributive depends on the existence (and value) of flat transfers and minimum pension guarantees, the degree to which benefits are earnings related, and the existence of ceilings on earnings subject to contributions. An individual's contribution history can be characterized by his or her age of entry into the labor force, contribution density, and decisions regarding the timing of retirement. To some degree, these three factors are influenced by the incentives embodied in the pension system. The tax and contribution system affects net replacement rates through the progressiveness of the income tax formula, which taxes (higher) income during a worker's active life more than it taxes (lower) pension benefits in retirement. In addition, social security levies (for pensions; unemployment; health care; and, at times, housing and family benefits) are typically reduced or eliminated altogether in retirement. These benefits are particularly important for low- to middle-income groups.

Benchmarks need to be established for the evaluation of the adequacy of the income replacement provided by the earnings-related pension schemes. Unfortunately, there is no consensus on what constitutes adequacy. According to one widely respected definition, pensions are adequate when they are sufficient to prevent poverty among the elderly and provide the vast majority of the population with a reliable mechanism for smoothing income over their lifetime. Even with a definition, however, establishing benchmarks is problematic, because attitudes vary across countries as a result of social and cultural perceptions. Moreover, benchmarks ignore the other factors that affect the welfare of the elderly—and that also vary across countries—including the existence and generosity of health insurance and long-term care, the cost of housing, the structure of traditional living arrangements, the presence of informal intrafamily or intergenerational sources of financial and nonfinancial support, and the availability and security of other mechanisms for people to save for their own retirement.

One reputable nine-country study (OECD 2001) observes that living standards are roughly comparable for people 10 years older than the normal retirement age and people 15 years younger than the normal retirement age when retirees have disposable income equal to roughly 80 percent of the disposable income of working-age people. In part, this is attributable to the fact that retirees have no work-related expenses (they do not have to commute or buy special clothing or uniforms, for example). This finding, however, does not imply that mandatory first-pillar pension schemes should actually target an 80 percent net replacement rate. To the contrary, in middle- and high-income countries, one can reasonably expect individuals to save for their own retirement—and the empirical evidence suggests that, in practice, they do so.[8] There is also some evidence to suggest that the ratio between pre- and postretirement income is somewhat independent of the income replacement mandate of the public pension system. Put simply, individuals tend to save more in countries with more modest mandates (and vice versa).

Because Romania has access to relatively well-developed financial markets, it would seem reasonable to expect middle- and higher-income workers to save enough to finance at least 25 percent, if not closer to 50 percent, of this 80 percent income replacement target. Given this, three benchmarks are provided: a 40 percent net replacement rate (which implies that individuals would be expected to save enough to finance half of the total income replacement target); a 60 percent net replacement rate (which implies that individuals would be expected to finance a quarter of the target); and an 80 percent net replacement rate (which implies that individuals, most of whom would be low-income earners, would not be expected to contribute anything toward the target).[9] In the following analysis, these three benchmarks are used to evaluate the adequacy of benefits in Romania compared with the average net replacement rate observed in 53 countries around the world, the average net replacement rate observed in selected countries in Europe and Central Asia, and the poverty line in Romania.

For an estimation of gross and net replacement rates, two critical dimensions—earnings levels and contribution periods—are considered, with the help of the Analysis of Pension Entitlements across Countries (APEX) model.[10] This model generates estimates for replacement rates under steady-state assumptions (that is, as if the rules of the reformed pension scheme had been in place over the entire active life of the individual). Because life expectancies at retirement are projected to increase over time—which will affect the benefits paid by defined-contribution pension schemes—a reference year must be chosen. The year 2040 is used here, because it provides a sufficiently long contribution period to approximate steady-state conditions.

The first critical task is to investigate levels of income replacement across a relevant spectrum of income. Income is represented as a percentage (50–200 percent) of average earnings. The second task is to investigate the impact on income replacement of differences in the duration, timing, and density of an individual's contribution history (density refers to the percentage of time an individual actually contributes over a given period). To facilitate the presentation of these multidimensional results, we compute replacement rates as a function of the age at which an individual exits the labor market. They are presented separately for full-career and partial-career workers.

Replacement rates for full-career workers Full-career workers are examined first. For the purpose of this analysis, a full career is defined as continuous employment from age 20 to the normal retirement age of 65 for men (effective in 2015). Replacement rates are simulated for an unmarried man working a hypothetical career path under the assumption that real wage growth is 2 percent, inflation is 2.5 percent, the rate of return on invested assets is 3.5 percent, and the worker retires at the statutory retirement age.

Gross replacement rates clearly show why the earnings-related pension schemes have been described as providing a strong link between benefits and contributions (figure 7.1). Irrespective of income, gross replacement rates are 72.9 percent, of which 45.0 percentage points are provided by the first pillar and 27.9 percentage are provided by the second pillar. The situation does not change significantly when taxes are taken into consideration (figure 7.2). As a result of the impact of taxes and contributions, net replacement rates vary somewhat by income.

Pensions for full-career workers in Romania can be considered adequate (figure 7.3). Replacement rates for all levels of preretirement income are substantially higher than the highest benchmark (and highest for middle-income workers), indicating that the pension system is smoothing consumption effectively from work into retirement. The objective of poverty alleviation is also being met, with levels of income replacement for full-career workers in Romania far higher than regional and world averages.[11]

Figure 7.1   Gross Replacement Rates in Romania, by Income Level

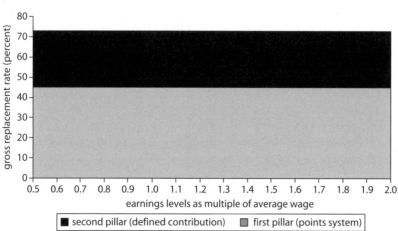

Source: APEX model.
Note: Figure shows projected replacement rate for 2040 as approximation of steady-state conditions.

Figure 7.2   Sources of Net Replacement Rates in Romania, by Income Level

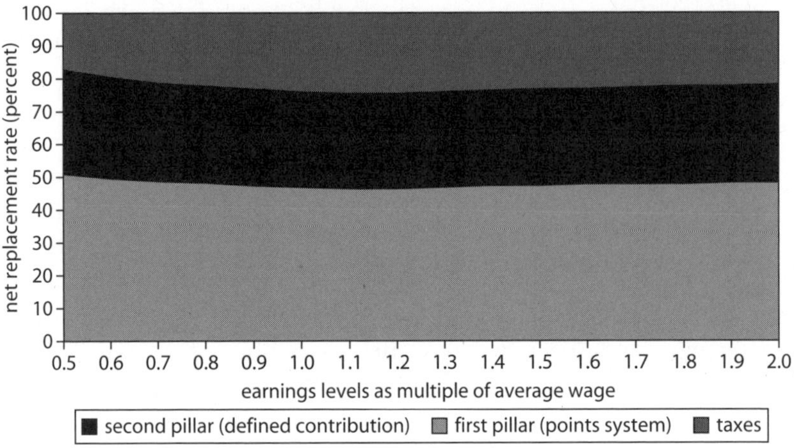

Source: APEX model.
Note: Figure shows projected replacement rate for 2040 as approximation of steady-state conditions.

Figure 7.3   Net Replacement Rates for Male Full-Career Workers in Romania, Europe and Central Asia, and the World

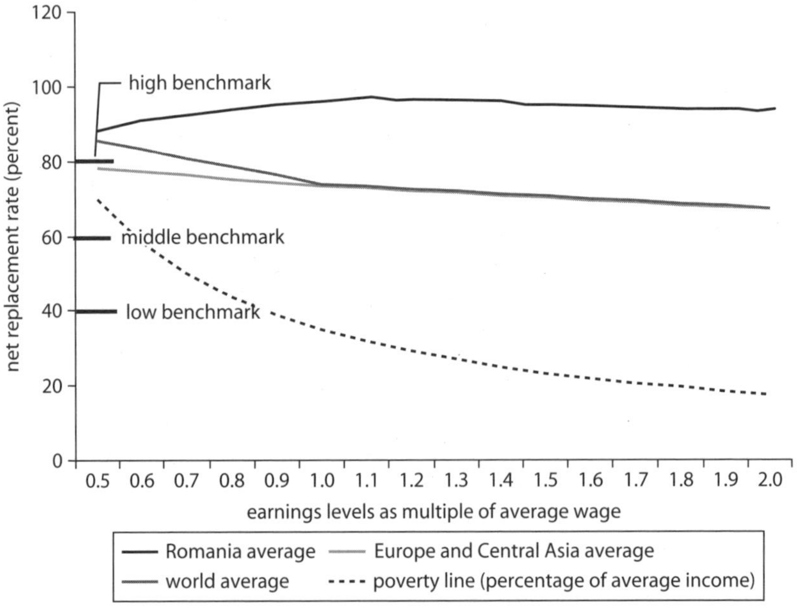

Source: Authors' calculations based on World Bank 2007a and the APEX model.
Note: Figure shows projected replacement rate for 2040 as approximation of steady-state conditions.

Replacement rates for partial-career workers. Not everyone works from age 20 to the statutory retirement age. Many individuals enter and exit the labor force (often at different ages and for different periods of time) and earn different wages while working (figure 7.4). To examine the adequacy of benefits for partial-career workers, we consider three stylized cases. These cases include career type A (someone entering the labor force at age 25 who works continuously for a period of years before leaving the workforce at some point between the ages of 50 and 70 and then claims a benefit); career type B (identical to career type A, except that the worker enters the workforce at age 30 and leaves no earlier than age 55); and career type C (identical to career type A, except that the individual contributes in only three years out of four while in the labor force). In cases where the withdrawal from the formal labor market occurs before the statutory retirement age, the pension is claimed (and the replacement rate calculated) only at the later age. For withdrawals after the statutory retirement age, the ages coincide.

Four conclusions can be drawn from examination of net replacement rates for middle-income partial-career workers.[12] First, almost all workers

Figure 7.4   Net Replacement Rates for Male Middle-Income Partial-Career Workers in Romania, by Career Type and Exit Age

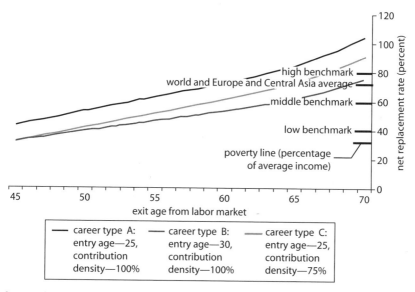

Source: Authors' calculations based on World Bank 2007a and the APEX model.
Note: Figure shows projected replacement rate for 2040 as approximation of steady-state conditions. See text for descriptions of career types.

receive levels of income replacement higher than the poverty line. Second, leaving the workforce very early can be costly. Someone retiring long before reaching the retirement age will receive levels of income replacement barely higher (and, in some cases, lower) than the lowest of the three benchmarks. Third, entering the workforce later in life is costly. Someone entering the workforce at age 30 receives a net replacement rate that is 11–13 percentage points lower than someone entering the workforce at age 25. Fourth, working intermittently is costly. Someone entering the workforce at the same age but who contributes only three years out of four will receive a net replacement rate that is 11–29 percentage points lower than someone who contributes continuously. Although career type A workers can attain the 80 percent benchmark before reaching the normal retirement age, career type B workers must work three years beyond the normal retirement age in order to attain this benchmark. Career type C workers will not be able to attain the 80 percent benchmark even if they work until age 70.

Fiscal Sustainability

The sustainability of a pay-as-you-go first-pillar pension scheme is best evaluated in actuarial terms by estimating the scheme's actuarial deficit as the difference between its assets and liabilities. If a large actuarial deficit exists, the scheme is financially unsustainable and needs policy actions that increase its assets, reduce its liabilities, or both. A good proxy for the actuarial deficit is the difference between the present value of the scheme's expected future revenues (that is, contributions and other income) and expected future expenditures (that is, benefit payments, administrative costs, and other expenses) over an extended projection period. The difference between these two values represents an unfunded liability (sometimes referred to as a financing gap) on the public-sector balance sheet. Because this study is also concerned with the time path of revenues and expenditures (and the resulting balance across the projection period ending in 2050), this more pragmatic approach has been taken. Projections of expenditures, revenues, and deficits are presented on the basis of available postreform fiscal projections.

Despite (and, in part, because of) the government 's reforms, the first-pillar scheme is projected to continue generating deficits, which are expected to grow for the next three decades relative to GDP before improving slightly (figure 7.5). Rising deficits are caused partly by the need to finance the transition to the second pillar. Revenues are projected to decline steadily, from 6.6 percent of GDP to 3.4 percent of GDP by 2050, as the number of contributors declines and an increasing share of

Figure 7.5   Projected Fiscal Balance of Romania's Public Pension System after Reform, 2008–50

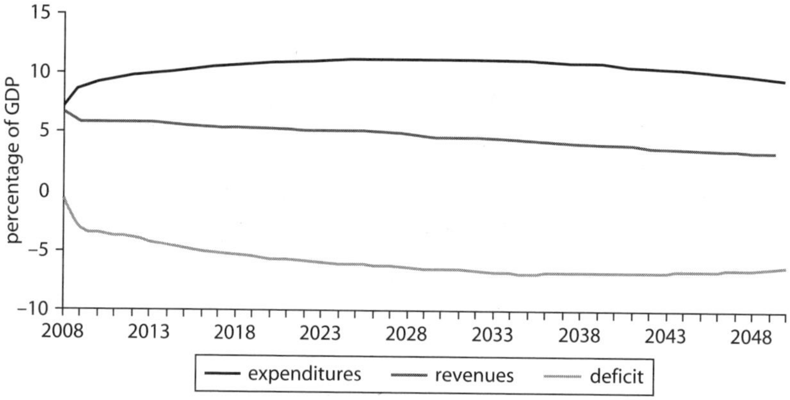

Source: Unpublished World Bank Pension Reform Options Simulation Toolkit (PROST) projections.

contributions is diverted from the first to the second pillar.[13] Over the same period, expenditures are projected to increase from 7.2 percent of GDP in 2008 to 9.6 percent of GDP by 2050 as the number of beneficiaries increases and benefits are indexed to wages. The net result is a projected deficit of 6.2 percent of GDP in 2050.

These projected deficits are also driven by the aging of the population. Romania's old-age dependency ratio is projected to increase from 23.6 percent in 2008 to 55.3 percent by 2050 (figure 7.6). The aging of the population, in turn, will raise the system dependency ratio (the number of people receiving a pension divided by the number of people contributing to the pension scheme) from 56.9 percent in 2008 to 95.9 percent by 2050.[14]

What options exist for restoring the system to fiscal balance? Unfortunately, for policy makers, the options are limited. Revenues can be increased by increasing the contribution rate. Alternatively—or in addition, because the options are not exclusive—expenditures can be reduced by cutting benefits, increasing the minimum number of years required to become eligible for benefits, or delaying the payment of benefits by raising the retirement age further. Because raising the contribution rate could threaten competitiveness and will likely strengthen incentives for tax evasion, it is typically not embraced. Raising the contribution rate would also represent a reversal of policy because Romania has been deliberately reducing the rate to dampen the adverse impact of high taxes on labor markets. This leaves policy makers with limited

Figure 7.6   Projected Old-Age and System Dependency Ratios in Romania, 2008–50

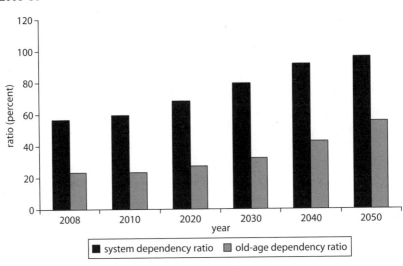

Sources: Unpublished World Bank Pension Reform Options Simulation Toolkit (PROST) projections; Reiterer 2008.

options: cutting benefits, tightening eligibility conditions, or raising the retirement age. Given that a major part of the deficit reflects the transition costs associated with the second pillar, the government may also consider financing part or all of these costs using general revenues. If it does otherwise, restoring sustainability may reduce the adequacy of benefits provided to future beneficiaries.

If retirement ages are left unchanged and the current structure of the system is retained, further cuts in benefits—on the order of a 59 percent reduction in the average benefit provided under the first pillar—will be required for the system to become sustainable (figure 7.7). If benefits are adjusted to maintain a similar fiscal balance in proportion to the overall size of the first-pillar scheme, full-career workers will receive replacement rates that are roughly 28 percentage points lower in 2050 than they are today.

Two conclusions can be drawn from comparing these new (lower) net replacement rates with the three benchmarks. First, a 59 percent reduction in first-pillar benefits would not cause income replacement for full-career workers to fall below the poverty line, except for those with very low incomes. This indicates that Romania's pension system would still broadly achieve its poverty alleviation objective. Second, the same reduction in benefits would still support the objective of smoothing

Figure 7.7   Net Replacement Rates for Male Workers in Romania before and after Benefit Adjustment

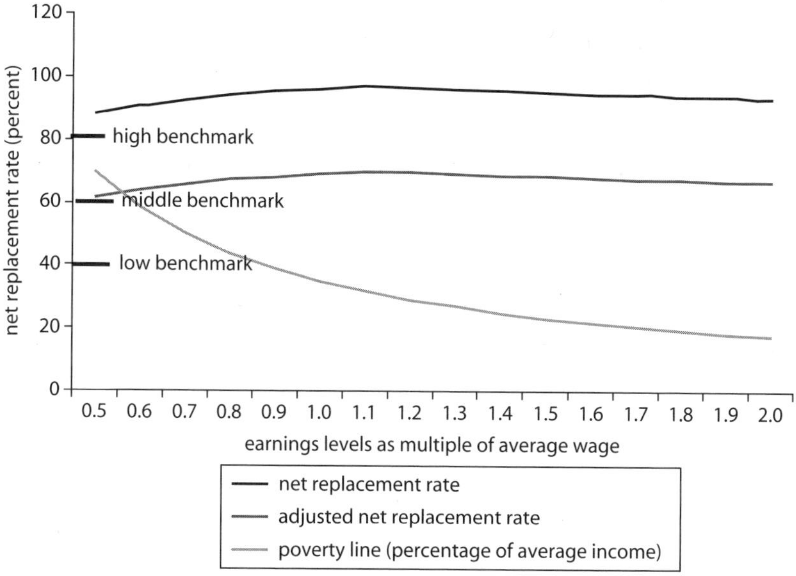

Source: Authors' calculations based on World Bank 2007a and the APEX model.

consumption for middle- and high-income full-career workers, because levels of income replacement are still equal to or higher than the middle 60 percent benchmark. Replacement rates for low-income workers, however, would fall substantially below the 80 percent benchmark.

This last observation is subject to three caveats. First, this analysis considers only full-career workers, while the average worker now contributes for only about 27–30 years, substantially less than the 45 years of a full career. Contributing to the pension scheme for only 35 years, for example, reduces net income replacement 23 percentage points for middle-income workers. This suggests that restoring the system to fiscal balance on the basis of benefit cuts alone may not provide many partial-career workers with adequate levels of income replacement. Second, if benefit cuts are combined with further increases in the retirement age, the benefit cuts will not need to be as steep to restore fiscal balance. Third, workers always have the option of saving outside of the first-pillar pension scheme. To increase income replacement by 1 percent, for example, a full-career worker would need to save only about 0.43 percent of his or her earnings from age 40 to the current age of retirement.[15]

Conclusions

Recognizing that a pension system that offers generous benefits, low retirement ages, and lax benefit eligibility conditions would not be sustainable over the long term as the population ages, Romania's government introduced substantial pension system reforms in 2000. These reforms raised retirement ages, extended the service period required to become eligible for a full pension, imposed new conditions on early retirement, and replaced the traditional defined-benefit formula with a new formula based on points. In 2006, the government also passed legislation to introduce a mandatory, fully funded, defined-contribution scheme, which became operational in May 2008.

The resulting gross and net replacement rates for full-career workers after reform are projected to be well above regional and world averages, especially for middle- and high-income workers (see chapter 1). Future net replacement rates for full-career workers are projected to be 88–97 percent across the analyzed income spectrum. The generosity of these initial replacement rates is enhanced by generous indexation policies, which will fully index first-pillar benefits to wages. As in other countries, workers with less than full careers—because they left the workforce before reaching retirement age, worked intermittently, or have gaps in their employment history—risk receiving a level of income replacement closer to the lower benchmark of 40 percent or possibly even lower.

Following reform, Romania's pension system is projected to generate ever-larger deficits relative to GDP for the next three decades before improving slightly to 6.2 percent of GDP by 2050. These deficits are driven by the aging of the population, as well as by the generous benefits in the reformed system (especially given recent large increases in benefits) and the transition costs associated with replacing part of the unfunded first-pillar scheme with a funded second-pillar scheme. Population aging by itself will reduce the number of contributors relative to the number of beneficiaries to such an extent that by 2050 the number of pension system beneficiaries will approach the number of contributors. The lower retirement age applied to women, in combination with their longer life expectancy, greatly increases their lifetime benefit costs relative to their contributions.

To restore long-term fiscal balance to the first-pillar scheme without recourse to general revenue financing, the government needs to raise retirement ages further—rough estimates suggest to well above age 70 by 2050. To realize the full fiscal impact of this measure, the government must maintain income replacement at levels associated with current retirement ages. Increasing the retirement age in step with increases in life expectancy at retirement is a natural choice, for both individuals and for policy makers, but it requires cross-sectoral policy reforms to enable elderly workers to continue to participate in the labor market.[16]

Other options for restoring fiscal balance including cutting first-pillar benefits at retirement, reducing the generosity of benefit indexation, or adopting some combination of the two. Rough estimates suggest that average first-pillar replacement rates would have to fall by about 28 percentage points. Moving from wage to price indexation would reduce average first-pillar benefits by some 25 percentage points. Reducing benefits by this amount would not compromise the objective of alleviating poverty among the elderly, because levels of income replacement would still not fall anywhere near the poverty line. Doing so may, however, compromise the objective of smoothing lifetime consumption for full-career workers of all income levels when measured against the highest of the three benchmarks examined here. Individuals who wish to defer more of their lifetime consumption into retirement would still have the option, of course, of participating in the voluntary third-pillar pension scheme.

Notes

1. The required contribution rate under the old system would have needed to be increased from 25.5 percent to 50 percent in the long term for the system to provide the same level of benefits provided now (World Bank 1998).

2. For more information regarding these population projections, see Reiterer (2008).

3. In 2007, the average number of points of existing pensioners was 1.38.

4. As a percentage of the gross average wage, the point value was about 31.0 percent in 2006, 37.5 percent in 2007, and 37.5 percent in 2008; it will rise to 45 percent in 2009. Existing pensions are revalued on the basis of changes in the point value by multiplying an individual's average points by the new point value. The increase in the point value over the past few years resulted in pensions rising faster than wages, because the point value, as a share of the average wage, increased from 30 percent to 45 percent (in 2009)—an increase of 50 percent.

5. In 2007, life expectancy at retirement age was 13.6 years for men and 20.9 years for women. These values are projected to increase to 16.0 years for men and 24.4 years for women by 2050. Lengthening life expectancy will substantially increase the average period over which benefits are paid. Many

pension systems worldwide are designed to provide individuals with 15 years of benefits in retirement (Schwarz 2006).

6. The law does not specify by how much first-pillar benefits will be reduced when contributions are made to the funded second-pillar scheme. This study assumes that the reduction will be proportional to the reduced share of contributions flowing to the first pillar.

7. The second-pillar pension scheme will eventually provide these benefits as well; many of the provisions governing the payment of benefits have yet to be determined.

8. In Chile, for instance, 70 percent of retirees from the mandatory public pension system own their home, which is a form of savings (Valdés-Prieto 2008).

9. These benchmarks approximate the standards developed by the International Labour Organization (ILO) (1952) and the Council of Europe (1990). ILO Convention 102 of 1952 sets a minimum benefit equal to 40 percent of the reference wage for married men of pensionable age. This amount was raised to 45 percent in 1968. The European Code of Security of 1990 sets a minimum standard for members of the Council of Europe equal to 65 percent for married people of a specific age.

10. The APEX model was developed by Axia Economics, with funding from the Organisation for Economic Co-operation and Development and the World Bank. The model codes detailed eligibility and benefit rules for first- and second-pillar schemes based on available public information that has been verified by country contacts. Because the details of the rules sometimes change on short notice (and limited public disclosure), the calculations presented here should be considered as best approximations only.

11. As a proxy for the poverty line, a figure of 35 percent of the average net wage is used, because this percentage broadly approximates a US$2.25-a-day poverty line converted into national currency, adjusted for purchasing power parity, expressed relative to the national average net wage, and averaged across the eight study countries.

12. Only middle-income, partial-career workers are examined because replacement rates are comparable for workers with lower and higher levels of pre-retirement income.

13. Projections reflect the 1.5 percentage point decrease in the contribution rate planned by the government as well as the diverting of contribution revenues to the second pillar.

14. Over the same period, the population is projected to decrease from 21.5 million to 17.1 million (Reiterer 2008).

15. This estimate is based on the assumption that real wage growth is 2.0 percent, the net real rate of return on invested assets is 3.5 percent, and benefits (from both the unfunded and the funded pillars) are price indexed.

16. See Holzmann, MacKellar, and Repansek (2009) for a conference volume that addresses these issues for the countries of southeastern Europe.

Bibliography

Council of Europe. 1990. *European Code of Social Security (Revised)*. Rome.

European Commission. 2007. Mutual Information System and Social Protection (MISSOC) database. http://ec.europa.eu/employment_social/.

GVG (Gesellschaft für Versicherungswissenschaft und -gestaltung) and European Commission. 2003. *Study on the Social Protection Systems in the 13 Applicant Countries: Romania Country Report*. Cologne.

Holzmann, R., and R. Hinz. 2005. *Old-Age Income Support in the 21st Century*. Washington, DC: World Bank.

Holzmann, R., L. MacKellar, and J. Repansek, eds. 2009. *Pension Reform in Southeastern Europe: Linking to Labor and Financial Market Reforms*. Washington, DC: World Bank.

ILO (International Labour Organisation). 1952. *ILO Convention 102*. Geneva: ILO.

———. 1967. *ILO Convention 128*. Geneva: ILO.

OECD (Organisation for Economic Co-operation and Development). n.d. Database. http://www.oecd.org/dataoecd/13/30/38708660.pdf.

———. 2001. *Ageing and Income: Financial Resources and Retirement in 9 OECD Countries*. OECD: Paris.

Reiterer, A. 2008. *Population Development and Age Structure in Southeastern Europe until 2050*. World Bank, Washington, DC.

Schwarz, A. 2006. Background paper for *Public Expenditure Review: Overview of Pension Sector in Serbia*. World Bank, Washington, DC.

U.S. Social Security Administration. 2006 *Social Security Systems throughout the World: Europe*. Washington, DC: Social Security Administration.

Valdés-Prieto, S. 2008. *Designs for the First Pillar Pensions and the 2008 Chilean Reform*. http://editorialexpress.com/cgi-bin/conference/download.cgi?db_name=SECHI2008&paper_id=130.

Whitehouse, E. 1999. *Tax Treatment of Funded Pensions*. Washington, DC: World Bank.

World Bank. 1998. *Romania: Pension Reform Note*. Washington, DC: World Bank.

———. 2003. *Romania Poverty Assessment*. Washington, DC: World Bank.

———. 2004. *The Pension System in Romania: Challenges of Pursuing an Integrated Reform Strategy*. Washington, DC: World Bank.

———. 2006. Background paper for the Romania Poverty Assessment. World Bank, Washington, DC.

————. 2007a. *Pensions Panorama*. Washington, DC: World Bank.

————. 2007b. Background paper for the *Romania Poverty Monitoring Analytical and Advisory Assistance Program*. World Bank, Washington, DC.

WHO (World Health Organization). 2000. *Healthcare Systems in Transition: Romania*. Copenhagen: WHO.

————. 2008. Database. http://www.who.int/research/en/.

CHAPTER 8

The Slovak Republic

Following the dissolution of Czechoslovakia in 1993, the Slovak Republic inherited a public pension system financed on a pay-as-you-go basis (meaning that contributions from current workers are used to pay benefits to current beneficiaries). The pension system effected considerable redistribution of income from the comparatively well-off population to those less fortunate. This loose connection between contributions and benefits, combined with the increased informality in labor markets, caused revenues to gradually decline, from an amount equivalent to 8 percent of gross domestic product (GDP) in the mid-1990s to about 7 percent by 2002. With expenditures hovering around 7.3 percent of GDP during this period, the fiscal condition of the pension system began to deteriorate.

In 1999, the system experienced its first deficit. Projections suggested the pension scheme would face even greater fiscal challenges in the future, as a result of the rapidly aging population, with deficits eventually reaching an amount equivalent to 10 percent of GDP.

Recognizing the need for reform, the government introduced major systemic changes to the existing pay-as-you-go scheme in 2004 intended to arrest growing deficits and restore fiscal balance. In 2005, it introduced a privately managed, fully funded defined-contribution scheme. Together, these reforms have considerably improved the fiscal health of the pension system. Projections suggest that deficits will reach 4.4 percent of GDP by 2050—less than half their previous level.

The aging of the Slovak population will almost certainly compel the government to enact further reforms. Further improvements will require that benefits be made less generous or retirement ages be raised further (or some combination of both), a tradeoff that will become even more pronounced as people live longer.

Against this backdrop, this chapter evaluates the Slovak Republic's pension system, focusing on fiscal sustainability and benefit adequacy. Adequacy is evaluated through the lens of statutory net replacement rates for different retirement ages, patterns of contributions, and income levels relative to international benchmarks.

This chapter is organized as follows. The next section discusses the motivation for the reforms. The following section describes the key characteristics of the reformed pension system. The third section assesses the adequacy of pension benefits and the fiscal sustainability of the system. The last section draws conclusions.

Motivation for Reform

Following independence from Czechoslovakia, the Slovak Republic underwent a difficult transition from central planning to a market economy. The difficulty of this transition was reflected in the fiscal balance of the pension system, which experienced declining contribution revenues (as a result of increasing informality in the labor markets, higher formal-sector unemployment, and stagnant—at times falling—average wages) and relatively constant expenditure (because the number of beneficiaries remained relatively flat).[1]

By 1999, the pension system began generating deficits (table 8.1). Although these deficits were not huge relative to GDP, projections suggested they would grow to unaffordable levels as a result of the aging of the population. By 2050, revenues were expected to hover around 6.5–7.0 percent of GDP while expenditures were expected to increase to 16.4 percent of GDP, resulting in deficits of roughly 10 percent of GDP (figure 8.1). For Slovak policy makers, this was the impetus for reform.

The aging of the Slovak population was largely behind these projections. The old-age dependency ratio (the population age 65 and older divided by the population age 20–64) was projected to increase from 18.3 percent in 2005 to 54.9 percent by 2050 (Reiterer 2008) (figure 8.2). The system dependency ratio was projected to increase from 52 percent

Table 8.1   Fiscal Balance of the Slovak Republic's Pension System before Reform, 1995–2002

(percentage of GDP)

Year	Revenues	Expenditures	Balance
1995	7.8	7.3	0.5
1996	8.1	7.3	0.8
1997	7.3	7.2	0.1
1998	7.3	7.3	0.0
1999	6.8	7.4	−0.6
2000	7.3	7.5	−0.2
2001	6.9	7.4	−0.5
2002	6.9	7.3	−0.4

Source: World Bank 2004.

Figure 8.1   Projected Fiscal Balance of the Slovak Republic's Public Pension Scheme before Reform, 2000–50

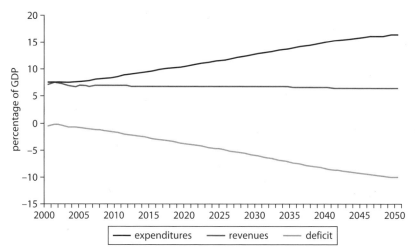

Source: Unpublished World Bank Pension Reform Options Simulation Toolkit (PROST) simulations.

in 2005 to 102 percent by 2050, suggesting that the number of beneficiaries would eventually exceed the number of contributors. Projections
suggested that 2.4 contributors were needed per beneficiary for the
scheme to be sustainable (World Bank 2004).

To address the problem, in 2004 the government redesigned the
parameters of the existing pay-as-you-go system by switching from a
defined-benefit formula for computing pension benefits to a system
based on points. Under a points system, individuals are awarded

Figure 8.2   Projected Old-Age and System Dependency Ratios in the Slovak Republic before Reform, 2005–50

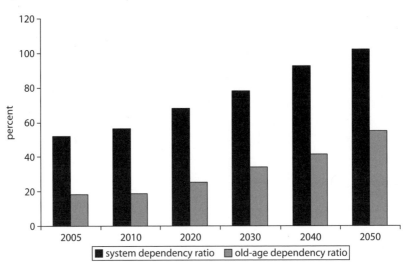

Sources: Reiterer 2008; unpublished World Bank Pension Reform Options Simulation Toolkit (PROST) simulations.

points for each year they contribute, where points are a function of the ratio of their earnings relative to the economywide average wage. At retirement, benefits are based on the total number of points accumulated. In 2005, the government introduced a mandatory fully funded defined-contribution scheme, whereby benefits depend on the amount of an individual's contributions and the rates of return earned on invested assets.

Characteristics of the Slovak Republic's Pension System

This section describes the main characteristics of the Slovak Republic's pension system. They include the design of the individual pillars of social insurance; the rules governing pension system taxation, institutional structure, and coverage; and the provisions governing old-age, disability, and survivorship pensions. The design of the pension system is assessed using a conceptual framework developed by the World Bank, which generally recommends including a funded component if conditions are appropriate but increasingly recognizes that a range of choices is available to policy makers to provide effective old-age protection in a manner that is fiscally responsible (see Holzmann and Hinz 2005).

In general, the World Bank supports pension systems composed of some combination of five basic pillars:

- a noncontributory (or zero) pillar (in the form of a demogrant, social pension, or social assistance benefit) intended to provide a minimal level of income protection;
- a first-pillar contributory system linked to earnings, which seeks to replace a portion of preretirement income;
- a mandatory second pillar (essentially, individual savings accounts), which can be designed in various ways;
- a voluntary third pillar, which is flexible and discretionary (this pillar, too, can take a variety of forms); and
- a fourth pillar of informal intrafamily or intergenerational sources of financial and nonfinancial support to the elderly, including access to health care and housing.

Pillar Design

The design of the Slovak pension system incorporates all five of the pillars recommended by the World Bank (table 8.2). The publicly managed non-contributory zero pillar, financed with general tax revenues, redistributes income to lower-income groups using means testing. The reference point for computing the amount of an individual's benefit is the minimum subsistence level, which implies that the noncontributory benefit is adjusted as the subsistence level is changed. Both the traditional publicly managed pay-as-you-go first pillar and the privately managed, fully funded second pillar are earnings-related schemes. First-pillar benefits are computed on the basis of the number of points accumulated over the course of an individual's career. Postretirement benefits are indexed using a combination of wage and price growth (Swiss indexation), whereby benefits increase with wages but at a lower rate. Second-pillar benefits are a function of an individual's contributions and investment earnings. At retirement, account balances are converted into annuities based on the accumulated capital in an individual's account and the individual's conditional life expectancy. Supplementing these earnings-related schemes is a voluntary privately managed third pillar, intended to provide individuals with a mechanism for adding to the benefits provided by the mandatory pillars. The fourth pillar provides health care to the elderly as part of the overall health care system.

The taxation of contributions and benefits varies across pillars. The zero, first, and fourth pillars are completely exempted from taxation. The

Table 8.2 Structure of the Slovak Pension System

Scheme type	Coverage	Type	Function	Financing	Generic benefit	Benefit indexation	Taxation		
							Contributions	Investment income/capital gains	Benefits
Zero pillar (public noncontributory)	Universal	Means tested	Redistributive	Tax revenues	Difference between minimum subsistence level and actual income	Minimum subsistence level (close to consumer price index)	n.a.	n.a.	Exempt
First pillar (public, earnings related)	Mandatory	Points	Insurance	Percentage of individual earnings	Based on the number of points earned	50 percent inflation, 50 percent nominal wage growth	Exempt	n.a.	Exempt
Second pillar (private, earnings related)	Mandatory	Defined contribution	Insurance	Percentage of individual earnings	Pension from capital accumulation	Depends on options chosen	Exempt	Taxed	Exempt
Third pillar (private, voluntary)	Voluntary	Defined contribution	Insurance	Voluntary contributions	Pension from capital accumulation	Depends on options chosen	Exempt[a]	Exempt	Taxed
Fourth pillar (public health care)	Mandatory	n.a.	Insurance	Percentage of individual earnings plus tax revenues	Basic health service package	n.a.	Exempt	n.a.	n.a.

Sources: European Commission 2007a, 2007b; World Bank 2004.

n.a. = Not applicable.

a. An amount up to 12,000 koruny annually is exempt from taxation.

second pillar is subject to an exempt-taxed-exempt regime, meaning that contributions are exempt from taxation, investment income is taxed, and benefits are exempt. The third pillar is subject to a classic expenditure tax (exempt-exempt-taxed) in which contributions (up to 12,000 koruny [SK] annually) and investment returns are exempt from taxation while benefits are taxed. (For a discussion of the taxation of retirement savings, see box 1.1 in chapter 1.)

Noncontributory scheme. In the Slovak Republic, the elderly are eligible for a noncontributory benefit as part of a general program of social assistance designed to provide a minimum level of income protection to the overall population irrespective of age. Both elderly pensioners and elderly people who are ineligible for a pension may apply for assistance. The amount of the benefit varies as a function of household income and size: higher benefits are paid to households with no other sources of income, while lower benefits are paid to households with modest income from other sources. The computation of the social assistance benefit for elderly people who contributed to the pension system for at least 25 years takes into account only 75 percent of their pension, with an additional 1 percent decrease with each additional year of contributions before retirement. Once a pensioner's benefit has been adjusted, the resulting figure is increased to ensure that total household income meets the minimum income thresholds established by law. At the end of 2007, social assistance benefits were paid to 182,479 beneficiaries, at a cost equivalent to 0.45 percent of GDP. There were 38,606 beneficiaries of pensionable age (21.2 percent of all beneficiaries).

Earnings-related schemes. Before reform, the Slovak pension system was highly redistributive, partly as a result of a cap on the accumulation of benefits. Although redistribution in a pension system is not necessarily a design flaw, the cap created an incentive for workers and employers to underreport earnings (which may have contributed to the fiscal problems of the pension system in the late 1990s, during the country's transition to a market economy). The reforms of 2004 eliminated the minimum pension, consistent with the separation of social insurance from social assistance. Social assistance benefits are now used to provide any needed redistribution, while the social insurance program is used as a contribution-based instrument of savings (World Bank 2004).

Under the reformed system, first-pillar benefits are now computed on the basis of the number of points accumulated throughout an individual's career, a change that ensures that benefits reflect lifetime wages. A point system effectively mimics a notional account approach to pension reform.[2] The former system, which used a complicated (and highly redistributive) formula based on the individual's best years of wages, was abolished. Contributions are now paid up to a wage of four times the average wage; benefits are computed on the basis of wages up to three times the average wage (under the old system benefits were based on a number of best years' wages).[3] Benefits are actuarially reduced for early retirement and increased for delayed retirement. Postretirement benefits are indexed using Swiss indexation. These reforms improved transparency and tightened the link between contributions and benefits, which reduced incentives for noncompliance.

Before reform, retirement ages were very low: life expectancy at retirement age was 16.8 years for men and 25.1 years for women (unpublished World Bank Pension Reform Options Simulation Toolkit [PROST] simulations). To combat the pressures created by these low retirement ages and gradually increasing life expectancies, retirement ages are gradually being increased to age 62 for both men and women (table 8.3). This will reduce the average period of benefit collection to 15.7 years for men and 20.8 years for women. The change will reduce benefit costs and increase pension system revenue, because workers will contribute to the scheme for more years. Even with these changes, however, retirement ages remain low, especially for women given their substantially higher life expectancy.

In 2005, the government introduced a mandatory fully funded defined-contribution scheme, consistent with its broader objective of moving away from a pension system based entirely on a single pillar.[4] In the new two-pillar structure, half of the contributions go to the newly established second scheme while the other half continue to finance first-pillar benefits.

Voluntary scheme. In 2005, the voluntary third-pillar pension scheme (previously available only to workers with an established employee–employer relationship) was opened to people over age 18 (table 8.4). Benefits are awarded to people over age 55 after a minimum of 10 years of contributions. Participation is encouraged through tax policy. Contributions made by employees to the scheme are deductible from personal income taxes up to an annual ceiling of Sk 12,000. Contributions made by employers on behalf of their employees are deductible from enterprise taxes up to 6 percent of wages. Part of an individual's account balance can be distributed as a lump sum upon reaching retirement, provided certain conditions are met.

Table 8.3 Parameters of Earnings-Related Schemes in the Slovak Republic before and after Reform

Scheme type	Period	Vesting period	Contribution rate	Contribution ceiling	Benefit rate	Pension assessment base	Retirement age
First pillar (earnings related)	Prereform	25 years	28 percent (21.6 percent by employer, 6.4 percent by employee)	Sk 32,000	2 percent accrual rate for first 25 years, 1 percent for next 17 years	Highest 5 of last 10 years average	60 for men, 53–57 for women depending on number of children
	Postreform	15 years	18 percent[a] (4 percent by employee, 14 percent by employer)	3 times average wage	1.19 percent per year	Lifetime average indexed to nominal wage growth	62 for all (men by 2007, women by 2016)
Second pillar (earnings related)	Prereform	n.a.	n.a.	n.a.	n.a.	n.a.	n.a.
	Postreform	10 years	9 percent by employer	3 times average wage	Pension from capital accumulation	Accumulated funds	62 for all

Sources: European Commission 2007a, 2007b; World Bank 2004.

n.a = Not applicable.

a. The total contribution for the old-age, disability, and survivors pensions reserve fund is 28.75 percent (18 percent for old-age reserve fund, 6 percent for disability reserve fund, and 4.75 percent for employer reserve fund). Individuals participating only in the first pillar pay 18 percent to the first pillar for old-age coverage (14 percent by employer, 4 by employee). Individuals participating in both the first and the second pillars pay 9 percent (5 percent by employer, 4 percent by employee) to the first pillar and 9 percent (entirely employer) to the second pillar for old-age coverage.

Table 8.4   Characteristics of the Voluntary Scheme in the Slovak Republic

Coverage	Vesting period	Retirement age	Tax advan- tages to par- ticipants	Contributions tax deductible by employers	Lump-sum payments possible in retirement
Anyone over age 18	10 years	55	Yes	Yes	Yes

Source: European Commission 2007b; U.S. Slovak Embassy Web site (http://www.slovakembassy-us.org).

In the event of disability, the account balance, including any investment earnings, is distributed to the participant or, in case of death, to his or her survivors. In 2006, assets of the scheme amounted to 1 percent of GDP. Some 673,352 people (17.4 percent of the working-age population) participated (Čillíková 2006).

Health care system. Health care in the Slovak Republic is provided primarily through the mandatory health insurance scheme, administered by one of five health insurance companies. It is financed primarily by contributions and by copayments for some medical services and pharmaceuticals. Voluntary health insurance is also available, although participation is negligible.

Contributions to the mandatory health insurance scheme from the economically active population constitute about 70 percent of the total; contributions from the government on behalf of the nonactive population (including pensioners) constitute 30 percent. The contribution rate of 14 percent (10 percentage points of which are paid by employers and 4 percentage points by employees) is levied on income between the minimum wage and a ceiling of three times the average wage. The government contributes 4 percent of the average wage on behalf of the nonactive population, which represents 60 percent of the total population (World Bank 2002). All insured people, including the elderly, have access to the same basic health care benefits specified by law.

In 2005, health expenditure accounted for 7.0 percent of GDP, 74.4 percent of which was public expenditure and 25.6 percent was private expenditure. Of the private expenditure, 88.1 percent was attributable to out-of-pocket expenditure (informal payments, direct payments, and copayments) (WHO 2008).

Institutional Structure and Coverage of Earnings-Related Schemes

The mandatory pillars of the Slovak pension system cover all salaried employees and the self-employed, including farmers. Voluntary participation is open to individuals older than age 16 and to the self-employed who earn less than the minimum wage. Special provisions are in place for the police corps, the Slovak information service, the national security authority, the prison and justice guard corps, railway police, and customs officers.

The Social Insurance Agency is responsible for administering the public system. It collects contributions for both the first and the second pillars, acting as a clearinghouse (meaning that it transfers second-pillar contributions to designated pension-fund management companies, thereby reducing the logistical burden on employers). Roughly 85.5 percent of the labor force (59.4 percent of the working-age population) contributes to the first pillar, of which 70 percent also participate in the second pillar.

In 2006, six pension-fund management companies were operating in the mandatory (second-pillar) pension fund market and four companies were operating in the voluntary (third-pillar) market. Private pension-fund management companies must be licensed by the National Bank of Slovakia, which oversees them. Pension fund management companies are required to offer three funds—a conservative fund, a balanced fund, and a growth fund—each governed by different portfolio investment guidelines. The conservative fund is limited to investing in bonds and money market instruments. The balanced fund can invest up to 50 percent of its assets in equities, while the growth fund can invest up to 80 percent in equities. Rules on external investment are liberal: only 30 percent of investments must remain in the country. Even this requirement is under review as potentially in conflict with European Union rules on the free flow of capital among member countries.

Structure of Benefits

The earnings-related pension schemes provide old-age, disability, and survivorship pensions. The provisions governing each of these types of benefits are discussed as follows.

Old-age benefits. In the first-pillar scheme, participants must have at least 15 years of service and must reach the minimum retirement age to be eligible for an old-age pension. Retirement ages for men were increased from 60 to 62 between 2004 and 2006, at the rate of 9 months per year. Under the old rules, the retirement age for women ranged from 53 to 58 (as a function of the number of children). Under the new rules, the age is being raised at the rate of 9 months per year, such that the retirement age for all women, regardless of the number of children, will be 62 by 2015.

Benefits from the first pillar are computed on the basis of a point system. People enrolled in the reformed first pillar (but not the second pillar), most of whom are older, accrue benefits at the rate of 1.19 percent per year of service. People enrolled in both the reformed first pillar and the new second pillar accrue benefits under the first pillar at half the rate (meaning their accrual rate is 0.6 percent); the remainder of their benefits come from their individual investment account (only half of their contributions are used to pay for the cost of their benefits under the first pillar).

People with at least 15 years of contributions may retire at any age before reaching the minimum retirement age, but their benefits are penalized by 6 percent per year until they reach the minimum retirement age. Early retirement is not permitted if the resulting pension is less than 1.2 times the subsistence income.

Retirement can be deferred after a person reaches the minimum retirement age. Benefits are increased by 6 percent for each year retirement is deferred. For pensioners who continue to work or who reenter the workforce after retiring once, the pension is recalculated when they retire the second time, with half of the points earned since their first retirement credited toward their pension.

Participants in the second pillar may elect to have some of the proceeds of their account paid in a lump sum or as a programmed withdrawal over a prespecified time period, as long as the remainder of their funds are sufficient to purchase a life annuity from an insurance company equal to or larger than 60 percent of the subsistence minimum. In the case of programmed withdrawals, the pension fund company must continue to invest assets in the account. Each year, as a function of the returns earned on invested assets, a monthly withdrawal amount is computed such that the account will be completely exhausted by the end of the term of the contract.

Disability benefits. Disability benefits are available to both individuals enrolled only in the first-pillar scheme and to those enrolled in both the first- and second-pillar schemes (table 8.5). Disabled people enrolled only in the first pillar are given credit for years lost to disability. Benefits are based on the worker's average wage at the time of disability. For people with 40–70 percent impairment, the pension is reduced by the extent of their disability. When the individual reaches the minimum retirement age, the disability pension is replaced by the old-age pension to which he or she would have been entitled. For fully disabled people who do not work after becoming disabled, the two pensions are equal, because their disability pension gives them credit for having worked a full career. For disabled people enrolled in both the first and second pillars, since January 2008 benefits have been determined by the first-pillar rules only, with years of disability excluded from the old-age pension calculation under the first pillar. As of January 2008, the disability fund stopped paying contributions to the second pillar, which now provides no disability benefits.

Survivor benefits. Survivor benefits are awarded under both the first and second pillars to the dependents of individuals who at the time of their death were receiving (or had met the criteria to receive) an old-age or disability pension (table 8.6). Eligible survivors include widows or widowers and orphaned children. Spouses receive 60 percent of the deceased's

Table 8.5   Eligibility Conditions for and Benefits Provided by Disability Pensions under the First-Pillar Earnings-Related Scheme in the Slovak Republic

Vesting period	Contributions	Eligibility	Benefit rate	Partial pension
Under age 20: less than 1 year Age 20–22: 1 year Age 22–24: 2 years Age 24–26: 3 years Age 26–28: 4 years Over age 28: 5 years	3 percent by employer, 3 percent by employee; ceiling of three times average wage	At least 40 percent loss of capacity to work	1.19 percent per year	Pension is prorated if disability is 40–70 percent

Sources: European Commission 2007a; World Bank 2004.

Table 8.6   Eligibility Conditions for and Benefits Provided by Survivor Pensions under the First-Pillar Earnings-Related Scheme in the Slovak Republic

Eligibility	Spouse replacement rate	Benefit duration	Remarriage test	Orphan age limit	Orphan replacement rate	Total family benefit
Eligibility of deceased for old-age or disability pension	60 percent of deceased's pension	For life, if spouse is 70 percent disabled, caring for a child, or at retirement age; otherwise, for one year	Pension ceases if survivor remarries	26	40 percent	100 percent, regardless of number of survivors

Source: European Commission 2007a.

pension, subject to rules governing remarriage and the duration of benefits. Irrespective of the number of orphans, total benefits paid to all survivors cannot exceed the total benefit to which the deceased was originally entitled. Survivors of individuals enrolled in the second pillar are entitled to the entire accumulated balance of the deceased's account. Survivors of old-age pensioners receive 60 percent of the annuity payable to the deceased plus any remaining balance in the deceased's account.

Assessment of the Performance of the Slovak Pension System

The World Bank has established four principles for evaluating public pension systems, which together should guide the process of pension reform (see Holzmann and Hinz 2005). Broadly speaking, these principles include the adequacy and security of benefits, the affordability of contributions, the sustainability of the system over time, and the robustness of the system in the face of demographic changes and macroeconomic shocks. This chapter focuses primarily on the adequacy of benefits and the financial sustainability of the earnings-related pension schemes. The remaining principles are mentioned only briefly. Adequacy is analyzed through the lens of net replacement rates. Financial sustainability is evaluated using projections of pension expenditure and revenues.

Benefit Adequacy

Replacement rates are a useful yardstick for measuring the adequacy of pension benefits, because they express benefits relative to preretirement earnings, thereby indicating the degree to which income is replaced when workers retire. Two variants are commonly used. Gross replacement rates compute income replacement as the ratio of benefits paid to pretax preretirement earnings. Net replacement rates compute income replacement as the ratio of benefits received (that is, after the payment of taxes and other levies, including contributions for social insurance) to posttax preretirement earnings. In general, net replacement rates are a more useful measure of benefit adequacy, because they capture the degree to which actual take-home pay is replaced when workers retire.

The level of income replacement at retirement is not the only measure of benefit adequacy. For a full assessment of benefit adequacy, it is also important to assess how postretirement indexation rules will affect replacement rates during retirement. Pension benefits in retirement are expected to be indexed to inflation so that their real value is maintained. In a growing economy with increasing real wages, mere price indexation of pensions, however, leads to a deterioration of the relative consumption position of the retirees. Individuals with otherwise identical work histories will receive different pensions depending on when they retire. For this reason, some countries, such as the Slovak Republic, have introduced mixed indexation of pensions with varying weights of inflation and wage growth in the indexation formula. In order to evaluate the effect of indexation on replacement rates in the Slovak Republic, the replacement rates are normalized to 100 and the assumptions for calculating the replacement rates are maintained (that is, inflation is 2.5 percent per year and real wage growth is 2 percent per year). The change in the replacement rate is measured in comparison with full wage indexation or compared to an active worker. The results of this analysis indicate that the relative income position of a retiree would deteriorate by 13 percent after 10 years in retirement and by 37 percent after 35 years in retirement. The evaluation of income replacement that follows considers replacement rates only at retirement; it does not take into account the impact of indexation policies on replacement rates during retirement.

Replacement rates are a function of the formula governing pension benefits; an individual's contribution history; and, in the case of net replacement rates, the rules of income tax, social security contributions, and other relevant levies. The benefit formula establishes the degree to which the system redistributes income across individuals of different levels of preretirement earnings. Progressive systems provide higher levels of income replacement to people with lower levels of preretirement income. In general, the degree to which a system is redistributive depends on the existence (and value) of flat transfers and minimum pension guarantees, the degree to which benefits are earnings related, and the existence of ceilings on earnings subject to contributions. An individual's contribution history can be characterized by his or her age of entry into the labor force, contribution density, and decisions regarding the timing of retirement. To some degree, these three factors are influenced by the incentives embodied in the pension system. The tax and contribution system influences net replacement rates through the progressiveness of the income tax formula, which taxes (higher) income during a worker's active life more so than it does (lower) pension benefits in retirement. In addition, social security levies (for pensions; unemployment; health care; and, at times, housing and family benefits) are typically reduced or eliminated altogether in retirement. These benefits are particularly important for low- to middle-income groups.

The adequacy of income replacement provided by the first-pillar earnings-related pension scheme in the Slovak Republic cannot be evaluated without first establishing benchmarks. Unfortunately, there is no consensus on what constitutes adequacy. According to one widely respected definition, pensions are adequate when they are sufficient to prevent poverty among the elderly and provide the vast majority of the population with a reliable mechanism for smoothing income over their lifetime. Even with the benefit of a definition, however, actually establishing benchmarks is problematic, because attitudes vary across countries as a result of social and cultural perceptions. Moreover, benchmarks ignore the existence of other factors that affect the welfare of the elderly—and that vary from country to country—including the existence and generosity of health insurance and long-term care, the cost of housing, the structure of traditional living arrangements, the presence of informal intrafamily or intergenerational sources of financial and nonfinancial support, and the availability and security of other mechanisms for people to save for their own retirement.

One reputable nine-country study (OECD 2001) observes that living standards are roughly comparable for people 10 years older than the normal retirement age and people 15 years younger than the normal retirement age when retirees have disposable income equal to roughly 80 percent of the disposable income of working-age people. In part, this is attributable to the fact that retirees have no work-related expenses (they do not have to commute or buy special clothing or uniforms, for example). This finding, however, does not imply that mandatory first-pillar pension schemes should actually target an 80 percent net replacement rate. To the contrary, in middle- and high-income countries, one can reasonably expect individuals to save for their own retirement—and the empirical evidence suggests that, in practice, they do so.[5] There is also some evidence to suggest that the ratio between pre- and postretirement income is somewhat independent of the income replacement mandate of the public pension system. Put simply, individuals tend to save more in countries with smaller mandates (and vice versa).

Because the Slovak Republic has access to relatively well-developed financial markets and investing outside the country is permitted with only modest restriction under the third-pillar voluntary pension scheme, it would seem reasonable to expect middle- and higher-income workers to save enough to finance at least 25 percent, if not closer to 50 percent, of this 80 percent income replacement target. Given this, three benchmarks are provided: a 40 percent net replacement rate (which implies that individuals would be expected to save enough to finance half of the total income replacement target); a 60 percent net replacement rate (which implies that individuals would be expected to finance a quarter of the target); and an 80 percent net replacement rate (which implies that individuals, most of whom would be low-income earners, would not be expected to contribute anything toward the target).[6] In the following analysis, these three benchmarks are used to evaluate the adequacy of benefits in the Slovak Republic compared with the average net replacement rate observed in 53 countries around the world, the average net replacement rate observed for selected countries in Europe and Central Asia, and the poverty line in the Slovak Republic.

To estimate gross and net replacement rates, we consider two critical dimensions—earnings levels and contribution periods—with the help of the Analysis of Pension Entitlements across Countries (APEX) model.[7] This model generates estimates for replacement rates under steady-state assumptions (that is, as if the rules of the reformed pension scheme had been in place over the entire active life of the individual). Because life expectancies at retirement are projected to increase over time—which will affect the benefits paid by defined-contribution pension schemes— a reference year must be chosen. For this study, 2040 is used, because it provides a sufficiently long contribution period over which to approximate steady-state conditions.

The first critical task is to investigate levels of income replacement across a relevant spectrum of income. Income is represented as a percentage (50–200 percent) of average earnings. The second task is to investigate the impact on income replacement of differences in the duration, timing, and density of an individual's contribution history (density refers to the percentage of time an individual actually contributes over a given period). To facilitate the presentation of these multidimensional results, we compute replacement rates as a function of the age at which an individual exits the labor market. They are presented separately for full-career and partial-career workers.

Replacement rates for full-career workers. Projected replacement rates for full-career workers in 2040 are examined first. For the purpose of this analysis, a full career is defined as continuous employment from age 20 to the current normal retirement age of 62. Gross replacement rates clearly show why the earnings-related pension scheme has been described as providing a strong link between benefits and contributions (figure 8.3). Gross replacements rates show a 56.7 percent gross replacement rate— 24.4 percentage points are provided by the points system, and 32.3 percentage points come from the defined-contribution scheme.

The situation changes when taxes are taken into consideration (figure 8.4). The impact of taxes and contributions on net replacement

Figure 8.3   Sources of Gross Replacement Rates in the Slovak Republic, by Income Level

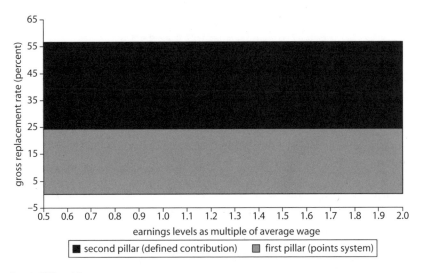

Source: APEX model.
Note: Figure shows projected replacement rate for 2040 as an approximation of steady-state conditions.

Figure 8.4   Sources of Net Replacement Rates in the Slovak Republic, by Income Level

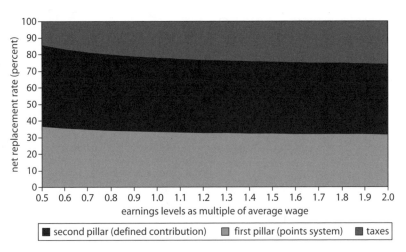

Source: APEX model.
Note: Figure shows projected replacement rate for 2040 as approximation of steady-state conditions.

rates increases as incomes rise. As a result, high-income workers receive higher net replacement rates than do low-income workers. This is attributable to the progressive nature of the tax code in the Slovak Republic, not to the design of the pension system.

Examination of net replacement rates by income level suggests that pensions for most full-career workers in the Slovak Republic can be considered adequate for middle- and high-income workers (figure 8.5).[8] Replacement rates for all levels of preretirement income are higher than the middle benchmark, suggesting that the pension system is effectively smoothing consumption from work into retirement for middle- and high-income workers. Replacement rates for low-income workers are lower than the 80 percent benchmark. Moreover, given that benefits for even very low–income full-career workers exceed the poverty line (except, marginally, at the lowest income levels), the objective of poverty alleviation is being met. Levels of income replacement for high-income workers in the Slovak Republic are higher than regional and world averages—and

Figure 8.5   Net Replacement Rates for Male Full-Career Workers in the Slovak Republic, Europe and Central Asia, and the World

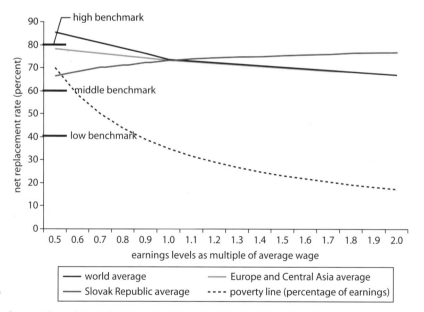

Source: Authors' calculations based on World Bank 2005, World Bank 2007a, and the APEX model.
Note: Figure shows projected replacement rate for 2040 as approximation of steady-state conditions.

replacement rates for low-income workers are lower than regional and world averages. These findings highlight the strong link between contributions and benefits and illuminate the fact that the Slovak pension system provides relatively little redistribution from the comparatively well-off population to those with lower levels of preretirement income.

Replacement rates for partial-career workers. Not everyone works from age 20 to the statutory retirement age. Many individuals enter and exit the labor force (often at different ages and for different periods of time) and earn different wages while working (figure 8.6.). To examine the adequacy of benefits for partial-career workers, we consider three styl-ized cases. (Only middle-income partial-career workers are examined because replacement rates are roughly comparable for workers with lower or higher levels of preretirement income.) These cases include career type A (someone entering the labor force at age 25 who works continu-ously for a period of years before leaving the workforce at some point between the ages of 50 and 70 and then claims a benefit); career type B (identical to career type A, except that the worker enters the workforce at age 30 and leaves no earlier than age 55); and career type C (identical

Figure 8.6   Net Replacement Rates for Male Middle-Income Partial-Career Workers in the Slovak Republic, by Career Type and Exit Age

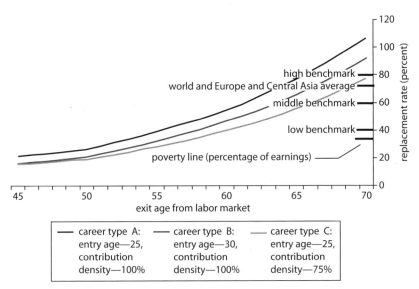

Source: Authors' calculations based on the APEX model.
Note: Figure shows projected replacement rate for 2040 as approximation of steady-state conditions. See text for descriptions of career types.

to career type A, except that the individual contributes in only three years out of four while in the labor force). In cases in which the withdrawal from the formal labor market occurs before the statutory retirement age, the pension is claimed (and the replacement rate calculated) only at the later age. For withdrawals after the statutory retirement age, the ages coincide.

Several conclusions can be drawn from figure 8.6. First, some workers are at risk of receiving levels of income replacement below the poverty line.[9] Second, leaving the workforce very early can be very costly. Someone retiring long before reaching the retirement age may not receive levels of income replacement higher than even the lowest of the three benchmarks. Third, entering the workforce later in life is costly. Someone entering the workforce at age 30 receives a net replacement rate that is 6–15 percentage points lower than someone entering the workforce at age 25. Fourth, working intermittently is costly. Someone who enters the workforce at the same age but who contributes only three years out of four will receive a net replacement rate that is 6–30 percentage points lower than someone who contributes continuously.

In all cases, net replacement rates grow faster the longer someone continues to work. This is encouraging, because it demonstrates that the pension system provides incentives for people to remain in the workforce. While career type A and B workers can attain the 40 percent benchmark before reaching the normal retirement age, career type C workers must work until the normal retirement age in order to do so. To replace 60 percent (or 80 percent) of their preretirement earnings, career type A and B workers must work for as many as eight years past the normal retirement age. Career type C workers cannot attain the 80 percent benchmark even if they work until age 70. This does not imply that the pension system is failing to achieve its poverty alleviation objective, however, because the Slovak pension system is supported by a program of social assistance that guarantees all individuals, including the elderly, income equal to the subsistence level.

Fiscal Sustainability

The sustainability of a pay-as-you-go first-pillar pension scheme is best evaluated in actuarial terms by estimating the scheme's actuarial deficit as the difference between its assets and liabilities. If a large actuarial deficit exists, the scheme is financially unsustainable and needs policy actions that increase its assets, reduce its liabilities, or both. A good proxy for the actuarial deficit is the difference between the present value of the scheme's expected future revenues (that is, contributions and other income) and the expected future expenditures (that is, benefit payments, administrative costs, and other expenses) over an extended projection period. The difference between these two values represents an unfunded liability (sometimes referred to as a financing gap) on the public-sector balance sheet. Because this study is also concerned with the time path of revenues and expenditures (and the resulting balance across the projection period ending in 2050), this more pragmatic approach has been taken. Projections of expenditures, revenues, and deficits are presented on the basis of available postreform fiscal projections.

Despite the huge improvement in the fiscal condition of the pension system attributable to the parametric reforms of 2004 and the introduction of the second pillar in 2005, the system remains in deficit (figure 8.7). The projected deficit is caused partly by the introduction of the second pillar and the loss of contribution revenues in the first pillar. Revenues are projected to hover around 6 percent of GDP for the entire projection period. Expenditures are projected to fall slightly between 2005 and 2015 but to rise thereafter, albeit at a rate far slower than was projected before the reforms. The growth in expenditures will be driven by the aging of the Slovak population. As a result of the imbalance between revenues and expenditures, deficits are projected to eventually reach levels equivalent to 4.4 percent of GDP by 2050.

What options exist for restoring the system to fiscal balance? Unfortunately, for policy makers, the options are limited. Revenues can be

Figure 8.7   Projected Fiscal Balance of the Slovak Republic's Public Pension Scheme after Reform, 2005–50

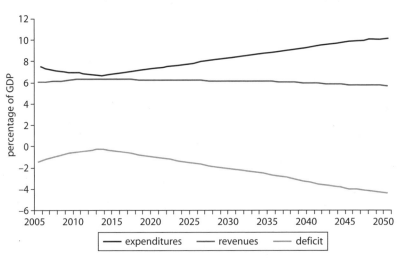

Source: Unpublished World Bank Pension Reform Options Simulation Toolkit (PROST) simulations.

increased by increasing the contribution rate and using general revenues to compensate partly or fully for the transition costs toward the funded second pillar. Alternatively—or in addition, because the options are not mutually exclusive—expenditures can be reduced by cutting benefits, increasing the minimum number of years required to become eligible for benefits, or delaying the payment of benefits by raising the retirement age further. Because raising the contribution rate could threaten competitiveness and will likely strengthen incentives for tax evasion, it is typically not embraced by policy makers. This leaves policy makers with limited options: cutting benefits, tightening eligibility conditions, or raising the retirement age. It also raises the question of whether restoring sustainability will exact a cost in terms of the adequacy of benefits provided to future beneficiaries. Increasing the retirement age further (commensurate with expected changes in life expectancy) would reduce the long-term deficit to 2.9 percent of GDP. Fully restoring long-term fiscal balance would require that retirement ages be gradually increased to 74 by 2050 (unpublished World Bank PROST simulations).

If retirement ages are left unchanged and the current structure of the system is retained, further cuts in benefits—on the order of a 36 percent reduction in the average benefit provided under the first pillar—will be required if the system is to become sustainable. Restoring sustainability will exact a cost in terms of the adequacy of benefits provided to future beneficiaries: if benefits are adjusted to maintain a fiscal balance similar to the current level in proportion to the overall size of the first-pillar scheme, full-career workers will receive replacement rates roughly 9 percentage points lower in 2050 than they receive today (figure 8.8).

Two observations emerge from a comparison of these new (and lower) net replacement rates against the three benchmarks. First, a 36 percent reduction in first-pillar benefits would not result in income replacement for full-career workers falling below the poverty line, except for very-low-income workers. This indicates that a sustainable first-pillar pension scheme in the Slovak Republic would still achieve its poverty alleviation objective. Second, a 36 percent reduction in benefits would still support the objective of smoothing lifetime consumption for middle- and high-income full-career workers, because levels of income replacement are still equal to or higher than the 60 percent benchmark. Low-income workers, however, would fall even further below the 80 percent benchmark.

This observation is subject to three caveats. First, this analysis considers only full-career workers, while the average worker now contributes for only about 27–30 years, substantially less than the 40 years expected of a

Figure 8.8   Net Male Replacement Rates in the Slovak Republic before and after Benefit Adjustment

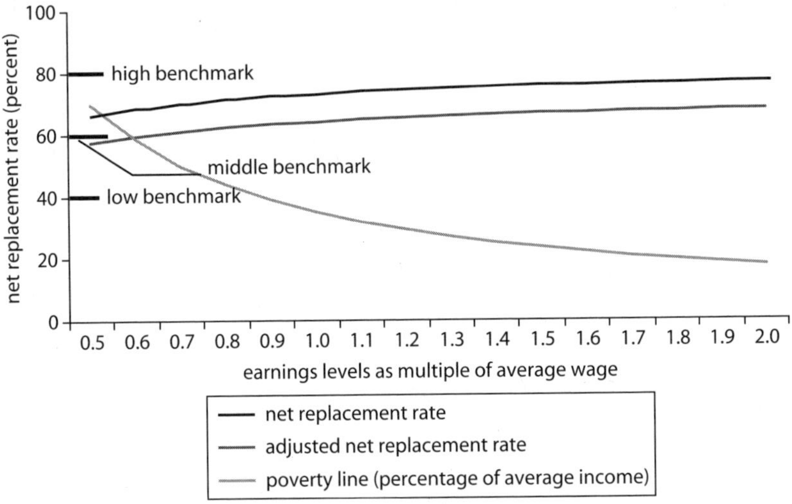

Source: Authors' calculations based on the APEX model.

full career'. Contributing to the pension scheme for only 30 years, for example, reduces net income replacement by 18 percentage points (for low-income workers) and by 22 percentage points (for high-income workers). Second, if benefit cuts are combined with further increases in the retirement age, the benefit cuts will not need to be as steep in order to restore fiscal balance. Third, workers always have the option of saving outside the first-pillar pension scheme. To increase income replacement by one percentage point, for example, a full-career worker would need to save only about 0.5 percent of his or her earnings from age 40 to the current age of retirement.[10]

Conclusions

In response to a looming crisis in the existing pay-as-you-go public pension system and the projections that suggested that the situation would gradually worsen as a result of the aging population, the Slovak Republic introduced significant parametric reforms to its first-pillar pension scheme in 2004. As a means of increasing revenues, retirement ages were increased to extend the period over which workers contribute to the system and the mechanism by which benefits are computed was changed to strengthen the link between preretirement contributions and postretirement benefits, thereby improving compliance incentives. So the growth in expenditure could be curtailed, average benefits were reduced. As a result of these reforms, the long-term fiscal position of the pension system improved substantially, with projected deficits for 2050 falling from 10.0 percent of GDP to 4.4 percent of GDP.

In 2005, the Slovak Republic introduced a mandatory second pillar to provide workers with a mechanism for diversifying their retirement income. Together with the first-pillar reforms, the introduction of the second pillar eliminated the highly redistributive provisions of the old pension system that had created incentives for evasion and the underreporting of income and strengthened incentives for people to remain in the workforce after reaching the minimum retirement age. The reform, however, also contributed to an increase in the cash deficit, because contribution revenues from the first pillar were diverted to second-pillar financing.

The resulting gross and net replacement rates for full-career workers are projected to be in line with regional and world averages (see chapter 1). The future net replacement rates for full-career workers are projected to be about 70–80 percent across the analyzed income spectrum. As in other countries, workers with less than full careers—because they left the workforce before reaching retirement age, worked intermittently, or have gaps in their employment history—risk receiving a level of income replacement closer to the lower benchmark of 40 percent, or possibly even lower.

To restore the long-term fiscal balance of the first-pillar pension scheme without recourse to general revenue financing, policy makers could raise retirement ages—rough estimates suggest to 74 by 2050. Realizing the full fiscal impact of this measure requires maintaining income replacement at levels now associated with the current retirement age. Increasing the retirement age in step with increases in life expectancy at retirement is a natural choice, for both individuals and policy makers, but it requires cross-sectoral policy reforms that would enable elderly workers to continue to participate in the labor market.[11]

Other options for restoring fiscal balance include cutting benefits at retirement, reducing the generosity of benefit indexation, or adopting some combination of the two. Rough estimates suggest that average replacement rates at retirement would have to fall by some 9 percentage points. Moving from Swiss indexation to full price indexation would reduce average first-pillar benefits by some 10 percentage points. Reducing benefits by this amount would not compromise the objective of smoothing lifetime consumption for middle- and high-income full-career workers or alleviating poverty among the elderly, because levels of income replacement would still not fall below the poverty line. Levels of income replacement for low-income individuals, however, would fall below the high benchmark following such a reduction. Individuals who wish to defer more of their lifetime consumption into retirement would still have the option, of course, of participating in the voluntary third-pillar pension scheme.

Notes

1. The number of contributors declined 14 percent between 1995 and 2002 (World Bank 2004).
2. A notional scheme computes benefits using a traditional defined-contribution formula (where the rate of return on the notional balance is computed using an economic proxy, such as the rate of growth in economywide wages) but finances those benefits using traditional pay-as-you-go financing. This approach tightens the connection between contributions and benefits without exposing participants to investment risks or imposing transition costs (see Holzmann and Palmer 2006).
3. Under the prereform rules, only the first Sk 2,500 was fully counted toward the pension assessment base. For earnings of Sk 2,501–SK 6,000, only a third were counted; for earnings of Sk 6,001–Sk 10,000, only a tenth were counted; earnings of more than Sk 10,000 were excluded. As a result, contributions on earnings of more than SK 10,000 were pure taxes (World Bank 2004).
4. Legislation states that the second pillar is not mandatory for new entrants. These projections assume that all new entrants elect to participate in the second pillar.
5. In Chile, for instance, 70 percent of retirees from the mandatory public pension system own their home, which is a form of savings (see Valdés-Prieto 2008).
6. These benchmarks approximate the standards developed by the International Labour Organization (ILO) (1952) and the Council of Europe (1990). ILO Convention 102 of 1952 sets a minimum benefit equal to 40 percent of the reference wage for married men of pensionable age. This amount was raised to 45 percent in 1968. The European Code of Security of 1990 sets a minimum standard for members of the Council of Europe equal to 65 percent for married people of a specific age.
7. The APEX model was developed by Axia Economics, with funding from the Organisation for Economic Co-operation and Development and the World Bank. The model codes detailed eligibility and benefit rules for first- and second-pillar schemes by using available public information that has been verified by country contacts. Because the details of the rules sometimes change on short notice (and limited public disclosure), the calculations presented here should be considered as best approximations only.

8. Replacement rates are simulated for an unmarried man working a hypothetical career path under the assumption that real wage growth is 2 percent, inflation is 2.5 percent, the rate of return on invested assets is 3.5 percent, and the worker retires at the statutory retirement age. Replacement rates shown do not consider the benefits received from occupational schemes.

9. A figure of 35 percent of the average net wage is used as a proxy for the poverty line, because this percentage very broadly approximates a US$2.25-a-day poverty line converted into national currency, adjusted for purchasing power parity, expressed relative to the national average net wage, and averaged across the eight study countries.

10. This estimate is based on the assumption that real wage growth is 2 percent, the net real rate of return on invested assets is 3.5 percent, and benefits (from both the unfunded and the funded pillars) are price indexed.

11. See Holzmann, MacKellar, and Repansek (2009) for a conference volume that addresses theses issues for the countries of southeastern Europe.

Bibliography

Čillíková, J. 2006. "Trends and Reforms in Slovakia." Paper presented at the CEE (Central and Eastern Europe) forum, Vienna, November 23. www.gvfw.at/files/slovakia.pdf.

Council of Europe. 1990. *European Code of Social Security (Revised)*. Rome.

European Commission. 2007a. Mutual Information System and Social Protection (MISSOC) database. ec.europa.eu/employment_social/.

———. 2007b. "Pension Schemes and Projection Models in EU-25 Member Countries." European Economy Occasional Paper 37, Economic Policy Committee and Directorate General for Economic and Financial Affairs, Brussels.

GVG (Gesellschaft für Versicherungswissenschaft und -gestaltung) and European Commission. 2003. *Study on the Social Protection Systems in the 13 Applicant Countries: Slovak Republic Country Report*. Cologne.

Hlavacka, S., R. Wagner, and A. Rosenberg. 2004. *Health Care Systems in Transition: Slovakia*. Geneva: World Health Organization.

Holzmann, R., and R. Hinz. 2005. *Old-Age Income Support in the 21st Century*. Washington, DC: World Bank.

Holzmann, R., L. MacKellar, and J. Repansek, eds. 2009. *Pension Reform in Southeastern Europe: Linking to Labor and Financial Market Reforms*. Washington, DC: World Bank.

Holzmann, R., and E. Palmer, eds. 2006. *Pension Reform: Issues and Prospects for Non-Financial Defined Contribution Schemes*. Washington, DC: World Bank.

ILO (International Labour Organisation). 1952. *ILO Convention 102*. Geneva: ILO.

──────. 1967. *ILO Convention 128*. Geneva: ILO.

INPRS (International Network of Pension Regulators and Supervisors). 2003. *Complementary and Private Pensions throughout the World*. Geneva: INPRS.

Institute of Financial Policy. 2006. *The Pension System in the Slovak Republic*. Bratislava.

Lesay, I. 2006. *Pension Reform in Slovakia: The Context of Economic Globalization*. Brussels: European Trade Union Institute.

Lindbeck, A., and M. Persson. 2003. "The Gains from Pension Reform." *Journal of Economic Literature* 41 (March): 74–112.

Ministry of Labor, Social Affairs and Family. 2005. *National Strategy Report on Adequate and Sustainable Pensions*. Bratislava.

Nalevanko, M. 2005. *Pension Reform in Slovakia: Why and How?* Bratislava: Ministry of Labor, Social Affairs and Family.

Natali, D. 2004. *The Reformed Pension System*. Observatoire Social Européen.

OECD (Organisation for Economic Co-operation and Development). 2001. *Ageing and Income: Financial Resources and Retirement in Nine OECD Countries*. Paris: OECD.

Queisser, M., and E. Whitehouse. 2006. *Neutral or Fair? Actuarial Concepts and Pension System Design*. Paris: Organisation for Economic Co-operation and Development.

Reiterer, A. 2008. *Population Development and Age Structure in Southeastern Europe until 2050*. World Bank, Washington, DC.

U.S. Social Security Administration. 2006. *Social Security Systems throughout the World: Europe*. Washington, DC: Social Security Administration.

Valdés-Prieto, S. 2008. *Designs for the First-Pillar Pensions and the 2008 Chilean Reform*. http://editorialexpress.com/cgi-bin/conference/download.cgi?db_name=SECHI2008&paper_id=130.

Whitehouse, E. 1999. *Tax Treatment of Funded Pensions*. Washington, DC: World Bank.

World Bank. 2002. *Slovak Development Policy Review*. Washington, DC: World Bank.

──────. 2004. *Slovak Republic: Pension Policy Reform Note*. Washington, DC: World Bank.

──────. 2005. *The Quest for Equitable Growth in the Slovak Republic*. Washington, DC: World Bank.

──────. 2007a. *Pensions Panorama*. Washington, DC: World Bank.

──────. 2007b. *Social Assistance in Central Europe and the Baltic States*. Washington, DC: World Bank.

WHO (World Health Organization). 2008. Database. http://www.who.int/research/en/.

CHAPTER 9

Slovenia

Slovenia inherited from the former Yugoslavia a traditional pension system financed on a pay-as-you-go basis (meaning that contributions from current workers are used to pay benefits to current beneficiaries). Following the transition from a state-planned economy to a market economy in 1991, the pension system began generating deficits, which, in 1992, were equivalent to 0.3 percent of gross domestic product (GDP). Pension expenditure increased as the number of retirees grew. In 1996, the government reduced the contribution rate, which led to a sharp drop in contribution revenues. By 1996, the fiscal deficit had reached 3.5 percent of GDP.

Deficits were projected to grow further as the population ages. The old-age dependency ratio (the population age 65 and older divided by the population age 20–64) was expected to increase from 23.5 percent in 2005 to 60.3 percent by 2050 (see Reiterer 2008).

Recognizing these challenges, Slovenian policy makers introduced several parametric changes to the existing public pension system. Rather than adopting a multipillar approach, as many other transition economies did, in 2000 Slovenia redesigned its existing pay-as-you-go pension system. Recognizing that benefits are expected to decrease following the reform of the public scheme, it also introduced a voluntary fully funded, defined-contribution scheme to provide individuals with additional savings options.

Despite these reforms, the aging of the population will continue to place stress on Slovenia's pension system. Projections suggest that deficits will reach 8.8 percent of GDP by 2050, which will almost certainly compel the government to introduce further reforms.

Against this backdrop, this chapter evaluates the Slovenian pension system, focusing on fiscal sustainability and benefit adequacy. Adequacy is evaluated through the lens of statutory net replacement rates for different retirement ages, patterns of contributions, and income levels with comparisons to international benchmarks.

This chapter is organized as follows. The next section discusses the motivation for the reforms. The following section describes the key characteristics of the reformed pension system. The third section assesses the adequacy of pension benefits and the fiscal sustainability of the system. The last section draws conclusions.

Motivation for Reform

Upon gaining independence in 1991, Slovenia inherited a socialist-era public pension system financed on a pay-as-you-go basis. The system suffered from a number of serious design flaws similar to those observed in other transition economies, including privileges for certain occupations, low retirement ages, generous benefits, and loose eligibility conditions. These characteristics affected both the revenues and the expenditures of the system, leading to fiscal imbalances beginning in 1992, when the system generated a deficit (table 9.1).

To address these issues, in 1992 Slovenia passed a reform law that included gradually raising the retirement age and restricting the criteria for early retirement. These changes came too late to prevent a large

Table 9.1   Fiscal Balance of Slovenia's Pension System before Reform, 1992–99

(percentage of GDP)

Year	Revenues	Expenditures	Balance
1992	13.5	13.8	−0.3
1993	13.9	14.4	−0.5
1994	13.1	14.4	−1.3
1995	12.9	14.7	−1.8
1996	11.0	14.5	−3.5
1997	10.1	14.4	−4.3
1998	10.2	14.3	−4.1
1999	9.9	14.4	−4.5

Source: ILO 2004.

number of early retirees from joining the benefit rolls from 1990 to early 1992.[1] Following a cut of 6.65 percentage points in the contribution rate paid by employers, the fiscal balance of the pension system deteriorated further, reaching 3.5 percent of GDP by 1996. By 1999, the deficit had reached 4.5 percent of GDP, despite the fact that contribution rates remained constant after 1996. In the absence of further reforms, expenditure was projected to eventually reach 26 percent of GDP (World Bank and IIASA 2001).

Recognizing these challenges, in 1999 the government introduced additional parametric reforms. These reforms included tightening the eligibility criteria for benefits, reducing accrual rates, and increasing the number of years of service required to collect benefits.

Characteristics of Slovenia's Pension System

This section describes the main characteristics of Slovenia's pension system. These include the design of the individual pillars of social insurance; the rules governing pension system taxation, institutional structure, and coverage; and the provisions governing old-age, disability, and survivorship pensions. The design of the pension system is assessed using a conceptual framework developed by the World Bank, which generally recommends including a funded component if conditions are appropriate but increasingly recognizes that a range of choices is available to policy makers to provide effective old-age protection in a manner that is fiscally responsible (see Holzmann and Hinz 2005).

In general, the World Bank supports pension systems composed of some combination of five basic pillars:

- a noncontributory (or zero) pillar (in the form of a demogrant, social pension, or social assistance benefit) intended to provide a minimal level of income protection;
- a first-pillar contributory system linked to earnings, which seeks to replace a portion of preretirement income;
- a mandatory second pillar (essentially, individual savings accounts), which can be designed in various ways;
- a voluntary third pillar, which is flexible and discretionary (this pillar, too, can take a variety of forms); and
- a fourth pillar of informal intrafamily or intergenerational sources of financial and nonfinancial support to the elderly, including access to health care and housing.

Pillar Design

The design of the Slovenian pension system incorporates four of the five pillars recommended by the World Bank (table 9.2). The publicly managed noncontributory zero pillar, financed with general tax revenues, redistributes income to lower income groups using means testing, such that eligible beneficiaries receive a benefit sufficient to ensure them of a total income equal to a third of the state-defined minimum pension assessment base. The mandatory first pillar is an earnings-related, defined-benefit pension scheme financed on a pay-as-you-go basis. There is no national second-pillar pension scheme.[2] The voluntary third pillar, introduced in 2000 to supplement the benefits of the mandatory first pillar, is a defined-contribution scheme in which benefits depend on an individual's contributions and investment earnings at the point of retirement. The mandatory fourth pillar, financed by a combination of contributions and copayments, provides health insurance to all people, including the elderly.

Benefits paid by the noncontributory zero pillar are exempt from taxation. Contributions to the first pillar are exempt from taxation, while benefits are taxed. The third pillar is subjected to a exempt-exempt-taxed (EET) regime, meaning that contributions are partially exempt from taxation, investment income is fully exempt, and benefits are taxed (see box 1.1 in chapter 1). This is similar to the tax regimes of most of the countries of the Organisation for Economic Co-operation and Development (OECD), which also take an EET approach. Contributions to the fourth pillar (the health care system) are exempt from taxation.

Noncontributory scheme. Individuals over age 65 who have lived in Slovenia for at least 30 years between the ages of 15 and 65 and who do not qualify for a pension from the first-pillar scheme are eligible for a means-tested noncontributory pension equal to a third of the minimum pension assessment base (European Commission 2007a). In 2006, such benefits were paid to 3.3 percent of people over age 65, at a cost equivalent to 0.3 percent of GDP.

Individuals who qualify for a pension from the first-pillar scheme but who receive very low benefits may apply for a pension income supplement, provided that their pension is lower than the minimum pension for a full contribution period and their household does not have other sources of income sufficient to exceed the minimum living standard. The supplement is calculated by multiplying a coefficient (which varies proportionally in relation to the length of the individual's contribution period)

Table 9.2 Structure of Slovenia's Pension System

Scheme type	Coverage	Type	Function	Financing	Generic benefit	Benefit indexation	Taxation Contributions	Taxation Investment income/capital gains	Taxation Benefits
Zero pillar (public non-contributory)	Universal	Means tested	Redistributive	Tax revenues	33.3 percent of minimum pension assessment base	Growth of minimum pension assessment base	n.a.	n.a.	Exempt
First pillar (public, earnings related)	Mandatory	Defined benefit	Insurance	Percentage of individual earnings	Benefit calculated on the basis of pension assessment base and accrual rate	Wage growth	Exempt	n.a.	Taxed
Third pillar (private, earnings related)	Voluntary	Defined contribution	Insurance	Voluntary contributions	Pension from capital accumulation	Depends on options chosen	Exempt[a]	Exempt	Taxed
Fourth pillar (public health care)	Mandatory	n.a.	Insurance	Percentage of individual earnings plus tax revenues	Specified basic health service package	n.a.	Exempt	n.a.	n.a.

Sources: European Commission 2007a, 2007b.

n.a. = Not applicable.

a. An amount up to 24 percent of contributions to the first pillar is tax exempt.

by the difference between the minimum pension for a full contribution period and the actual pension the individual receives.

Earnings-related schemes. Slovenia's traditional mandatory single-pillar earnings-related, pay-as-you-go, public pension scheme provides old-age, disability, and survivor benefits.[3] One of the major reforms of 2000 was to change the benefit formula (table 9.3).

Before reform, the minimum level of income replacement for 15 years of service was 35 percent for men and 40 percent for women. The accrual rate for each additional year of service was 2 percent, with an income replacement ceiling of 85 percent. Women were awarded 3 percent per

Table 9.3   Parameters of First-Pillar Earnings-Related Scheme in Slovenia before and after Reform

Period	Vesting period	Contribution rate	Contribution ceiling	Benefit rate	Pension assessment base	Retirement age
Prereform	15 years	31 percent (15.5 percent by employer, 15.5 percent by employee)	No maximum	40 percent for men and 35 percent for women for first 15 years, 2 percent thereafter	10 best consecutive years	58 for men, 53 for women
Postreform	15 years	24.35 percent (15.50 percent by employee, 8.85 percent by employer)	No maximum	35 percent for men and 38 percent for women for first 15 years, 1.5 percent per year beyond 15 years	Gradually increased to reach best 18 years in 2008 Wages are valorized using coefficients determined from growth of wages and pensions in preceding years	Gradually increased to reach 63 for men in 2009 and 61 for women in 2023

Sources: European Commission 2007a, 2007b; World Bank and IIASA 2001.

year up to 20 years of service. As a result, women could qualify for the maximum replacement rate with 35 years of service while men needed 40 years. The pension assessment base was calculated based on the 10 best consecutive years of service. The reforms changed this such that accrual rates for both men and women are now 1.5 percent per year. The minimum replacement rate for 15 years of service is maintained at 35 percent for men but is reduced to 38 percent for women, equalizing the replacement rate for a full-service career (defined as 40 years for men and 38 years women) at 72.5 percent. For ease of transition, contribution periods before 1999 are still evaluated using prereform provisions.

Before the reforms of 2000, the pension assessment base was calculated using an individual's 10 best years of earnings. The reforms gradually changed this to the 18 best years of earnings, effective as of 2008. Wages are valorized using coefficients determined from the growth of wages and pensions in the preceding years. The value of the revaluation coefficient is established yearly by ministerial decree; depending on the year, values are 77–80 percent of the growth of nominal wages.[4] A minimum and a maximum are applied to the pension assessment base. If the actual pension assessment base is lower than the statutory minimum assessment base, the pension is calculated using the statutory minimum.[5] The maximum pension assessment base is four times the minimum.

The reforms also raised retirement ages. The retirement age for men was increased by six months per year to reach 63 by 2009. The retirement age for women was increased by four months per year to reach 61 by 2023. The years of service required to become eligible for a full pension were also gradually increased, to 40 for men and 38 for women. Postretirement pensions are indexed to wages, with indexation conducted twice a year. Benefits are financed by contributions from employers and employees. The contribution rate is 15.50 percent for employers and 8.85 percent for employees, for a total levy of 24.35 percent. There is no ceiling on wages for contributions.

Voluntary scheme. The voluntary, defined-contribution, third-pillar pension scheme was introduced in 2001 to supplement the benefits provided under the mandatory first pillar (table 9.4). To be eligible for benefits, workers must have claimed their old-age pension from the first pillar, be at least 58 years old, and have contributed to the voluntary scheme for a minimum of 120 months. Investments are guaranteed to earn at least 40 percent of the average annual interest rate paid on fixed-income government securities with a maturity of more than

Table 9.4   Characteristics of the Voluntary Scheme in Slovenia

Coverage	Vesting period	Retirement age	Tax advantages to participants	Contributions tax deductible by employers	Lump-sum payments possible in retirement
Individuals covered under the public scheme	10 years	58	Yes	Yes	Yes

Source: European Commission 2007a.

one year. The Insurance Act regulates investments and gives pension fund managers wide latitude to purchase securities, make loans, purchase real estate, and make bank deposits. There are restrictions on asset class allocation and foreign investments. The voluntary pension scheme is administered by mutual funds, pension fund companies, and insurance companies authorized to sell life insurance. Mutual funds are licensed by the Securities Market Agency; pension fund and insurance companies are licensed by the Insurance Supervision Agency.

Individuals can enroll either individually or collectively through an employer. They may elect to join a fund individually while paying their contributions through an employer. In 2006, 196,883 participants (17 percent of the labor force) were contributing to four pension fund companies. The total assets of the scheme amounted to 22.9 billion tolars (SIT) (0.3 percent of GDP) (Insurance Supervision Agency 2006).[6]

Health care system. Health care in Slovenia is provided primarily by a mandatory health insurance scheme administered by the Health Insurance Institute of Slovenia. The scheme is financed mainly by contributions from the covered population. The contribution rate for insured employees is 12.92 percent of payroll (6.56 percentage points of which are paid by employers and 6.36 percentage points of which are paid by employees). Pensioners pay 5.65 percent of their gross pension. Self-employed workers contribute 12.92 percent and farmers contribute 6.36 percent of their net income. Individuals with no income are registered in municipalities, which are obliged to pay a fixed contribution (Albreht and others 2002; U.S. Social Security Administration 2006).

In 2005, health expenditure accounted for 8.5 percent of GDP, 71.9 percent of which was public expenditure and 28.1 percent was private expenditure. Of the private expenditure, 88.1 percent was attributable to out-of-pocket expenditure (informal payments, direct payments, and copayments) (WHO database).

The benefit package provided by the mandatory health insurance scheme covers almost all services, including preventive services, diagnostic procedures, ambulatory care, and long-term nursing care. Almost all services require copayments, which are 5–50 percent of the cost of the service. Individuals may make copayments directly or purchase copayment insurance (which is becoming quasi-mandatory). The government recently proposed a bill to Parliament relating to the provision of coverage for people of low income.

Institutional Structure and Coverage of Earnings-Related Schemes

The Pensions and Disability Insurance Institute (PDII) administers the first-pillar scheme, using a centralized database and payment system. The PDII also has regional offices, which play a purely administrative role. Legal supervision of the PDII is carried out by the Ministry of Labor, Family and Social Affairs. Contributions and personal income taxes are collected simultaneously by a separate agency. The first pillar is mandatory for both employees with an established employer relationship and the self-employed. Voluntary participation is permitted for certain categories of people, as defined in the law. In 2006, 857,922 individuals were contributing to the first-pillar scheme (about 61 percent of the total working-age population and 83 percent of the labor force) and 536,887 individuals (about 27 percent of the population) were receiving pensions.

Structure of Benefits

The first-pillar earnings-related pension scheme provides old-age, disability, and survivorship pensions. The provisions governing each of these types of benefits are discussed as follows.

Old-age benefits. To be eligible for an old-age pension, individuals must have at least 15 years of service. The minimum old-age pension is 35 percent of the minimum pension assessment base for men and 38 percent for women. For years of service beyond 15, the accrual rate is 1.5 percent per year. Pensions of eligible individuals with very low earnings are computed using the statutory-minimum pension assessment base (set at about 64 percent of the average wage in 2003). Pensions of individuals with very high earnings are computed using the maximum pension assessment base (equal to four times the minimum assessment base).

Retirement ages are being gradually increased to 63 for men (by 2009) and 61 for women (by 2023). The number of years of service required to become eligible for a full pension is also being increased, to 40 years for men and 38 years for women. Once this requirement is met, workers will be able to retire at age 58. Men and women with 20 years of service may retire at 63 and 61, respectively. Men and women with 15 years of service may retire at 65 and 63, respectively. Both mothers and fathers may retire earlier as a function of the number of children they have.[7] The retirement age is reduced by eight months for one child, 20 months for two children, 36 months for three children, and 36 months plus an additional 20 months per child beyond three. The minimum retirement age for women with children is 56.

Higher accrual rates are provided to men who reach age 63 and women who reach age 61 and who are eligible for benefits but elect to defer their retirement.[8] These rates (which vary by year) are provided for a maximum of four years, after which additional benefits accrue at the rate of 1.5 percent a year. Penalties apply to men age 58–63 who have less than 40 years of contributions and to women age 58–63 who have less than 38 years of contributions. The severity of the penalty varies depending on the age of the individual.[9]

Disability benefits. Disability benefits in Slovenia are based on the cause of the disability (table 9.5). For occupational diseases or work-related injuries, benefits are paid regardless of the individual's period of contributions. If the disability results from other causes, individuals must have paid contributions for at least a third of the period between age 20 and the date of their disability to be eligible for benefits. Disability benefits are calculated in a manner similar to that used to calculate old-age pensions, but benefits cannot be lower than 45 percent

Table 9.5 Eligibility Conditions for and Benefits Provided by Disability Pensions in Slovenia under the First-Pillar Earnings-Related Scheme

Vesting period	Contributions	Eligibility	Benefit rate	Partial pension
Individual must have contributed at least one-third of the period between age 20 and the time of disability	No specific contributions for disability	At least 30 percent loss of capacity to work	Based on level of disability; 10–24 percent of minimum pension for full pension qualifying period	Prorated based on level of disability

Source: European Commission 2007a.

for men and 48 percent for women of the minimum pension assessment base.

Survivor benefits. Survivor benefits are awarded to the dependents of individuals who at the time of death were receiving (or had met the criteria to receive) an old-age or disability pension (table 9.6). The minimum eligibility age for widows and widowers is 53. If a widow or widower is incapable of working, becomes incapable of working within a year of the individual's death, or has dependent children, survivor pensions are awarded irrespective of age.

Survivor benefits are set at at least 45 percent of the deceased's pension assessment base. Widow and widower benefits are 70 percent of the higher of the old-age or disability pension, provided there are no other survivors. If the spousal survivor is already receiving an old-age or disability pension, the maximum replacement rate is 15 percent of the deceased's pension, not to exceed the average monthly pension in Slovenia the previous year. Orphans below age 15 (26 for students) are eligible for orphans' benefits. If the orphan is incapable of working, benefits are paid for life. Dependent parents, grandchildren, and siblings of the deceased are also eligible for benefits under certain conditions. Benefits are provided to dependent parents regardless of age if they are incapable of working. Total survivor benefits paid to all survivors cannot exceed 100 percent of the deceased's pension.

Table 9.6   Eligibility Conditions for and Benefits Provided by Survivor Pensions in Slovenia under the First-Pillar Earnings-Related Scheme

Eligibility	Spouse replacement rate	Benefit duration	Remarriage test	Orphan age limit	Orphan replacement rate	Total family benefit
Eligibility of deceased for old-age or disability pension	70 percent of deceased's pension if sole beneficiary; 15 percent of deceased's pension if receiving own pension	For life if spouse is 70 percent disabled, is taking care of a child, or has reached retirement age; otherwise, one year	Benefits cease if survivor remarries before reaching retirement age unless incapable of working	15 (26 for students)	70 percent if sole beneficiary	100 percent regardless of number of survivors

Source: European Commission 2007a.

Assessment of the Performance of Slovenia's Pension System

The World Bank has established four principles for evaluating public pension systems, which together should guide the process of pension reform (see Holzmann and Hinz 2005). Broadly speaking, these principles include the adequacy and security of benefits, the affordability of contributions, the sustainability of the system over time, and the robustness of the system in the face of demographic changes and macroeconomic shocks. This chapter focuses primarily on the adequacy of benefits and financial sustainability of the first-pillar, earnings-related pension scheme. The remaining principles are mentioned only briefly. Adequacy is analyzed through the lens of net replacement rates. Financial sustainability is evaluated using projections of pension expenditure and revenues.

Benefit Adequacy

Replacement rates are a useful yardstick for measuring the adequacy of pension benefits, because they express benefits relative to preretirement earnings, thereby indicating the degree to which income is replaced when workers retire. Two variants are commonly used. Gross replacement rates compute income replacement as the ratio of benefits paid to pretax preretirement earnings. Net replacement rates compute income replacement as the ratio of benefits received (that is, after the payment of taxes and other levies, including contributions for social insurance) to posttax preretirement earnings. In general, net replacement rates are a more useful measure of benefit adequacy, because they capture the degree to which actual take-home pay is replaced when workers retire.

The level of income replacement at retirement is not the only measure of benefit adequacy. To fully assess benefit adequacy, it is also important to determine how postretirement indexation rules will affect replacement rates during retirement. Pension benefits in retirement are expected to be indexed to inflation, so that their real value is maintained. In a growing economy with rising real wages, however, mere price indexation of pensions leads to a deterioration of the relative consumption position of the retirees. Individuals with otherwise identical work histories will receive different pensions depending on when they retire. For this reason, some countries have introduced mixed indexation of pensions that use varying weights of inflation and wage growth in the indexation formula. For an evaluation of the effect of indexation on replacement rates in Slovenia, the replacement rates are normalized to 100 and the assumptions for calculating the replacement rates are maintained (that is, inflation is 2.5 percent per year and real wage growth is 2 percent per year). The change in the replacement rate is measured in comparison to full wage indexation or an active worker. The results of the analysis indicate that the relative income position of retirees will be maintained because pensions are indexed to wage growth in Slovenia. The evaluation of income replacement that follows considers replacement rates only at retirement. Given Slovenia's indexation policies, however, replacement rates are preserved in retirement.

Replacement rates are a function of the formula governing pension benefits; an individual's contribution history; and, in the case of the net replacement rates, the rules of income tax, social security contributions, and other relevant levies. The benefit formula establishes the degree to which the system redistributes income across individuals of different levels of preretirement earnings. Progressive systems provide higher levels of income replacement to people with lower levels of preretirement income. In general, the degree to which a system is redistributive depends on the existence (and value) of flat transfers and minimum pension guarantees, the degree to which benefits are earnings-related, and the existence of ceilings on earnings subject to contributions. An individual's contribution history can be characterized by his or her age of entry into the labor force, contribution density, and decisions regarding the timing of retirement. To some degree, these three factors are influenced by the incentives embodied in the pension system. The tax and contribution system influences net replacement rates through the typical progressiveness of the income tax formula, which taxes higher income during a worker's active life more so than it does lower pension benefits in retirement. In addition, social security levies (for pensions; unemployment; health care; and, at times, housing and family benefits) are typically reduced or eliminated altogether in retirement. These benefits are particularly important for low- to middle-income groups.

The adequacy of income replacement provided by the first-pillar earnings-related pension scheme in Slovenia cannot be evaluated without first establishing benchmarks. Unfortunately, there is no consensus for what constitutes adequacy. According to one widely respected definition, pensions are adequate when they are sufficient to prevent poverty among the elderly and provide the vast majority of the population with a reliable mechanism for smoothing income over their lifetime. Even with the benefit of a definition, however, establishing benchmarks is problematic, because attitudes vary from one country to another as a function of social and cultural perceptions. Moreover, benchmarks ignore the existence of other factors that affect the welfare of the elderly—and that vary from country to country—including the existence and generosity of health insurance and long-term care, the cost of housing, the structure of traditional living arrangements, the presence of informal intrafamily or intergenerational sources of financial and nonfinancial support, and the availability and security of other mechanisms for saving for one's own retirement.

One reputable nine-country study (OECD 2001) observes that living standards are roughly comparable for people 10 years older than the normal retirement age and people 15 years younger than the normal retirement age when retirees have disposable income equal to roughly 80 percent of the disposable income of working-age people. In part, this is attributable to the fact that retirees have no work-related expenses (they do not have to commute or buy special clothing or uniforms, for example). This finding, however, does not imply that mandatory first-pillar pension schemes should actually target an 80 percent net replacement rate. To the contrary, in middle- and high-income countries, one can reasonably expect individuals to save for their own retirement—and the empirical evidence suggests that in practice they do so.[10] There is also some evidence to suggest that the ratio between pre- and postretirement income is somewhat independent of the income replacement mandate of the public pension system. Put simply, individuals tend to save more in countries with more modest mandates (and vice versa).

Because Slovenia enjoys a relatively well-developed banking sector, has access to established financial markets, and permits external investments under the third pillar with only modest restrictions, it would seem reasonable to expect middle- and higher-income workers to save enough to finance at least 25 percent, if not closer to 50 percent, of this 80 percent income replacement target. Given this, three benchmarks are provided: a 40 percent net replacement rate (by implication, individuals would be expected to save enough to finance half of the total income replacement target), a 60 percent net replacement rate (individuals would be expected to finance a quarter of the target), and an 80 percent net replacement rate (individuals, most of whom would be low income earners, would not be expected to contribute anything toward the target).[11] In the following analysis, these three benchmarks are used to evaluate the adequacy of benefits in Slovenia compared with the average net replacement rate observed in 53 countries around the world, the average net replacement rate observed for selected countries in Europe and Central Asia, and the poverty line in Slovenia.[12]

To estimate gross and net replacement rates, we use the Analysis of Entitlements across Countries (APEX) model to consider two critical dimensions: earnings levels and contribution periods.[13] This model generates estimates for replacement rates under steady-state assumptions (that is, as if the rules of the reformed pension scheme had been in place over the whole active life of the individual). Because life expectancies at retirement are projected to increase over time—which will influence the benefits paid by defined-contribution pension schemes—a reference year must be chosen. For the purpose of this study, 2040 is used, because it provides a sufficiently long contribution period over which to approximate steady-state conditions.

The first critical task is to investigate levels of income replacement across a relevant spectrum of income. Income is represented as a percentage (50–200 percent) of average earnings. The second task is to investigate the impact on income replacement of differences in the duration, timing, and density of an individual's contribution history (density refers to the percentage of time an individual actually contributes over a given period). To facilitate the presentation of these multidimensional results, we compute replacement rates as a function of the age at which an individual exits the labor market. They are presented separately for full-career and partial-career workers.

Replacement rates for full-career workers. Full-career workers are examined first.[14] Gross replacement rates indicate that the earnings-related pension scheme is progressive (that is, it provides higher levels of income replacement to people with lower levels of preretirement income) (figure 9.1). The level of gross income replacement provided to someone earning half the average wage is 17 percentage points higher than that provided to someone earning twice the average wage.

The situation does not change significantly when taxes are taken into consideration. The impact of taxes on net replacement rates increases as incomes rise (figure 9.2). As a result, the proportional increase from gross to net replacement rates is slightly higher for high-income workers than for low-income workers.

Examination of net replacement rates by income level suggests that pensions for full-career workers in Slovenia can be considered adequate (figure 9.3).[15] Net replacement rates decrease with income, indicating the progressiveness of the scheme. Replacement rates for all levels of preretirement income are higher than the middle benchmark, and replacement rates for low- and middle-income workers are higher than

Figure 9.1   Sources of Gross Replacement Rates in Slovenia, by Income Level

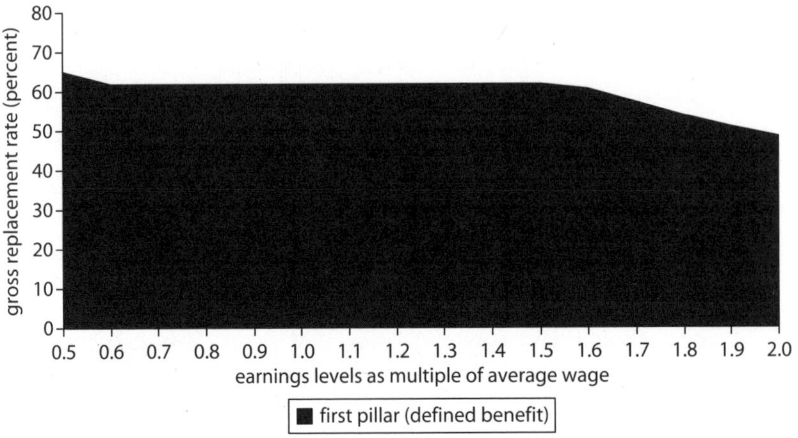

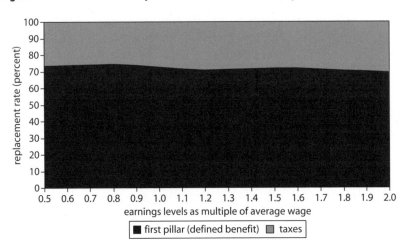

Source: APEX model.
Note: Figure shows projected replacement rate for 2040 as approximation of steady-state conditions.

Figure 9.2   Sources of Net Replacement Rates in Slovenia, by Income Level

Source: APEX model.
Note: Figure shows projected replacement rate for 2040 as approximation of steady-state conditions.

the highest benchmark. Given that benefits for the lowest full-career workers significantly exceed the poverty line, the objective of poverty alleviation is being met. Income replacement levels for all workers are higher than regional and world averages, suggesting that the Slovenian pension system provides relatively generous benefits.

Figure 9.3   Net Replacement Rates for Male Full-Career Workers in Slovenia, Europe and Central Asia, and the World

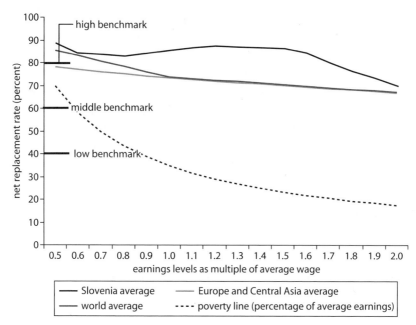

Source: Authors' calculations based on World Bank 2007 and the APEX model.
Note: Figure shows projected replacement rate for 2040 as approximation of steady-state conditions.

Replacement rates for partial-career workers. Not everyone works from age 20 to the statutory retirement age. Many individuals enter and exit the labor force (often at different ages and for different periods of time) and earn different wages while working (figure 9.4). To examine the adequacy of benefits for partial-career workers, we consider three stylized cases.[16] These cases include career type A (someone entering the labor force at age 25 who works continuously for a period of years before leaving the workforce at some point between the ages of 50 and 70 and then claims a benefit); career type B (identical to career type A, except that the worker enters the workforce at age 30 and leaves no earlier than age 55); and career type C (identical to career type A, except that the individual contributes in only three years out of four while in the labor force). In cases where the withdrawal from the formal labor market occurs before the statutory retirement age, the pension is claimed (and the replacement rate calculated) only at the later age. For withdrawals after the statutory retirement age, the ages coincide.

Figure 9.4   Net Replacement Rates for Male Middle-Income Partial-Career Workers in Slovenia, by Career Type and Exit Age

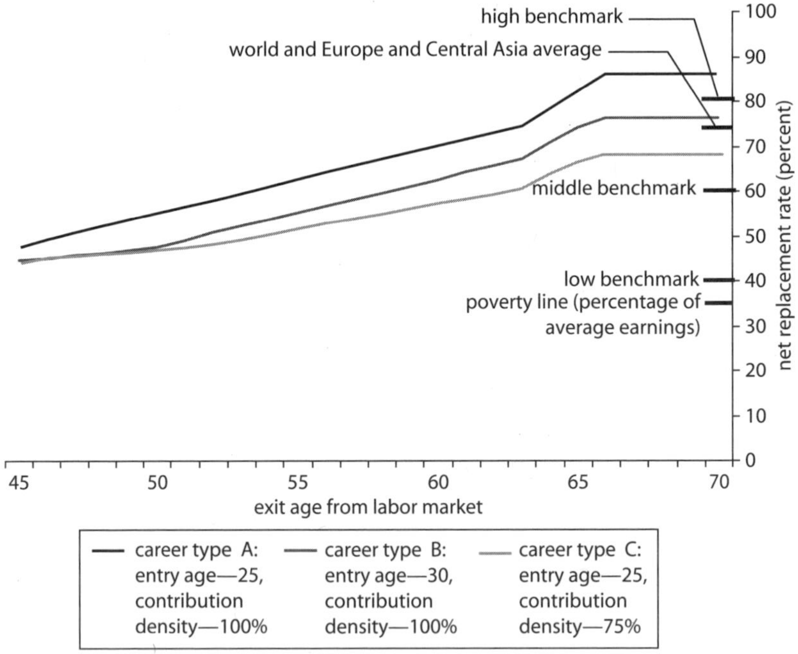

Source: Authors' calculations based on World Bank 2007 and the APEX model.
Note: Figure shows projected replacement rate for 2040 as approximation of steady-state conditions. See text for description of career types.

Several conclusions can be drawn from figure 9.4. First, all workers receive levels of income replacement higher than the poverty line. Second, leaving the workforce early is costly, because partial-career workers who retire long before the retirement age may receive income replacement slightly below the middle of the three benchmarks. Third, entering the workforce later in life is costly, because entering the workforce at age 30 results in a net replacement rate 3–10 percentage points lower than entering at age 25. Fourth, working intermittently is costly, because the net replacement rate of a worker who contributes three out of four years will be 4–18 percentage points lower than that of a worker who contributes continuously. In all cases, net replacement rates grow faster the longer someone continues to work past normal retirement age for up to four years after which replacement rates become flat. The increase in replacement rates beyond the normal retirement age becomes steeper, because of higher accrual rates awarded for up to four years of delayed retirement. This implies that the scheme provides an incentive to defer retirement. Although career type A and B workers can attain the 60 percent benchmark before reaching the normal retirement age, career type C workers must work until the normal retirement age to attain this benchmark. To replace 80 percent of their preretirement earnings, career type A workers must work for two years past the normal retirement age. Career type B and C workers cannot attain the 80 percent benchmark, even if they work until age 70.

Fiscal Sustainability

The sustainability of a pay-as-you-go first-pillar pension scheme is best evaluated in actuarial terms by estimating the scheme's actuarial deficit as the difference between its assets and liabilities. If a large actuarial deficit exists, the scheme is financially unsustainable and needs policy actions that increase its assets, reduce its liabilities, or both. A good proxy for the actuarial deficit is the difference between the present value of the scheme's expected future revenues (that is, contributions and other income) and expected future expenditures (that is, benefit payments, administrative costs, and other expenses) over an extended projection period. The difference between these two values represents an unfunded liability (sometimes referred to as a financing gap) on the public-sector balance sheet. Because this study is also concerned with the time path of revenues and expenditures (and the resulting balance across the projection period ending in 2050), this more pragmatic approach has been taken. Projections of expenditures, revenues, and deficits are presented on the basis of available postreform fiscal projections.

Reforms reduced the deficits of the first-pillar pension scheme from 4.5 percent of GDP in 1999 to 1.5 percent of GDP in 2005. The system remains unsustainable in the long term, however. Pension expenditures are projected to stabilize at about 11.2 percent of GDP for the next few years before rising gradually to 18.5 percent of GDP by 2050, driven by the wage indexation of pensions and the aging of the population.[17] Revenues are projected to remain flat, at about 10.0 percent of GDP over the same period, resulting in a deficit of 8.8 percent by 2050 (figure 9.5).

The aging of the Slovene population is driving these projections. Like other countries in the region, Slovenia will experience rapid aging over the next few decades as a result of low fertility rates and increased life expectancy. As a result, the old-age dependency ratio is projected to increase from 23.8 percent in 2005 to 60.3 percent by 2050 (figure 9.6).

Figure 9.5   Projected Fiscal Balance of Slovenia's Public Pension Scheme, 2005–50

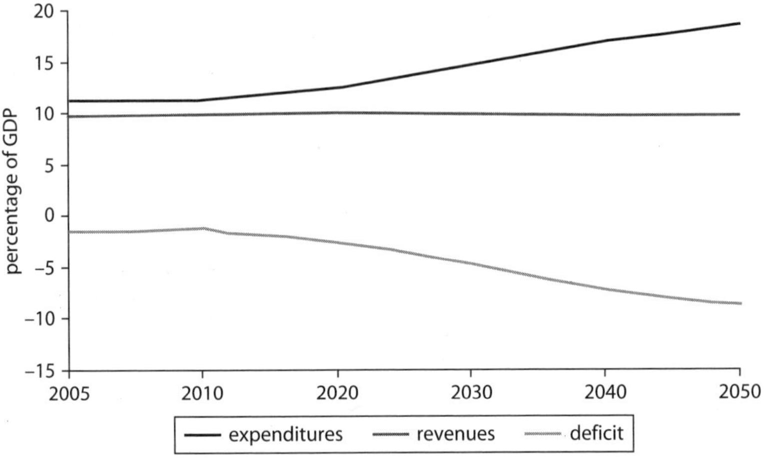

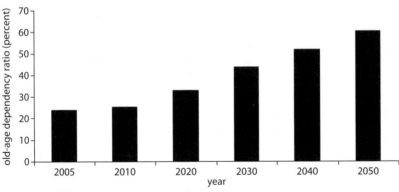

Sources: European Commission 2007b; Institute of Macroeconomic Analysis and Development 2007.

Figure 9.6   Projected Old-Age Dependency Ratio in Slovenia, 2005–50

Source: Reiterer 2008.

What options exist for restoring the system to fiscal balance? Unfortunately, for policy makers, the options are limited. Revenues can be increased by raising the contribution rate. Alternatively—or in addition, because the options are not mutually exclusive—expenditures can be reduced by cutting benefits, increasing the minimum number of years required to become eligible for benefits, or delaying the payment of benefits by raising the retirement age further. Because raising the contribution rate could threaten competitiveness and will likely strengthen incentives for tax evasion, it is typically not embraced by policy makers. This leaves policy makers with limited options: cutting benefits, tightening eligibility conditions, or raising the retirement age. An informal analysis suggests that retirement ages for men and women will have to be increased to at least 70 by 2050 to restore long-term fiscal balance.[18] Restoring sustainability may reduce the adequacy of benefits provided to future beneficiaries.

If retirement ages are left unchanged and the current structure of the system is retained, further cuts in benefits—on the order of a 56 percent reduction in the average benefit provided under the first pillar—will be required for the system to become sustainable (figure 9.7). If benefits are adjusted to maintain a fiscal balance to the current level, full-career workers will receive replacement rates 27–34 percentage points lower in 2050 than they receive today, depending on their relative level of preretirement income.

Two observations emerge from comparing these new (and lower) net replacement rates against the three benchmarks. First, a 56 percent reduction in benefits would result in levels of income replacement for full-career workers that are below the poverty line, indicating that the pension scheme would not achieve its poverty alleviation objective for low-income

Figure 9.7   Net Replacement Rates for Male Workers in Slovenia before and after Benefit Adjustment

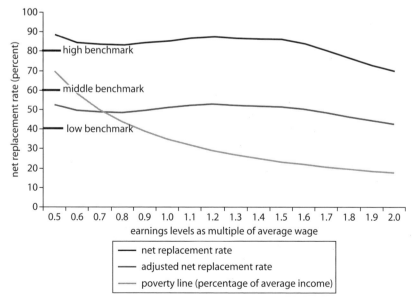

Source: Authors' calculations based on the APEX model.

workers. Second, the same reduction in benefits would likely frustrate the objective of smoothing consumption for all but high-income full-career workers. Replacement rates for middle-income workers are below the middle 60 percent benchmark, while rates for low-income workers are substantially below the 80 percent benchmark.

This last observation is subject to three caveats. First, this analysis applies only to full-career workers, while the average worker now contributes for only 27–30 years, substantially less than the 43 years defining a full career. Contributing to the pension scheme for 33 years (10 years short of a full career) reduces net income replacement by 6 percentage points for low-income workers and 12 percentage points for high-income workers. As a result, reducing benefits to restore the scheme to fiscal balance would make it very difficult for the scheme to effectively smooth consumption for virtually all partial-career workers and for most full-career low- and middle-income workers. Second, if benefit cuts are combined with further increases in the retirement age, the cuts need not be as large to restore fiscal balance. Third, all workers have the option of saving outside of the first-pillar pension scheme. To increase income replacement by 1 percentage point, for example, a full-career worker would need to save only about 0.5 percent of his or her earnings from age 40 to the current age of retirement.[19]

Conclusions

The reforms of 2000 improved the fiscal condition of Slovenia's pension system, but they failed to make the first-pillar scheme sustainable. Levels of net replacement for full-career workers remain well above 80 percent— quite high relative to regional and global benchmarks for workers of all income levels (see chapter 1). As in other countries, however, workers with less than full careers—because they left the workforce before reaching the retirement age, worked intermittently, or have gaps in their employment history—risk receiving a level of income replacement closer to the lower benchmark of 40 percent. The generosity of replacement rates at retirement is enhanced by generous indexation practices, which fully link pensions to wages. Moreover, the reforms failed to adequately address the aging of the population, which will steadily raise the ratio of pensioners to workers over time. As a result, the pension scheme is projected to generate a deficit equivalent to 8.8 percent of GDP by 2050.

To restore the long-term fiscal balance of the pension scheme without recourse to general revenue financing, policy makers could raise retirement ages further—rough estimates suggest an age well above 70 by 2050. To realize the full fiscal impact of this measure, income replacement must be maintained at levels now associated with the current retirement age. Increasing the retirement age in step with increases in life expectancy at retirement is a natural choice, both for individuals and for policy makers, but it requires cross-sectoral policy reforms to enable elderly workers to continue to participate in the labor market.[20]

Other options for restoring fiscal balance include cutting benefits at retirement or reducing the generosity of benefit indexation (or some combination thereof). Rough estimates suggest that average first-pillar replacement rates at retirement would have to fall some 30 percentage points. Moving from wage indexation to price indexation would reduce average first-pillar benefits by some 25 percentage points. Reducing benefits by such magnitudes would, however, likely compromise the objective of smoothing lifetime consumption for full-career low- and middle-income workers when measured against the three benchmarks used here. It would also likely frustrate the objective of alleviating poverty among elderly people with low preretirement income, because levels of income replacement would fall below the poverty line.

This suggests that policy makers in Slovenia will have to either support the pension scheme with funds from the general budget or enact further reforms to restore fiscal balance. Given the magnitude of projected deficits, restoring fiscal balance through benefit cuts alone may frustrate the objective of smoothing consumption. Raising retirement ages further and cutting benefits may be the only viable option. Even if benefits are reduced, individuals have the option of supplementing their benefits by saving outside the mandatory first-pillar scheme. Given that participation in the voluntary third-pillar scheme remains small, an opportunity exists for broadening the reach of the scheme.

Notes

1. The number of pensioners rose 18 percent between 1990 and 1992, as a result of the provision in the pre-1992 law that allowed older contributors to pay lower rates for missing years of contributions and then claim old-age pensions (Novak 2004). To ease the economic transition, the government shifted some of the costs to the pension system by allowing mass early retirement (Verbic, Majcen, and Nieuwkoop 2005).

2. There are two mandatory closed-end second-pillar schemes: one for employees working in hazardous occupations and (since April 2004) one for government

employees. Both are financed by small contributions paid by employers only. The scheme for government employees was introduced to address wage demands by public employees while still complying with the Maastricht criteria in the run-up to adopting the euro. Because these two schemes do not apply to all employees, they are excluded in the system characterization and analysis.

3. Mandatory defined-contribution schemes provide early retirement benefits for certain occupations, including miners, police officers, military personnel, and artists, who are assumed to work under harsh work conditions. Upon reaching age 58, qualified workers are entitled to an old-age pension from the pay-as-you-go scheme in addition to a pension from their occupational scheme. Employers are required to pay additional contributions of 4.2–12.6 percent (depending on the occupation) to finance these occupational pensions. The schemes are administered by the state-owned pension management fund.

4. In 2006, for example, the revalorization coefficient applied to wages earned in 1990 was only 78 percent of actual nominal wage growth over the period 1990–2005.

5. The minimum pension assessment base is set nominally. It was about 64 percent of the average wage in 2003.

6. For a critical view of the regulatory framework, see Berk (2008).

7. This provision was reportedly used largely by men in recent years.

8. The accrual rate is 3 percent the first year, 2.6 percent the second year, 2.2 percent the third year, and 1.8 percent the fourth year after the retirement age of 63 for men and 61 for women. If an individual does not fulfill the entire qualifying period and continues to work after the retirement age, the accrual rate is 0.3 percent per month the first year, 0.2 percent the second year, and 0.1 percent the third year.

9. The reduction is 0.3 percent per month at age 58, 0.25 percent per month at age 59, 0.2 percent per month at age 60, 0.15 percent per month at age 61, and 0.1 percent per month at age 62.

10. In Chile, for instance, 70 percent of retirees from the mandatory public pension system own their home, which is a form of savings (see Valdés-Prieto 2008).

11. These benchmarks approximate the standards developed by the International Labour Organization (ILO) and the Council of Europe (1990). ILO Convention 102 of 1952 sets a minimum benefit equal to 40 percent of the reference wage for married men of pensionable age. This amount was subsequently increased to 45 percent in 1968. The European Code of Security of 1990 sets a minimum standard for members of the Council of Europe equal to 65 percent for married people of a specific age.

12. As a proxy for the poverty line, this study uses 35 percent of the average net wage, which very broadly approximates a US$2.25-a-day poverty line

converted into national currency, adjusted for purchasing power parity, expressed relative to the national average net wage, and averaged across the eight study countries. Such an approach enables valid comparisons to be made across the sample (see chapter 1 of this volume).

13. The APEX model was developed by Axia Economics, with funding from the OECD and the World Bank. The model codes detailed eligibility and benefit rules for first- and second-pillar schemes based on available public information that has been verified by country contacts. Because the details of the rules sometimes change on short notice (and limited public disclosure), the calculations presented here should be considered as best approximations only.

14. For this analysis, a full career is defined as continuous employment from age 20 to the current normal retirement age of 63.

15. Replacements rates are simulated for an unmarried male working a hypothetical career path under the assumption that real wage growth is 2 percent, inflation is 2.5 percent, the rate of return on invested assets is 3.5 percent, and the worker retires at the statutory retirement age.

16. Only male middle-income, partial-career workers are examined. Although replacement rates across income levels vary, the results of the analysis are similar.

17. For projections of different policy scenarios using an overlapping generational model, see Majcen and Verbic (2008).

18. This estimate is based on the World Bank's baseline demographic projections. It assumes that everyone over age 70 receives a pension, everyone age 20–70 contributes, and all pensioners receive the replacement rate awarded to the median worker (62 percent).

19. This estimate is based on the assumption that real wage growth is 2 percent, the net real rate of return on invested assets is 3.5 percent, and benefits (from both the unfunded and the funded pillars) are price indexed.

20. See Holzmann, MacKellar, and Repansek (2009) for a conference volume that addresses these issues for the countries of southeastern Europe.

Bibliography

Albreht, T., M. Cesen, D. Hindle, E. Jakubowski, B. Kramberger, V. Kerstin Petric, M. Premik, and M. Toth. 2002. *Healthcare Systems in Transition: Slovenia.* World Health Organization Regional Office for Europe, Copenhagen.

Berk, A. 2008. "Contemporary Issues and Challenges in a Supplementary Pension System: The Case of Slovenia." In *Pension Reform in Southeastern Europe: Linking to Labor and Financial Market Reforms*, ed. R. Holzmann, L. MacKellar, and J. Repansek, 209–25. Washington, DC: World Bank.

Council of Europe. 1990. *European Code of Social Security (Revised)*. Rome.

European Commission. 2007a. Mutual Information System and Social Protection (MISSOC) database. http://ec.europa.eu/employment_social/.

———. 2007b. "Pension Schemes and Projection Models in EU-25 Member Countries." European Economy Occasional Paper 37, Economic Policy Committee and Directorate General for Economic and Financial Affairs, Brussels.

GVG (Gesellschaft für Versicherungswissenschaft und -gestaltung) and European Commission. 2003. *Study on the Social Protection Systems in the 13 Applicant Countries: Slovenia Country Report*. Cologne.

Holzmann, R., and R. Hinz. 2005. *Old-Age Income Support in the 21st Century*. Washington, DC: World Bank.

Holzmann, R., L. MacKellar, and J. Repansek, eds. 2009. *Pension Reform in Southeastern Europe: Linking to Labor and Financial Market Reforms*. Washington, DC: World Bank.

Institute of Macroeconomic Analysis and Development. 2007. *Pension Expenditures and Revenues*. Government of Slovenia, Slovenia Country Fische, Economic Policy Committee Aging Group, Ljubljana.

Insurance Supervision Agency. *2006. Annual Report*. Ljubljana.

ILO (International Labour Organization). 1952. *ILO Convention 102*. Geneva: ILO.

———. 1967. *ILO Convention 128*. Geneva: ILO.

———. 2004. *The Collection of Pension Contributions: Trends, Issues, and Problems in Central and Eastern Europe*. Subregional Office for Central and Eastern Europe, Budapest.

Majcen, B., and M. Verbic. 2009. "Slovenian Pension System in the Context of Upcoming Demographic Development." In *Pension Reform in Southeastern Europe: Linking to Labor and Financial Market Reforms*, ed. R. Holzmann, L. MacKellar, and J. Repansek, 73–88. Washington, DC: World Bank.

Novak, A. 2004. *Pension Reform in Slovenia*. University of Glasgow.

OECD (Organisation for Economic Co-operation and Development). 2001. Ageing and Income: Financial Resources and Retirement in Nine OECD Countries, Paris: OECD.

Reiterer, A. 2008. *Population Development and Age Structure in Southeastern Europe until 2050*. World Bank, Washington, DC.

U.S. Social Security Administration. 2006. *Social Security Systems throughout the World: Europe*. Washington, DC: Social Security Administration.

Valdés-Prieto, S. 2008. *Designs for the First-Pillar Pensions and the 2008 Chilean Reform*. http://editorialexpress.com/cgi-bin/conference/download.cgi?db_name=SECHI2008&paper_id=130.

Verbic, M., B. Majcen, and R. van Nieuwkoop. 2005. *Sustainability of the Slovenian Pension System: An Analysis with an Overlapping-Generations General Equilibrium Model.* Ljubljana: Institute of Economic Research.

Whitehouse, E. 1999. *Tax Treatment of Funded Pensions.* Washington, DC: World Bank.

World Bank. 2007. *Pensions Panorama.* Washington, DC: World Bank.

World Bank and IIASA (International Institute for Applied Systems Analysis). 2001. "The Slovenian Pension System and Reform." Paper presented at the World Bank–IIASA conference, Vienna.

WHO (World Health Organization). 2008. Database. http://www.who.int/research/en/.

Index

Boxes, figures, notes, and tables are indicated by b, f, n, and t following the page number.

A

age for receiving benefits
  See also headings starting with "replacement rates"
  Bulgaria, 19, 26, 49, 69, 72, 85
  Croatia, 26, 49, 94, 96, 98, 100, 111
  Czech Republic, 26, 117, 120, 125, 136, 137, 140–41
  general discussion of, 5, 20–24t, 26, 34, 49, 51
  Hungary, 19, 26, 49, 154, 160, 168–69, 171, 174, 176n6
  Poland, 26, 49, 182, 193
  recommendation to increase, 55
  Romania, 26, 49, 212, 216, 220, 234–35
  Slovak Republic, 26, 49, 246, 250, 263
  Slovenia, 19, 26, 49, 268, 270, 273, 275, 287, 289
Agency for the Supervision of Financial Services (Croatia), 97–98
age-related social pension. *See* pension income supplement; social assistance benefits
Agricultural Social Insurance Fund (Poland), 192

Albania, 7
Analysis of Pension Entitlements across Countries (APEX) model, 39–40, 57n9
annuities
  Bulgaria, 69
  Croatia, 96, 99
  Czech Republic, 123
  disability payments, 30
  Hungary, 151, 154, 158, 160
  Poland, 185, 191, 193
  Slovak Republic, 243, 250
Armenia, 7
assessment of performance of pension system
  Bulgaria, 73–84
  Croatia, 100–110
  Czech Republic, 127–41
  general discussion of, 37–52
  Hungary, 162–73
  Poland, 195–204
  recommendations to improve performance, 56
  Romania, 223–34
  Slovak Republic, 252–62
  Slovenia, 278–88

Averting the Old-Age Crisis (World Bank), 6
Azerbaijan, 7

B

benchmarks for adequacy analysis.
    See benefit adequacy
benefit adequacy
    Bulgaria, 62, 73–81
    Croatia, 102–9
    Czech Republic, 129–38
    general discussion of, 37–48
    Hungary, 163–69
    indexation and, 27
    Poland, 195–203
    reforms not focusing on, 2
    Romania, 223–30
    Slovak Republic, 252–59
    Slovenia, 278–84, 290n12
benefit calculations, 20–24t, 26
benefit indexation. *See* indexation
best years of wages as basis for benefits
    Hungary, 157
    Poland, 191
    Slovak Republic, 246
    Slovenia, 273
Bosnia, 7
Bulgaria, 61–85
    age for receiving benefits in, 26, 49, 69,
        72, 85
    annuities in, 69
    assessment of performance of pension
        system in, 73–84
        benefit adequacy, 62, 73–81
        fiscal sustainability, 49, 50f, 62,
            81–84, 82f, 84f, 87n16
        replacement rates for full-career
            workers, 40, 41f, 43, 43f, 52,
            78–79, 78–80f, 87n14
        replacement rates for partial-career
            workers, 45f, 79–81, 81f
    benefit calculations in, 20t, 26
    characteristics of pension system in, 8t,
        64–73
        earnings-related schemes, 65, 67–69,
            68t, 70–71
        health care system, 36t, 65, 69–70,
            86n3
        noncontributory scheme, 67
        pillar design, 12t, 65–70, 66t
        voluntary scheme, 35t, 65, 69, 70t,
            85, 86n4

contribution ceilings in, 20t, 26
contribution rates in, 20t, 25
cutting benefits to increase fiscal
    sustainability in, 51, 82–83
deferment of retirement in, 83
deficits anticipated in, 62, 83, 85
defined-benefit scheme in, 61
early retirement in, 63, 72
farmers' pensions in, 70
guaranteed minimum income program
    in, 65, 67, 72
indexation in, 27, 47f, 75, 85
life expectancy in, 77, 85
lump-sum payments in, 69
motivation for reform in, 62–64
    fiscal balance prior to reform, 4f,
        61–62, 63f, 63t
occupational pension schemes in, 63,
    67–69, 86n4
old-age and system dependency ratios,
    62, 64f
pension fund management companies
    in, 69
point systems for pension calculation in,
    67, 71
police pensions in, 72
poverty alleviation in, 53, 78, 83
self-employed in, 70
social assistance benefits in, 17t, 53
structure of benefits in, 71–73
    disability benefits, 28t, 69, 72t,
        72–73, 86n8
    old-age benefits, 20t, 71–72, 86n6,
        86n9
    survivor benefits, 30, 31t, 73, 74t, 86n8
tax exemptions in, 69
universal pension schemes in, 67–69,
    86n4
women and pensions in, 49, 67, 69, 71, 83

C

capital gains treatment
    Poland, 192
    Slovak Republic, 16
Central Administration of National Pension
    Insurance (Hungary), 159
Central Registry of Insured People
    (REGOS, Croatia), 97–98
characteristics of pension system
    Bulgaria, 8t, 64–73
    Croatia, 8t, 91–100

Czech Republic, 117–27
    general discussion of, 10–37
    Hungary, 8t, 150–62
    Poland, 9t, 184–95
    Romania, 9t, 213–23
    Slovak Republic, 9t, 242–52
    Slovenia, 269–77
Chile
    financial market development in, 6
    home ownership in, 56n6
    pillar model of, 7, 10
contribution ceilings, 20–24t, 25–26, 38
contribution rates, 20–24t, 25, 51
Council of Europe, minimum benefit set
        by, 56n7
Croatia, 89–111
    age for receiving benefits in, 26, 49, 94,
        96, 98, 100, 111
    annuities in, 96, 99
    assessment of performance of pension
        system in, 100–110
        benefit adequacy, 102–9
        fiscal sustainability, 49, 50f, 109–10,
            110f, 112nn16–17
        replacement rates for full-career
            workers, 40, 41, 41f, 42, 43f, 52,
            105f, 105–7, 106f, 107f,
            112nn11–12
        replacement rates for partial-career
            workers, 45f, 107–9, 108f, 110–11,
            112nn13–15
    benefit calculations in, 20t, 26
    characteristics of pension system in, 8t,
        91–100
        earnings-related schemes, 94, 95t,
            97–98
        health care system, 36t, 96–97
        noncontributory scheme, 94
        pillar design, 12t, 92–97, 93t
        voluntary scheme, 35t, 94–96, 96t
    contribution ceilings in, 20t, 25
    contribution rates in, 20t, 25
    deficits anticipated in, 89, 109, 111
    early retirement in, 98, 108–9, 112n15
    flat-rate benefit formula in, 20t, 98,
        106–7
    guaranteed minimum income program
        in, 17t
    indexation in, 27, 42, 47f, 48, 102
    life expectancy in, 92, 99, 112n2
    lump-sum payments in, 96
    motivation for reform in, 90–91

fiscal balance prior to reform, 4f,
        90, 90t
    old-age dependency ratio in, 91, 91f
    pension fund management companies
        in, 91, 98
    point systems for pension calculation in,
        7, 11, 89, 91, 94, 98–99, 110,
        112nn3–4
    poverty alleviation in, 53, 107
    replacement of defined-benefit scheme
        in, 11, 89, 91, 94, 110
    social assistance benefits in, 53
    state-provided matching contributions
        in, 111
    structure of benefits in, 96–100
        disability benefits, 28t, 99t, 99–100
        old-age benefits, 20t, 98–99,
            112nn3–6
        survivor benefits, 31t, 100, 101t
    tax deductions in, 34, 96
    women and pensions in, 49, 94, 98, 100,
        112n2
Croatian Institute for Health Insurance
        (HZZO), 96–97
Croatian Pension Insurance Institute, 97, 100
Croatian Tax Administration, 97
cutting benefits to increase fiscal
        sustainability
    Bulgaria, 51, 82–83
    Czech Republic, 51, 140
    general discussion of, 51, 54, 55
    Hungary, 51, 171
    Romania, 51, 231, 232, 235
    Slovak Republic, 261, 262–63
    Slovenia, 51, 286–87, 289
Czech National Bank, 123
Czech Republic, 2–3, 115–43
    age for receiving benefits in, 26, 117,
        120, 125, 136, 137, 140–41
    annuities in, 123
    assessment of performance of pension
        system in, 127–41
        benefit adequacy, 129–38
        fiscal sustainability, 49, 50f, 138–41,
            139f, 144nn16–17
        replacement rates for full-career
            workers, 40, 41, 41f, 42, 43, 43f,
            52, 132f, 132–33, 133f, 134f, 140,
            141f, 142, 144nn11–12
        replacement rates for partial-career
            workers, 45f, 133–38, 135f, 136f,
            137f, 142

benefit calculations in, 21t, 26
characteristics of pension system in,
    117–27
  earnings-related schemes, 120–22,
    121t, 125, 143nn4–5
  health care system, 36t, 124–25
  noncontributory scheme, 120, 143n2
  pillar design, 7, 12t, 118–25, 119t
  voluntary scheme, 35t, 122–23, 123t
contribution ceilings in, 21t, 25
contribution rates in, 21t, 25
cutting benefits to increase fiscal
    sustainability in, 51, 140
deferment of retirement in, 126, 135
deficits anticipated in, 116, 138, 142
early retirement in, 117, 120, 126
flat-rate benefit formula in, 21t, 116,
    117, 120, 143n3
guaranteed minimum income program
    in, 17t, 118, 120
indexation in, 27, 47, 47f, 129
life expectancy in, 139
lump-sum payments in, 123, 143n6
motivation for reform in, 116–17
  fiscal balance prior to reform, 4f, 117,
    117t
occupational pension schemes in, 117
old-age and system dependency ratios
    in, 116, 139f, 139–40, 144nn14–15
parametric reforms in, 115, 117, 141–42
pension fund management companies
    in, 123
poverty alleviation in, 53, 133, 138, 140
prepaid expenditure taxes in, 16
self-employed in, 124, 125
social assistance benefits in, 53
state-provided matching contributions
    in, 122–23, 143, 143n7
structure of benefits in, 125–27
  disability benefits, 28t, 126t, 126–27
  old-age benefits, 21t, 125–26, 143n2
  survivor benefits, 31t, 127, 128t
tax deductions in, 122–23
tax exemptions in, 122
weakness of parametric reform in, 142
women and pensions in, 120, 125, 140

D

deferment of retirement
  Bulgaria, 83
  Czech Republic, 126, 135

Hungary, 171, 175
Poland, 193, 203
Romania, 231, 235
Slovak Republic, 246, 250, 261, 264
Slovenia, 276, 285
deficits anticipated
  See also fiscal sustainability
  Bulgaria, 62, 83, 85
  Croatia, 89, 109, 111
  Czech Republic, 116, 138, 142
  Hungary, 147, 170, 171, 173,
    177nn16–17
  Poland, 181, 182, 204
  Romania, 230–31, 234
  Slovak Republic, 239, 240, 260–61, 263
  Slovenia, 267, 268, 288
defined-benefit schemes
  See also pillar design
  Bulgaria, 61
  Croatia, replacement of, 11, 89, 91, 94,
    110
  Czech Republic, 11, 116, 120
  general discussion of, 11
  Hungary, 11, 147, 148, 154, 173
  Poland, replacement of, 11, 188, 205
  Romania, replacement of, 11, 211, 213,
    216, 234
  Slovak Republic, replacement of, 11, 241
  Slovenia, 11, 270
defined-contribution schemes
  See also fully-funded defined-contribution
    scheme; notional defined-
    contribution (NDC) scheme
  benefit calculations in, 26
  general discussion of, 13
  vesting in, 25
delaying retirement. See deferment of
    retirement
demographics. See old-age and system
    dependency ratios
dependents. See survivor benefits
disability benefits
  Bulgaria, 28t, 69, 72t, 72–73, 86n8
  Croatia, 28t, 99t, 99–100
  Czech Republic, 28t, 117, 126t, 126–27
  general discussion of, 27, 28–29t, 30
  Hungary, 28t, 160–61, 161t
  Poland, 29t, 194t, 194–95
  Romania, 29t, 212, 218–19, 220–21, 221t
  Slovak Republic, 29t, 248, 250–51, 251t
  Slovenia, 29t, 276t, 276–77
  vesting and, 27, 28–29t

E

early retirement
  Bulgaria, 63, 72
  Croatia, 98, 108–9, 112n15
  Czech Republic, 117, 120, 126
  Hungary, 148, 160, 168
  Poland, 193, 206n5
  Romania, 212, 213, 220, 234
  Slovak Republic, 246, 250
  Slovenia, 268–69, 289n1, 290n3
earnings-related schemes
  Bulgaria, 65, 67–69, 68t, 70–71
  Croatia, 94, 95t, 97–98
  Czech Republic, 120–22, 121t, 125,
    143nn4–5
  general discussion of, 13, 38
  Hungary, 154–57, 155–56t, 159–62
  Poland, 188–91, 189–90t, 192–93,
    206n5
  Romania, 216–17, 217t, 219–20, 236n6
  Slovak Republic, 245–46, 247t, 248–49,
    264nn2–4
  Slovenia, 272t, 272–73, 275, 290nn4–5
  taxation and, 13
Estonia, 8t
European System of National Accounts, 54
exempt-exempt-taxed (EET) regime, 15b
  See also tax exemptions

F

farmers' pensions
  Bulgaria, 70
  general discussion, 6
  Hungary, 159
  Poland, 192
  Romania, 219
  Slovak Republic, 248
  Slovenia, 274
financial instruments available for individ-
    ual investment, 6, 39
Financial Supervision Commission
    (Bulgaria), 71, 86n2
Financial Supervision Commission
    (Poland), 191, 193
financial system reform, 6, 10
financing gap, defined, 48
fiscal balance prior to reform
  Bulgaria, 4f, 61–62, 63f, 63t
  Croatia, 4f, 90, 90t
  Czech Republic, 4f, 117, 117t
  general discussion of, 3, 4f

  Hungary, 4f, 148, 149t, 150f
  Poland, 4f, 182, 183f, 183t
  Romania, 4f, 212, 213t
  Slovak Republic, 4f, 240, 241f, 241t
  Slovenia, 4f, 268, 268t
fiscal sustainability
  Bulgaria, 49, 50f, 62, 81–84, 82f, 84f,
    87n16
  Croatia, 49, 50f, 109–10, 110f,
    112nn16–17
  Czech Republic, 49, 50f, 138–41, 139f,
    144nn16–17
  general discussion of, 48–52, 50f
  Hungary, 49, 50f, 169–73, 170f,
    177nn18–19
  indexation and, 27
  as motivation for reform in, 1–2, 3
  Poland, 49, 50f, 203–4, 204f
  Romania, 49, 50f, 230–33, 231f,
    236nn13–15
  Slovak Republic, 49, 50f, 259–62, 260f,
    265n10
  Slovenia, 49, 50f, 285–88, 286f,
    291nn17–19
flat-rate benefit formula
  Croatia, 20t, 98, 106–7
  Czech Republic, 21t, 116, 117, 120,
    127, 143n3
French system as example for point
    system, 7
full-career workers, replacement rates for.
    See replacement rates for
    full-career workers
fully-funded defined-contribution scheme
  Hungary, 148, 149, 154, 173
  Poland, 185, 205
  Romania, 211, 213, 218, 234
  Slovak Republic, 239, 246
  Slovenia, 267

G

General Health Insurance Fund
    (Czech Republic), 124
German system as example for point
    system, 7
guaranteed minimum income program
  Bulgaria, 65, 67, 72
  Croatia, 17t
  Czech Republic, 17t, 118, 120
  general discussion of, 16
  Poland, 17t, 191, 193

Romania, 18*t*, 214, 216
Slovak Republic, 18*t*, 245

H

hazardous occupations, workers in
    Bulgaria, pension schemes for, 63
    Slovenia, 289*n*2
health care system
    Bulgaria, 36*t*, 65, 69–70, 86*n*3
    Croatia, 36*t*, 96–97
    Czech Republic, 36*t*, 124–25
    general discussion of, 13, 34, 36*t*, 37,
        56*n*5
    Hungary, 36*t*, 158–59
    Poland, 36*t*, 192, 206*n*6
    Romania, 36*t*, 219
    Slovak Republic, 36*t*, 248
    Slovenia, 36*t*, 274–75
Health Insurance Fund (Hungary), 159
Health Insurance Institute of Slovenia, 274
Herzegovina, 7
home ownership in Chile, 56*n*6
Hungarian Financial Supervisory Authority,
    158, 159
Hungary, 147–75
    age for receiving benefits in, 49
    annuities in, 151, 154, 158, 160
    assessment of performance of pension
        system in, 162–73
        benefit adequacy, 163–69
        fiscal sustainability, 49, 50*f*, 169–73,
            170*f*, 177*nn*18–19
        replacement rates for full-career
            workers, 41, 41*f*, 42, 43, 43*f*, 53,
            166–67*f*, 166–68, 172*f*
        replacement rates for partial-career
            workers, 45*f*, 168–69, 169*f*
    benefit calculations in, 21*t*, 26
    characteristics of pension system in, 8*t*,
        150–62
        earnings-related schemes, 154–57,
            155–56*t*, 159–62
        health care system, 36*t*, 158–59
        noncontributory scheme, 154
        pillar design, 7, 12*t*, 151–59, 152–53*t*
        voluntary scheme, 35*t*, 157–58, 158*t*
    contribution ceilings in, 21*t*, 26
    cutting benefits to increase fiscal
        sustainability in, 51, 171
    deferment of retirement in, 171, 175
    deficits anticipated in, 147, 170, 171,
        173, 177*nn*16–17

defined-benefit scheme in, 11, 147, 148,
    154, 173
early retirement in, 148, 160, 168
farmers' pensions in, 159
fully-funded defined-contribution
    scheme in, 148, 149, 154, 173
indexation in, 27, 157, 163, 174–75,
    176*n*8
life expectancy in, 175*n*2, 176*n*6
"lost generation" in, 174
lump-sum payments in, 158, 160
motivation for reform in, 148–50
    fiscal balance prior to reform, 4*f*, 148,
        149*t*, 150*f*
    old-age and system dependency ratios
        in, 149, 150*f*
    parametric reforms in, 148, 149, 154, 173
    pension fund management companies
        in, 159
    poverty alleviation in, 53, 168, 172
    prepaid expenditure taxes in, 16
    self-employed in, 158, 159
    social assistance benefits in, 53
    structure of benefits in, 159–62
        disability benefits, 28*t*, 160–61, 161*t*
        old-age benefits, 17*t*, 21*t*, 159–60
        survivor benefits, 32*t*, 161–62, 162*t*
    tax deductions in, 158
    tax exemptions in, 154
    unemployment in, 175
    women and pensions in, 49, 154, 160,
        171, 175*n*2

I

increasing age of retirement. *See* deferment
    of retirement
indexation
    Bulgaria, 27, 47*f*, 75, 85
    Croatia, 27, 42, 47*f*, 48, 102
    Czech Republic, 27, 47, 47*f*, 129
    general discussion of, 3, 20–24*t*, 26–27,
        46–48, 47*f*
    Hungary, 27, 157, 163, 174–75, 176*n*8
    Poland, 27, 47, 47*f*, 48, 197, 207*n*7
    recommendation of, 54–55
    Romania, 46, 47*f*, 57*n*12, 224, 234, 235
    Slovak Republic, 27, 47*f*, 48, 246, 253,
        263
    Slovenia, 27, 47, 47*f*, 48, 273, 278–79,
        289
individual retirement accounts, 39, 52
    See also voluntary scheme

Insurance Act (Slovenia), 274
Insurance and Pension Funds Supervisory
    Commission (Poland), 191
Insurance Supervision Agency (Slovenia),
    274
international investment of Kosovo
    scheme, 10
International Labour Organization (ILO),
    minimum benefit set by, 7, 56n7

K

Kazakhstan, 7, 8t, 10
Kosovo, 8t, 10
Kyrgyz Republic, 7

L

last years of wages as basis for benefits
    See also best years of wages as basis for
        benefits
    Romania, 212, 216
Latin American examples, 6, 7
    See also Chile
Latvia, 7, 8t
life annuities. See annuities
life expectancy at retirement
    Bulgaria, 77, 85
    Croatia, 92, 99, 112n2
    Czech Republic, 139
    general discussion of, 40, 41–42
    Hungary, 175n2, 176n6
    Poland, 205
    Romania, 234, 235n5
    Slovak Republic, 246, 261
    Slovenia, 285
Lithuania, 8t
"lost generation," 55, 174
lump-sum payments
    Bulgaria, 69
    Croatia, 96
    Czech Republic, 123, 143n6
    disability benefits, 30
    Hungary, 158, 160
    Poland, 191, 195
    Romania, 221, 223
    Slovak Republic, 246, 250
    survivor benefits, 30
    voluntary old-age benefits, 34

M

Macedonia, 9t
mandatory funded schemes. See pillar design

military pensions
    Poland, 192
    Romania, 219
    Slovenia, 290n3
minimum-income guarantee program.
    See guaranteed minimum income
        program
Ministry of Finance (Czech Republic), 123,
    124, 144n13
Ministry of Labor, Family and Social Affairs
    (Slovenia), 275
Ministry of Labor and Social Affairs
    (Czech Republic), 125, 144n13
Ministry of Social Affairs (Czech
    Republic), 124
Montenegro, 7
motivation for reform
    See also fiscal balance prior to reform
    Bulgaria, 62–64
    Croatia, 90–91
    Czech Republic, 116–17
    general discussion of, 3–10
    Hungary, 148–50
    Poland, 182–84
    Romania, 212–13, 235n1
    Slovak Republic, 240–42
    Slovenia, 268–69, 289n1

N

National Bank of Slovakia, 249
National Health Fund (Poland), 192
National Health Insurance Fund (Bulgaria),
    70
National Health Insurance Fund
    (Romania), 219
National Health Insurance Fund
    Administration (NHIFA, Hungary),
    158
National House of Pensions (Romania),
    220
National Revenue Agency (Bulgaria), 71
National Social Security Institute (NSSI,
    Bulgaria), 70–71, 86n7
noncontributory scheme
    Bulgaria, 67
    Croatia, 94
    Czech Republic, 120, 143n2
    Hungary, 154
    Poland, 188
    Romania, 216
    Slovak Republic, 245
    Slovenia, 270–72

notional defined-contribution (NDC)
    scheme
  in Poland, 2, 11, 42, 57n13, 181–82,
    185, 188, 191, 193, 205, 206n2
  in Sweden, 7

O

occupational pension schemes
  Bulgaria, 63, 67–69, 86n4
  Czech Republic, 117
  Poland, 206n3
  Romania, 212, 219
  Slovenia, 290n3
old-age allowance in Hungary, 17t, 154
old-age and system dependency ratios
  Bulgaria, 62, 64f
  Croatia, 91, 91f
  Czech Republic, 116, 139f, 139–40,
    144nn14–15
  general description of problem related
    to, 2, 5, 5f
  Hungary, 149, 150f, 175nn3–5
  Poland, 182–83, 184f
  Romania, 213, 231–32, 232f
  Slovak Republic, 240–41, 242f
  Slovenia, 285, 286f, 290nn8–9
old-age benefits
  Bulgaria, 20t, 71–72, 86n6, 86n9
  Croatia, 20t, 98–99, 112nn3–6
  Czech Republic, 21t, 125–26, 143n2
  general discussion of, 16, 17t, 19–27
  Hungary, 21t, 159–60
  Poland, 22t, 193–95, 207n7
  Romania, 22–23t, 220
  Slovak Republic, 23t, 249–50
  Slovenia, 24t, 275–76
Orbán, G., 177n16
Organisation for Economic Co-operation
    and Development (OECD)
    countries
  health insurance programs in, 37
  study on living standards for people 10
    years older and people 15 years
    younger than normal retirement
    age, 39
orphans. See survivor benefits

P

Palotai, D., 177n16
parametric reforms
  adjustment in second half of 1990s, 3

Croatia, 2
Czech Republic, 115, 117, 141–42
  general discussion of, 2, 7
Hungary, 148, 149, 154, 173
Romania, 2
Slovak Republic, 2, 260, 263
Slovenia, 267, 269
partial-career workers, replacement rates
    for. See replacement rates for
    partial-career workers
pay-as-you-go structure. See pillar design
Pension and Old-Age Round Table, 177n16
pension fund management companies
  Bulgaria, 69
  Croatia, 91, 98
  Czech Republic, 123
  Hungary, 159
  Poland, 193
  Romania, 219
  Slovak Republic, 249
  Slovenia, 274, 290n3
pension income supplement in Slovenia,
    53, 270
Pensions and Disability Insurance Institute
    (PDII, Slovenia), 275
performance assessment. See assessment of
    performance of pension system
pillar design
  Bulgaria, 12t, 65–70, 66t
  Croatia, 12t, 92–97, 93t
  Czech Republic, 7, 12t, 118–25, 119t
  general discussion of, 7, 10, 11–13, 12t
  Hungary, 7, 12t, 151–59, 152–53t
  Poland, 7, 12t, 185–92, 186–87t
  Romania, 12t, 214–19, 215t
  Slovak Republic, 12t, 243–48, 244t
  Slovenia, 7, 12t, 270–75, 271t, 289n2
point systems for pension calculation
  Bulgaria, 67, 71
  Croatia, 7, 11, 89, 91, 94, 98–99, 110,
    112nn3–4
  general discussion of, 2
  Romania, 7, 11, 211, 213, 216, 220,
    235nn3–4
  Slovak Republic, 7, 11, 241–42, 250
Poland, 181–206
  age for receiving benefits in, 26, 49, 182,
    193
  annuities in, 185, 191, 193
  assessment of performance of pension
    system in, 25, 195–204
  benefit adequacy, 195–203

fiscal sustainability, 49, 50*f*, 203–4, 204*f*
replacement rates for full-career workers, 40, 41*f*, 43, 43*f*, 53, 200–201, 200–202*f*
replacement rates for partial-career workers, 45*f*, 201–3, 203*f*, 205
benefit calculations in, 22*t*, 26
"bridging pensions" in, 206*n*5
characteristics of pension system in, 9*t*, 184–95
earnings-related schemes, 188–91, 189–90*t*, 192–93, 206*n*5
health care system, 36*t*, 192
noncontributory scheme, 188
pillar design, 7, 12*t*, 185–92, 186–87*t*
voluntary scheme, 35*t*, 191–92, 192*t*
contribution ceilings in, 22*t*, 26
contribution rates in, 22*t*, 25
deferment of retirement in, 193, 203
early retirement in, 193, 206*n*5
farmers' pensions in, 192
fully-funded defined-contribution scheme in, 185, 205
guaranteed minimum income program in, 17*t*, 191, 193
indexation in, 27, 47, 47*f*, 48, 197, 207*n*7
life expectancy in, 205
lump-sum payments in, 191, 195
military pensions in, 192
motivation for reform in, 182–84
fiscal balance prior to reform, 4*f*, 182, 183*f*, 183*t*
notional defined-contribution (NDC) scheme in, 2, 11, 42, 57*n*13, 181–82, 185, 188, 191, 193, 205, 206*n*2
occupations and pension schemes in, 206*n*3
old-age and system dependency ratios in, 182–83, 184*f*
pension fund management companies in, 193
police pensions in, 192
poverty alleviation in, 53, 198, 200–201
replacement of defined-benefit scheme in, 11, 188, 205
"Security through Diversity" reform program, 205, 206*n*1
self-employed in, 192, 206*n*6
social assistance benefits in, 53, 188

structure of benefits in, 193–95
disability benefits, 29*t*, 194*t*, 194–95
old-age benefits, 22*t*, 193–95
old-age benefits in, 207*n*7
survivor benefits, 32*t*, 195, 196*t*
women and pensions in, 25, 49, 191, 193, 194, 205
police pensions
Bulgaria, 72
Poland, 192
Slovak Republic, 249
Slovenia, 290*n*3
poverty
alleviation
Bulgaria, 53, 78, 83
Croatia, 53, 107
Czech Republic, 53, 133, 138, 140
general discussion of, 16, 53
Hungary, 53, 168, 172
Poland, 53, 198, 200–201
Romania, 53, 227, 232, 235
Slovak Republic, 53, 257, 259, 261
Slovenia, 53, 282, 287
poverty line, proxy for, 57*n*8
promoting formal sector employment, 54
purpose of reforms, 1–2

R

ratio of population age 65 and older to population age 15–64. *See* old-age and system dependency ratios
replacement rates for full-career workers
Bulgaria, 40, 41*f*, 43, 43*f*, 52, 78–79, 78–80*f*, 87*n*14
Croatia, 40, 41, 41*f*, 42, 43*f*, 52, 105*f*, 105–7, 106*f*, 107*f*, 112*nn*11–12
Czech Republic, 40, 41, 41*f*, 42, 43, 43*f*, 52, 132*f*, 132–33, 133*f*, 134*f*, 140, 141*f*, 142, 144*nn*11–12
general discussion of, 40–43, 41*f*, 43*f*, 52–53, 57*n*10
Hungary, 41, 41*f*, 42, 43, 43*f*, 53, 166–67*f*, 166–68, 167*f*, 172*f*, 173, 176*nn*12–15
Poland, 40, 41*f*, 43, 43*f*, 53, 200–201, 200–202*f*, 207*nn*11–13
Romania, 40, 41*f*, 43, 43*f*, 53, 227, 227–28*f*, 234, 236*n*11
Slovak Republic, 40, 41*f*, 42, 43, 43*f*, 53, 255–58, 256–57*f*, 261, 262*f*, 265*n*8

Slovenia, 41, 41*f*, 43, 43*f*, 53, 273,
281–83, 282–83*f*, 287*f*,
291*nn*14–15
replacement rates for partial-career workers
Bulgaria, 45*f*, 79–81, 81*f*
Croatia, 45*f*, 107–9, 108*f*, 110–11,
112*nn*13–15
Czech Republic, 45*f*, 133–38, 135*f*, 136*f*,
137*f*, 142
general discussion of, 43–46, 45*f*, 53,
57*n*11
Hungary, 45*f*, 168–69, 169*f*, 173–74
Poland, 45*f*, 201–3, 203*f*, 205
Romania, 45*f*, 229*f*, 229–30, 236*n*12
Slovak Republic, 45*f*, 258*f*, 258–59,
265*n*9
Slovenia, 44, 45*f*, 283–85, 284*f*
Romania, 211–35
age for receiving benefits in, 26, 49, 212,
216, 220, 234–35
assessment of performance of pension
system in, 223–34
benefit adequacy, 223–30
fiscal sustainability, 49, 50*f*, 216–17,
217*t*, 219–20, 236*n*6
replacement rates for full-career
workers, 40, 41*f*, 43, 43*f*, 53, 227,
227–28*f*, 234, 236*n*11
replacement rates for partial-career
workers, 45*f*, 229*f*, 229–30, 236*n*12
benefit calculations in, 22–23*t*, 26
characteristics of pension system in, 9*t*,
213–23
earnings-related schemes, 216–17,
217*t*, 219–20, 236*n*6
health care system, 36*t*, 219
noncontributory scheme, 216
pillar design, 12*t*, 214–19, 215*t*
voluntary scheme, 35*t*, 218*t*, 218–19
contribution ceilings in, 22–23*t*, 25
contribution rates in, 22–23*t*, 25
cutting benefits to increase fiscal
sustainability in, 51, 231,
232, 235
deferment of retirement in, 231, 235
deficits anticipated in, 230–31, 234
early retirement in, 212, 213, 220, 234
farmers' pensions in, 219
fully-funded defined-contribution
scheme in, 211, 213, 218, 234
guaranteed minimum income program
in, 18*t*, 214, 216

indexation in, 46, 47*f*, 57*n*12, 224, 234,
235
last years of wages as basis for benefits
in, 212, 216
life expectancy in, 234, 235*n*5
lump-sum payments in, 221, 223
military pensions in, 219
motivation for reform in, 212–13, 235*n*1
fiscal balance prior to reform, 4*f*, 212,
213*t*
old-age and system dependency ratios
in, 213, 231–32, 232*f*
pension fund management companies
in, 219
point systems for pension calculation in,
7, 11, 211, 213, 216, 220,
235*nn*3–4
poverty alleviation in, 53, 227, 232, 235
replacement of defined-benefit scheme
in, 11, 211, 213, 216, 234
self-employed in, 219
structure of benefits in, 220–23
disability benefits, 29*t*, 212, 218–19,
220–21, 221*t*
old-age benefits, 22–23*t*, 220
survivor benefits, 32*t*, 221–23, 222*t*
tax deductions in, 218
women and pensions in, 49, 216, 218,
220, 234
Romanian Private Pension System
Supervision Commission, 220
Russia, 7, 9*t*

S

Securities Market Agency (Slovenia), 274
"Security through Diversity" reform
program (Poland), 205, 206*n*1
self-employed persons and pensions
Bulgaria, 70
Czech Republic, 124, 125
general discussion of, 6
Hungary, 158, 159
Poland, 192, 206*n*6
Romania, 219
Slovak Republic, 248–49
Slovenia, 274, 275
Serbia, 7
Slovak Republic, 239–64
age for receiving benefits in, 26, 49, 246,
250, 263
annuities in, 243, 250

assessment of performance of pension
system in, 252–62
benefit adequacy, 252–59
fiscal sustainability, 49, 50f, 259–62,
260f
replacement rates for full-career
workers, 40, 41f, 42, 43, 43f, 53,
255–58, 256–57f, 262f
replacement rates for partial-career
workers, 45f, 258f, 258–59
benefit calculations in, 23t, 26
best years of wages as basis for benefits
in, 246
capital gains treatment in, 16
characteristics of pension system in, 9t,
242–52
earnings-related schemes, 245–46,
247t, 248–49
health care system, 36t, 248
noncontributory scheme, 245
pillar design, 12t, 243–48, 244t
voluntary scheme, 35t, 246–48, 248t
contribution ceilings in, 23t, 26
contribution rates in, 23t, 25
cutting benefits to increase fiscal
sustainability in, 261, 262–63
deferment of retirement in, 246, 250,
261, 264
deficits anticipated in, 239, 240,
260–61, 263
early retirement in, 246, 250
farmers' pensions in, 248
fully-funded defined-contribution
scheme in, 239, 246
guaranteed minimum income program
in, 18t, 245
indexation in, 27, 47f, 48, 246, 253, 263
life expectancy in, 246, 261
lump-sum payments in, 246, 250
motivation for reform in, 240–42
fiscal balance prior to reform, 4f, 240,
241f, 241t
old-age and system dependency ratios,
240–41, 242f
pension fund management companies
in, 249
point systems for pension calculation in,
7, 11, 241–42, 250
police pensions in, 249
poverty alleviation in, 53, 257, 259, 261
replacement of defined-benefit scheme
in, 11, 241

self-employed in, 248–49
social assistance benefits in, 53
structure of benefits in, 249–52
disability benefits, 29t, 248, 250–51,
251t
old-age benefits, 23t, 249–50
survivor benefits, 33t, 251t, 251–52
tax deductions in, 246
tax exemptions in, 16, 245
women and pensions in, 49, 246, 249
Slovenia, 3, 267–89
age for receiving benefits in, 26, 49, 268,
270, 273, 275, 287, 289
assessment of performance of pension
system in, 278–88
benefit adequacy, 278–84, 290n12
fiscal sustainability, 49, 50f, 285–88,
286f, 291nn17–19
replacement rates for full-career
workers, 41, 41f, 43, 43f, 53,
281–83, 282–83f, 287f,
291nn14–15
replacement rates for partial-career
workers, 44, 45f, 283–85, 284f,
291n16
benefit calculations in, 24t, 26
best years of wages as basis for benefits
in, 273
characteristics of pension system in,
269–77
earnings-related schemes, 272t,
272–73, 275
health care system, 36t, 274–75
noncontributory scheme, 270–72
pillar design, 7, 12t, 270–75, 271t,
289n2
voluntary scheme, 35t, 273–74, 274t
contribution ceilings in, 24t, 25
contribution rates in, 24t, 25
cutting benefits to increase fiscal
sustainability in, 51, 286–87, 289
deferment of retirement in, 276, 285,
289
deficits anticipated in, 267, 268, 288
defined-benefit scheme in, 11, 270
early retirement in, 268–69, 289n1,
290n3
farmers' pensions in, 274
fully-funded defined-contribution
scheme in, 267
hazardous occupations workers in,
289n2

indexation in, 27, 47, 47*f,* 48, 273, 278–79, 289
life expectancy in, 285
military pensions in, 290*n*3
motivation for reform in, 268–69, 289*n*1
  fiscal balance prior to reform, 4*f,* 268, 268*t*
occupational pension schemes in, 290*n*3
old-age and system dependency ratios in, 285, 286*f,* 290*nn*8–9
parametric reforms in, 267, 269
pension fund management companies in, 274, 290*n*3
pension income supplement in, 53, 270
police pensions in, 290*n*3
poverty alleviation in, 53, 282, 287
self-employed in, 274, 275
state pension in, 18*t*
structure of benefits in, 275–77
  disability benefits, 29*t,* 276*t,* 276–77
  old-age benefits, 24*t,* 275–76, 290*nn*8–9
  survivor benefits, 33*t,* 277, 277*t*
women and pensions in, 49, 272–73, 275–76
social assistance benefits
  See also pension income supplement in Slovenia
Bulgaria, 53, 67, 70
Croatia, 53, 94
Czech Republic, 53, 120, 124
general discussion of, 2, 16, 19
Hungary, 53, 154
Poland, 53, 188
Slovak Republic, 53, 245, 259
Social Insurance Agency (Slovak Republic), 249
Social Insurance Institution (ZUS, Poland), 192–93
social pensions in Bulgaria, 17*t,* 19
  See also social assistance benefits
Social Security Administration (Czech Republic), 125
state pension in Slovenia, 18*t,* 270, 290*n*3
state-provided matching contributions
Croatia, 111
Czech Republic, 122–23, 143, 143*n*7
State Tax Collection Agency (Hungary), 159

structure of benefits
  See also disability benefits; health care system; old-age benefits
Bulgaria, 71–73
Croatia, 96–100
Czech Republic, 125–27
Hungary, 159–62
Poland, 193–95
Romania, 220–23
Slovak Republic, 249–52
Slovenia, 275–77
survivor benefits
Bulgaria, 30, 31*t,* 73, 74*t,* 86*n*8
Croatia, 31*t,* 100, 101*t*
Czech Republic, 30, 31*t,* 127, 128*t*
general discussion of, 30, 31–33*t*
Hungary, 30, 32*t,* 161–62, 162*t*
Poland, 30, 32*t,* 195, 196*t*
Romania, 32*t,* 221–23, 222*t*
Slovak Republic, 33*t,* 251*t,* 251–52
Slovenia, 33*t,* 277, 277*t*
Sweden as example of NDCs, 7
Swiss indexation. *See* indexation

T

taxation of contributions and benefits, 13–16, 14*t,* 15*b*
  See also tax deductions; tax exemptions
tax deductions
Croatia, 34, 96
Czech Republic, 122–23
general discussion of, 34
Hungary, 158
Romania, 218
Slovak Republic, 246
tax exemptions
Bulgaria, 16, 69
Czech Republic, 122
exempt-exempt-taxed (EET) regime, 15*b*
Hungary, 154
noncontributory scheme benefits, 56*n*2
Slovak Republic, 16, 245
taxed-exempt-exempt (TEE) regime, 15*b*
Turkmenistan, 7

U

Ukraine, 7, 9*t*
universal pension schemes in Bulgaria, 67–69, 86*n*4

V

vesting periods
  disability benefits, 27, 28–29*t*
  old-age benefits, 19, 20–24*t*, 25
voluntary scheme
  Bulgaria, 35*t*, 65, 69, 70*t*, 85, 86*n*4
  Croatia, 35*t*, 94–96, 96*t*
  Czech Republic, 35*t*, 122–23, 123*t*
  general discussion of, 1, 13, 34, 35*t*, 39,
    52, 53, 57*n*15
  Hungary, 35*t*, 157–58, 158*t*, 175
  Poland, 35*t*, 191–92, 192*t*
  Romania, 35*t*, 218*t*, 218–19
  Slovak Republic, 35*t*, 246–48, 248*t*
  Slovenia, 35*t*, 273–74, 274*t*

W

widows/widowers. *See* survivor benefits
women and pensions
  Bulgaria, 49, 67, 69, 71, 83
  Croatia, 49, 94, 98, 100, 112*n*2
  Czech Republic, 120, 125, 140
  Hungary, 49, 154, 160, 171,
    175*n*2
  Poland, 25, 49, 191, 193,
    194, 205
  Romania, 49, 216, 218, 220, 234
  Slovak Republic, 49, 246, 249
  Slovenia, 49, 272–73, 275–76
  survivor benefits, 30
World Bank
  assessment principles for evaluating
    pension systems, 37
    See also assessment of performance of
    pension system
  Averting the Old-Age Crisis, 6
  conceptual framework of pension
    systems by, 10
    See also pillar design
  influence on pension reform,
    56*n*1